Law and Justice in the Courts of Classical Athens

In *Law and Justice in the Courts of Classical Athens*, Adriaan Lanni draws on contemporary legal thinking to present a new model of the legal system of classical Athens. She analyzes the Athenians' preference in most cases for *ad hoc*, discretionary decision making, as opposed to what moderns would call the rule of law. Lanni argues that the Athenians consciously employed different approaches to legal decision making in different types of courts. The varied approaches to the legal process stem from a deep tension in Athenian practice and thinking, between the demand for flexibility of legal interpretation consistent with the exercise of democratic power by Athenian jurors and the advantages of consistency and predictability. Lanni presents classical Athens as a case study of a sophisticated legal system with an extraordinarily individualized and discretionary approach to justice.

Adriaan Lanni is assistant professor of law at Harvard Law School. A former member of the Harvard Society of Fellows, she holds a law degree from Yale Law School and a Ph.D. in ancient history from the University of Michigan. She is a scholar of ancient law and modern criminal law and procedure.

LAW AND JUSTICE IN THE COURTS OF CLASSICAL ATHENS

ADRIAAN LANNI

HARVARD LAW SCHOOL

CAMBRIDGE
UNIVERSITY PRESS

CAMBRIDGE UNIVERSITY PRESS
Cambridge, New York, Melbourne, Madrid, Cape Town, Singapore,
São Paulo, Delhi, Dubai, Tokyo, Mexico City

Cambridge University Press
32 Avenue of the Americas, New York, NY 10013-2473, USA

www.cambridge.org
Information on this title: www.cambridge.org/9780521733014

First published 2006
Reprinted 2008
First paperback edition 2008

A catalog record for this publication is available from the British Library

Library of Congress Cataloging in Publication data

Lanni, Adriaan, 1972–
Law and justice in the courts of classical Athens / Adriaan Lanni.
    p. cm.
Includes bibliographical references and index.
ISBN-13: 978-0-521-85759-8 (hardback)
ISBN-10: 0-521-85759-7 (hardback)
1. Justice, Administration of (Greek law)   2. Courts – Greece – Athens – History.   3.
Judicial process – Greece – Athens – History.   I. Title.
KL4345.L36   2006
347.495'12 –dc 22   2005032402

ISBN 978-0-521-85759-8 Hardback
ISBN 978-0-521-73301-4 Paperback

To the memory of
Mike Lanni
1941–1992

CONTENTS

Acknowledgments

This book, which began as a dissertation at the University of Michigan, has been shaped by many teachers and colleagues. I benefited from an excellent dissertation committee, including Sara Forsdyke, Raymond Van Dam, and James Boyd White. I could not have asked for better advisors and editors than my dissertation co-chairs, Bruce Frier and Thomas Green. I would also like to thank several former teachers from the University of Cambridge and Yale Law School who, though not directly involved in this book, have influenced my thinking on Athenian law in important ways: Paul Cartledge, Peter Garnsey, Simon Goldhill, Robert Gordon, Keith Hopkins, Paul Millett, Dorothy Thompson, and James Whitman.

The Greek law community is an uncommonly generous one. Over the years I have benefited from conversations with many classicists, including Danielle Allen, Alan Boegehold, Eva Cantarella, Michael DeBrauw, Matthew Christ, David Cohen, Edward Cohen, Craig Cooper, Edward Harris, Steven Johnstone, Josiah Ober, David Phillips, Lene Rubinstein, Adele Scafuro, Gerhard Thür, Stephen Todd, and Robert Wallace. Michael Gagarin deserves individual mention; he read drafts of every chapter and offered valuable corrections and suggestions regarding both technical matters and the overall argument.

Both the dissertation and book manuscript were written at Harvard. While at the Society of Fellows I received many useful comments from junior and senior Fellows, particularly Bernard Bailyn, Oren Bar-Gill, Michael Gordin, Martha Minow, and Gregory Nagy. I would also like to thank my colleagues at Harvard Law School for their valuable comments and advice, particularly Charles Donahue, Morton Horwitz, Kenneth Mack, Martha Minow, and William Stuntz. Two law students, Karl Chang and Rita Lomio, provided excellent research assistance. The project was greatly improved by suggestions I received while presenting part of this work to the law faculties at Columbia, Cornell, Harvard, the University of Michigan, the University of Minnesota, New York University, the University of San Diego, the University of Southern California, and Willamette. I am also grateful to Cambridge University Press's two referees for their helpful suggestions.

Although this book is not directly comparative, the ideas in it are informed by my background as a lawyer. I was lucky enough to clerk for two judges who have earned a place in history: Judge Stephen Reinhardt of the U.S. Court of Appeals for the Ninth Circuit and Justice Dana Fabe of the Alaska Supreme Court. My approach to all legal questions reflects their influence.

I owe a special debt to Victor Bers, who introduced me to Athenian law in an undergraduate class in Yale College more than a decade ago and has served since then as mentor, friend, and marriage officiant. He commented on several versions of the dissertation and manuscript and was an invaluable resource throughout the project.

Finally, I would like to thank Wes Kelman, a partner in this project as in all things. The dedication refers to my father, a union leader who pointed out to me at an early age the distinction between law and social justice that is central to the thesis of this book.

1 INTRODUCTION

WHAT ROLE DID THE LAW COURTS PLAY IN THE WORLD'S FIRST WELL-DOCUMENTED democracy?[1] Ancient Athens is celebrated for its democratic political institutions, but its law courts have been largely ignored by lawyers and legal historians. This neglect is not mysterious. Athenian law has failed to attract the interest of legal historians because it was run by amateurs and did not generate jurisprudential texts. It has not helped that the best-known example of Athenian justice is an outrage: the trial and execution of Socrates.

Classicists have begun to remedy this neglect, but much of their work has emphasized the arbitrariness and anti-legal aspects of Athenian litigation. Most of what we know of Athenian law comes from court speeches, and these scholars have focused on the fact that these speeches contain information – boasts of their family's public services, character attacks, appeals to pity – that would be considered irrelevant or inadmissible in a modern courtroom. On this basis, they argue that the aims and ideals of the Athenian courts were radically different from those of modern courts. On this view, the Athenian courts did not attempt to resolve disputes according to established rules and principles equally and impartially applied but rather served primarily a social or political role.[2] According to this approach, litigation was not aimed chiefly at the final resolution of the dispute or the discovery of truth; rather, the courts provided an arena for the parties to publicly define, contest, and evaluate their social relations to one another, and the hierarchies of their society.[3] The law under which the suit was brought mattered little to either the litigants or the jurors; the statute was merely a procedural mechanism for moving the feud or competition onto a public stage.[4] Extra-legal

---

[1] Robinson (1997:16–25) discusses possible examples of early democracies outside of Athens, some of which predate the Athenian democracy. Our sources for these possible early democracies are too thin to permit meaningful analysis of these political systems.

[2] D. Cohen 1995:87–88; Osborne 1985a:52.

[3] D. Cohen 1995:87–88. Cohen argues that Athenian judges and litigants acknowledged that litigation was primarily a form of feuding behavior.

[4] D. Cohen 1995:90. However, the choice of whether to bring a private suit or to style the prosecution as a public suit, which would mean a higher profile and more severe penalties, had important consequences in the game of honor (Osborne 1985a:52–53).

I

considerations trumped law in a process that bore little relation to the functioning of modern court systems – or so the argument goes.

This approach to the Athenian legal system has been challenged by two different academic camps, both of which credit Athens with attempting to implement a rule of law. First, institutional historians argue that reforms in the late fifth and early fourth century curtailed the lawmaking powers of the popular Assembly, and created a moderate democracy committed to a rule of law.[5] Second, other scholars analyze the surviving court speeches and argue that "legal" reasoning – citations to, and exegesis of, the applicable statutes – played a much greater role in Athenian litigation than is commonly thought.[6] They tend to dismiss the extra-legal arguments in the surviving speeches as stray comments reflecting only the amateurism and informality of the system.[7]

This book offers a different account of the aims and ideals of the Athenian courts. Rather than approaching Athenian courts as a homogeneous entity (as most historians have to date), this book focuses on the differences between ordinary cases tried in the Athenian popular courts, on the one hand, and the homicide and maritime cases that were tried in special courts with their own procedures, on the other. The Athenians handled these cases quite differently, and the juxtaposition illuminates a key feature of the Athenian concept of law. Most interestingly, the Athenians understood the desirability of a regular application of abstract principles to particular cases, but made this the dominant ideal only in the homicide and maritime cases.

Popular courts tried the vast majority of trials in the Athenian court system, and they are the focus of modern scholarship on the nature of Athenian litigation. In these cases, litigants regularly discuss matters that are extraneous to the application of the relevant statute to the event in question. For example, popular court litigants

---

[5] Ostwald 1986:497–524; Sealey 1987:146–148. In the fourth century, the Athenians distinguished between general laws passed by a Board of Lawgivers and short-term decrees of the popular Assembly that could not contradict existing laws (Hansen 1999:161–177).

[6] Meyer-Laurin 1965; E. Harris 2000; Meineke 1971. Meyer-Laurin and Meineke argue that Athenian litigants and jurors applied the law strictly, while Harris suggests that the open texture of Athenian law left room for creative statutory interpretation. All three share the view that litigants and jurors considered themselves bound by the law and that the goal of the system approximated modern notions of a rule of law. E. Harris (2000:78 & n. 85), for example, argues that "litigants pay careful attention to substantive issues and questions about the interpretation of law" and jurors "considered themselves bound to adhere to the letter of the law."

[7] E. Harris 1994a:137.

make arguments based on their opponents' actions in the course of the litigation process, or the financial or other effects a conviction would have on the defendant and his innocent family. I argue that these extra-legal arguments were vital to making a case in an Athenian popular court rather than aberrations in an essentially modern legal system. However, the prevalence of extra-legal argumentation does not indicate that the triggering event and legal charge were mere subterfuge in a game aimed at evaluating the relative honor and prestige of the litigants. Rather, both legal and extra-legal argumentation were considered relevant and important to the jury's decision because Athenian juries aimed at reaching a just verdict that took into account the broader context of the dispute and the particular circumstances of the individual case.[8] Even the relative importance of legal and contextual information in any individual case was open to dispute by the litigants.[9]

Homicide and maritime cases, by contrast, followed a perceptibly more formal, legal approach. The homicide courts employed a rule prohibiting statements "outside the issue." A written contract was required to bring a maritime suit, and speeches in this type of case tend to focus more narrowly on the terms of the contract and less on arguments from fairness and the broader context of the dispute than comparable non-maritime commercial cases.

Do the homicide and maritime procedures suggest that Athens was gradually discovering the rule of law, and would have eventually insisted that popular courts resolve disputes based exclusively on the application of set legal principles? The short answer is no. Although maritime procedures were introduced toward the end of the classical period, the more formal homicide procedures were developed sometime *before* the popular courts came into being. The jarring differences in the level of formality between the homicide courts and the popular courts were therefore the product not of progress but of ambivalence. In the spectrum of

---

[8] Of course, some litigants were undoubtedly motivated by a desire to gain honor or to pursue personal enmity. Moreover, I do not doubt that the courts at times functioned in a manner far from the ideal, or that popular court trials may have also served a variety of social or ideological roles in society. I am concerned with the *primary* aim of the popular courts, as it was understood by the majority of the participants. I argue that litigants and jurors by and large considered the purpose of the trial to be the arrival at a just resolution to the dispute. The primary goal was to resolve the specific dispute that gave rise to the litigation, using social context as an instrument toward that end.

[9] My contention that Athenian jurors attempted to reach a "fair" or "just" decision based on the evidence before it rather than strictly applying the laws to the case is in accord with the views expressed by Christ (1998b:195–196); Scafuro (1997:50–66), and Humphreys (1983:248). These scholars do not distinguish between approaches taken in different types of suit.

Athenian approaches to law, we find, in the first legal system we know very much about, the fissure between following generalized rules and doing justice in the particular case that has haunted the law ever since.

The varied approach to the legal process stems from a deep tension in the Athenian system between a desire for flexibility and wide-ranging jury discretion on the one hand, and consistency and predictability on the other. The special rules and procedures of the homicide and maritime courts indicate that the Athenians could imagine (and, to a lesser extent, implement) a legal process in which abstract rules were applied without reference to the social context of the dispute, but rejected such an approach in the vast majority of cases. This choice reflects not only a normative belief that a wide variety of contextual information was often relevant to reaching a just decision, but also a political commitment to maximizing the discretion wielded by popular juries. In other cases, however, such as commercial suits, where the practical importance of predictable verdicts was high, the Athenians employed rules of admissibility and relevance that limited jury discretion. Classical Athens thus provides a valuable case study of a legal system that favored equity and discretion over the strict application of generalized rules, but managed to do so in a way that did not destroy predictability and legal certainty in the parts of the system where it was most needed.

SOURCES AND METHOD

There is no surviving statement of Athenian democratic legal theory. The theoretical texts that we have – principally the works of Plato and Aristotle – are hostile to the democracy and offer little insight into the aims of the court system. We are forced to draw inferences from the structure and practices of the courts themselves. Although the Athenians liked to tell themselves that their legal system and laws were the product of a single intelligence – "the lawgiver" of the distant past – Athenian court procedures developed from a combination of laws passed at different times by the popular assembly and an accumulation of custom and practice. There was, of course, no single, unified vision of the aims of the Athenian courts or procedures.[10] But whatever their hodge-podge origins, the practices

---

[10] It is not my contention that every, or even most, aspects of Athenian law fit into a coherent and logical system. As Christ (1994) points out, viewing Athenian law as a system with a "latent logic" may lead one to underestimate the impact of piecemeal legislation and to overlook the eclecticism of Athenian law.

of the courts constituted an Athenian tradition that reflected a shared under-standing of how justice was and should be done. The Athenian courts can tell us something about the "Athenian mind" that is more than the historian's convenient fiction: the product of many generations and many hands may bear the imprint of the collective more deeply than that of any individual's work; that a group's tradi-tions may be arbitrary in origin does not make them less valuable in assessing the group's peculiar understanding of the world. I am seeking to uncover the values and concerns that seem to underlie the practices and procedures of the Athe-nian courts – values and concerns that the various individual participants in the legal system may have been more or less consciously aware of at any given time.

The Athenian law courts are remarkably well attested, at least by the standards of ancient history: roughly 100 forensic speeches survive from the period between 430 and 323 B.C.E. These speeches represent not an official record of the trial proceedings, but the speech written by a speechwriter (*logographos*) for his client (or, at times, for himself) and later published, in some cases with revisions.[11] Only speeches that were attributed to one of the ten Attic orators later formed into a canon were preserved.[12] The ten Attic orators are: Aeschines (ca. 395–ca. 322); Andocides (ca. 440–ca. 390); Antiphon (ca. 480–411); Demosthenes (384–322); Dinarchus (ca. 360–ca. 290); Hyperides (390–322); Isaeus (ca. 415–ca. 340); Isocrates (436–338); Lycurgus (ca. 390–ca. 324); and Lysias (ca. 445–ca. 380).[13] The speeches in the corpus run the gamut, and are from politically charged treason

Indeed, as we will see, the association of the homicide courts with a more formal, legal approach stems as much from historical accident followed by path dependency as from any "latent logic" related to the nature of the crime of homicide. Nevertheless, the differences between procedures can tell us something about the goals of the Athenian courts.

[11] Demosthenes and Aeschines, for example, both revised their published speeches in the case over the Crown in response to each other's courtroom presentations (Yunis 2001:26–7). On revision for publication more generally, see, e.g., Trevett 1996; Worthington 1991.

[12] See, e.g., Smith 1995; Worthington 1994b:244.

[13] Not all of the "Attic" orators were Athenian citizens; some were resident aliens. For a very brief summary of the life and work of each of the orators, see Gagarin 1998b:xii–xv. It is suspected that several of the speeches in the corpus were written by other, lesser-known classical logographers and falsely attributed to a member of the canon, perhaps by ancient publishers hoping to sell more books. Most scholars agree, for example, that seven of the speeches in the Demosthenic corpus were in fact written by Apollodorus. For discussion of Apollodorus' career and speeches, see Trevett 1992. Since the issues I explore in this book are not affected by the authorship of any individual speech, I use the traditional citation system for the Attic orations and do not mark speeches that I believe are spurious with square brackets.

trials and violent crime trials to inheritance cases and property disputes between neighbors.

Despite their copiousness, these sources are not without their problems. The surviving cases are those in which at least one litigant was wealthy enough to hire a famous logographer, and as a result involve primarily members of the elite.[14] The Attic orations were preserved not as legal documents but as tools for teaching boys and young men the art of rhetoric in the Hellenistic and Roman periods. As a result, the information a legal historian would most like to know about any particular case is generally lost. We almost never have speeches from both sides of a legal contest;[15] we rarely know the outcome of the case. Citations of laws and witness testimony are often omitted or regarded as inauthentic later additions. Most important, any statement we meet in the speeches regarding the law or legal procedures may be a misleading characterization designed to help the litigant's case.[16] As is often pointed out, however, a litigant who wished to be successful would presumably limit himself to statements and arguments that were likely to be accepted by a jury; speakers may at times give us a self-serving account of the law, but their arguments generally remain within the realm of plausible interpretations of the legal situation in question.[17]

In addition to court speeches, the sources for the Athenian legal system include the *Constitution of the Athenians*, a partial history and description of Athenian political and legal institutions probably written by Aristotle or his students. The comic plays of Aristophanes include several references to the law courts; the central character of the comedy *The Wasps* is an elderly Athenian juror. Some laws, most notably Draco's law on homicide, survive in the form of stone inscriptions, but they represent only a tiny percentage of the body of Athenian statutes. The nature of our sources presents not only challenges but also opportunities: from the beginning, the study of Athenian law has been of necessity a study not of law on the books but of law in action.

---

[14] Lysias 24 *For the Invalid* is a notable exception, though some scholars have argued that this speech is merely a rhetorical exercise for a fictional case. It is unclear whether Athenian litigation was dominated by the wealthy, or whether the widespread participation of ordinary Athenians is simply not reflected in the historical record. For a discussion of who litigated in Athens, see Chapter 2.

[15] Only two pairs of speeches survive: Demosthenes 19 and Aeschines 2 (*On the Embassy*); Aeschines 3 and Demosthenes 18 (*On the Crown*). In two other instances we have imperfectly matched speeches on both sides of a particular issue: Lysias 6 and Andocides 1; Demosthenes 43 and Isaeus 11.

[16] On how to deal with apparent outliers in our sources, see Bers 2002.

[17] Dover 1974:8–14.

My approach is, for the most part, synchronic. This approach is dictated by the distribution of our surviving speeches. There is little evidence for the early development of the legal system; the classical court system was fully formed by the time of our earliest preserved orations. With a few important exceptions,[18] the practices and procedures of the courts remained largely unchanged throughout the classical period. It therefore makes sense to treat the popular court system from 430–323 B.C.E. as a single unit for analytical purposes. A synchronic organization also highlights the dynamic tension between different notions of legal process present throughout the classical period.

RELEVANCE AND DISCRETION

In exploring the aims and ideals of the courts, a key focus will be on relevance – that is, notions of what types of information and arguments should be presented to a jury and given weight in reaching a verdict. I refer to information and argumentation in the court speeches that do not bear on the application of the formal charge to the facts of the case as "extra-legal."

In categorizing some types of argumentation as "legal" or "extra-legal" and choosing relevance as my primary focus, I am not using a modern metric foreign to the Athenian mindset. The Athenians were themselves concerned with what sort of information was considered on or off the point (ἐις τὸ πρᾶγμα/ ἔξω τοῦ πράγματος), and employed a relevancy rule prohibiting statements "outside the issue" in the homicide courts. Chapters 3, 4, and 6 explore the distinctive notions of relevance employed in, respectively, the popular courts, homicide courts, and maritime cases. Although I am primarily interested in comparing the approaches to relevance taken by various Athenian courts to each other rather than to modern courts, a brief discussion of modern notions of relevance and admissibility may help to clarify what is at stake in how a society decides to approach this issue.

In contemporary American courts, statutes and/or case law provide for a list of criteria (often called "elements") that must be met for a prosecutor or

---

[18] The two most important changes were the transition from oral to written indictments and witness evidence in the early fourth century and the revision of the laws and law-making process at the end of the fifth century. The Athenians repeatedly tinkered with the system during the fourth century by adding new actions, changing the process of jury selection, etc., but the basic structure and procedures of the popular courts remained unchanged.

plaintiff to prevail under a particular criminal charge or civil cause of action. Any information that tends to make it more likely than not that any of these legal elements are (or are not) present is "relevant" to the case,[19] though some classes of relevant information may be inadmissible because, for example, it is deemed to be overly time consuming or prejudicial.[20] I discuss Athenian notions of evidence that should be presented to a jury as "relevant" rather than "admissible" because Athenian litigants explaining why they are making certain arguments speak in terms of whether the evidence is relevant (literally, on or off the issue or point). In modern courts, much of this extra-legal argumentation is considered relevant but inadmissible.

Of course, determining which information is relevant is not as straightforward as it sounds. How one frames the legal case – how the rich context of lived experience is translated and trimmed to fit into fixed, abstract legal categories – is often crucial to the outcome.[21] In many trials, each party attempts to broaden or narrow the scope of the story the jury is to hear. A battered woman charged with murdering her husband will argue for a "wide-angle"[22] perspective, one that takes in the history of the couple's relationship, while the state will focus on the killing itself.[23] Where the rules of evidence impose restrictions on what is relevant and how a party frames the case, for instance, the federal rule excluding evidence of a rape victim's sexual history,[24] these rules encapsulate more or less explicit value judgments.[25] Beyond this, there is information that lacks even a theoretical connection to factual guilt – such as the charitable activities of a defendant's

---

[19] As is evidence that tends to disprove the opponent's case, as, for example, evidence impeaching the reliability of an opponent's witness.

[20] Rule 403 of the Federal Rules of Evidence, for example, provides: "Although relevant, evidence may be excluded if its probative value is substantially outweighed by the danger of unfair prejudice, confusion of the issues, or misleading the jury, or by considerations of undue delay, waste of time, or needless presentation of cumulative evidence." For a summary of the legal doctrine of relevance and its relation to the "received view" of the modern trial as "the institutional device for the actualization of the Rule of Law," see Burns 1999:21–23.

[21] On the difficulties involved in framing a case, see Frier 1985:214–215; White 1990:179–201, 257–269.

[22] Scheppele 1989:2096.

[23] Armour 1996.

[24] Federal Rules of Evidence, Rule 412.

[25] See Weyrauch (1978:706): "Many judicial references to relevance are substantive dispositions in the guise of rules of evidence"; Scheppele (1989:2097) "standards of legal relevance, appearing to limit the gathering of evidence neutrally to just 'what happened' at the time of 'the trouble' may have the effect of excluding the key materials of outsiders' stories."

parents, a common type of evidence in Athenian courts – that we unquestionably exclude as irrelevant to proving the elements of the legal charge.

In practice, modern trial lawyers are often able to impart to the jury some information that, strictly speaking, is not relevant to proving the charge. Witnesses, for example, are routinely asked at the beginning of their testimony to describe their occupation and home address, information that may improperly influence the jurors' perception of the testimony. In the presentation of evidence concerning the specific event in question, it is inevitable that a fair amount of extraneous material about the milieu of the parties will incidentally be heard by the jury as well. A botched drug deal that ended in violence may look very different to a jury if it involved gang members in an urban housing project rather than college kids meeting a dealer in a motel room. A skillful trial attorney will exploit the flexibility in the rules of evidence to his advantage, and may even be able to suggest surreptitiously in his opening and closing statements that the verdict should hinge on legally irrelevant factors – from the race or class of one of the parties to the relative importance of a money judgment to the family of a poor tort victim as opposed to a wealthy corporate defendant.[26] Even under the most cynical view of modern trial practice, however, contemporary evidence regimes are different from that of ancient Athens in one vital respect: while the Athenians openly recognized the relevance of extra-legal information, in modern courts the law's status as the authoritative rule of decision is certain and arguments based on extra-legal factors are always couched in terms that permit the presiding judge and court of appeals to accept the verdict as the jury's application of the law based solely on the legally relevant evidence presented at trial.[27]

In the Athenian popular courts, there was effectively no rule of relevance limiting litigants to information and arguments related to the legal charge.[28] How "the case" should be framed was precisely what was at issue in many Athenian suits: litigants presented jurors with a wide variety of legal and extra-legal arguments,

---

[26] In a recent book, Burns (1999:29–30, 36–37, 201) makes a detailed case for what courtwatchers have long maintained, namely that in practice there is enough flexibility in the modern American rules of evidence to permit an attorney to argue for a verdict based on extra-legal norms. He argues that in many trials, the jury's task is to decide between a variety of conflicting norms – legal, economic, moral, political, and professional.

[27] Burns 1999:36–37.

[28] Cf. Arist. *Ath.Pol.* 67.1. For discussion, see Chapter 3. Abbreviations of classical texts follow the style of the *Oxford Classical Dictionary* (2d edition).

and it was up to the jury to decide which types of information were most important in reaching a just outcome to the particular case. The result was a highly flexible – but also highly unpredictable – ad hoc system that permitted litigants to describe the dispute in their own voice and on their own terms. Of course, litigants (and their speechwriters) were limited by the expectations of the jurors; we will see that even in the absence of a rule of relevance, several types of argument recur, indicating that speechwriters believed that jurors would find these arguments persuasive. It is therefore possible to speak of broad categories of evidence that were considered particularly relevant in the popular courts. Nevertheless, litigants could choose from a variety of legal and extra-legal arguments within these broad categories and had much more flexibility in telling their stories than modern litigants.

One example may help to illustrate how the Athenian conception of relevance in the popular courts altered the nature of the jurors' task. The Athenian popular courts drew no distinction between evidence relevant to guilt and evidence relevant to sentencing. Unlike the practice generally employed in American courts of withholding from the trial jury information about the likely penalty and arguments regarding the appropriate sentence, Athenian litigants at trial regularly discuss potential penalties and make what a modern would regard as sentencing arguments – from comments about the defendant's character and prior record to appeals for mercy and discussion of the disastrous financial consequences a conviction would have on the defendant's innocent family. The trial verdict thus encompassed much more than a decision as to factual guilt, as the jury considered, as part of their decision at the guilt stage, whether the likely penalty was justified in light of the circumstances of the offense, the character of the offender, and the effects of the penalty on the offender, his family, and society. Arguments relating to the application of the relevant statute were no more authoritative than information regarding the concrete effects a conviction would have on the offender, and the relative weight to be accorded to the various types of extra-legal or legal argument presented in each case was left to the discretion of the jury.

This unusual approach to relevance was not the only example of the Athenian system's extraordinary flexibility. In designing a legal system, all societies must address the inevitable tension between consistency and flexibility. A legal system's flexibility can be enhanced or limited by adjusting one of three elements: the precision of the rules; the definition of relevance; and the degree of discretion extended to the state prosecutor (where there is one), the judge, or jury (including the provision for appeal). We will see that in all three respects the Athenian popular courts favored flexibility to a remarkable degree. Athens thus offers an example of a sophisticated system that managed to function and maintain legitimacy without relying on the regular application of generalized rules, but rather employed a highly discretionary form of justice.[29]

PLAN OF THE BOOK

Chapter 2 provides non-specialist readers with a general introduction to the history of Athenian democracy and a sketch of Athenian society, with particular emphasis on the moral values and obligations of citizens. Because Athenian jurors in the popular courts made highly individualized, ad hoc decisions, I do not attempt to describe a "substantive law" of Athens. Nonetheless, although popular court jurors operated without general, authoritative rules of decision, in reaching a verdict they drew upon commonly shared norms and values. The discussion of these values is intended to help the reader better understand the various legal and extra-legal arguments to which Athenian litigants appeal as we encounter them in this study. Chapter 2 also introduces the institutions, structure, and procedures of the classical Athenian legal system.

Chapter 3 examines the broad notion of relevance employed in the popular courts. Three categories of extra-legal argumentation were commonly used in our surviving speeches: discussion of the broader background and context of the dispute, including the past relationship and interaction between the parties and their approach to litigation and settlement; defense appeals to the jury's pity based on the harmful effects of an adverse verdict; and arguments based on the character of the parties. I argue that both extra-legal and legal argumentation were considered relevant and important to the jury's decision because Athenian juries sought to reach a just verdict taking into account the particular circumstances of the individual case.

Chapter 4 focuses on the homicide courts, which served as a notional antithesis to the flexible approach of the popular courts. I argue that the unusual procedures of these courts, particularly a rule prohibiting irrelevant statements, made these courts (in theory, and, to a lesser extent, in practice) more congenial to formal legal

---

[29] Ad hoc legal systems, such as those in a variety of traditional societies, generally draw their legitimacy from the reputation of the judge for legal expertise or wisdom. For the various ways in which the Athenian courts maintained legitimacy in the absence of expert judges, see Chapter 5.

argument. I examine in detail the evidence for the real and perceived differences between the homicide and popular courts with respect to composition, legal argumentation, and the approach to relevance. The chapter goes on to address two more general questions: (1) why were homicide cases treated differently? and (2) what do these differences reveal about the Athenian conception of judicial process? I argue that it is the peculiar development of homicide law in the archaic period, not a sense that homicide was more serious or in some way different from other charges, that accounts for the unusual character of the homicide courts in the classical period.[30] The unusual homicide procedures suggest that the Athenians were capable of imagining a more formal legal approach, but reserved this austere approach for only a tiny minority of cases. At the same time, the idealization of the homicide courts indicates anxiety over the dangers of broad notions of relevance and wide-ranging jury discretion in the popular courts, particularly the potential misuse of character evidence.

Chapter 5 explores another source of ambivalence, namely the inevitable reduction in legal consistency and predictability that accompanies an ad hoc system like the one developed in Athens. Legal insecurity increased the risk and cost of many private transactions because men could not confidently conform their conduct to the law. Nevertheless, a variety of mechanisms, from informal means of social control to elaborate legal fictions, permitted the system to function and maintain authority. I also describe a short-lived attempt to foster enhanced consistency and predictability – the legal reforms at the end of the fifth century. Chapters 4 and 5 thus illustrate the two disadvantages inherent in any legal system that favors context and flexibility: (1) the possibility of verdicts based on prejudice and motives completely unrelated to the issue in dispute, and (2) reduced consistency and predictability.

In Chapter 6, I discuss the special procedures used for maritime cases beginning in the middle of the fourth century. A written contract was required to bring a maritime suit, and speeches in this type of case tend to focus more narrowly on the contractual dispute and less on the character of the litigants than similar non-maritime commercial cases. I argue that these differences stem from a need to facilitate trade by offering a predictable procedure for enforcing contracts, and thereby to attract foreign merchants to Athens. Further, in judging claims of

---

[30] The homicide courts do, however, appear to have a distinctive religious coloring. For discussion, see Chapter 4.

non-citizens, who made up a significant portion of the litigants in maritime cases, Athenian jurors would be less eager to look beyond the terms of the contract to enforce social norms of fair dealing and good conduct. In this one area of the law, the costs associated with flexible justice outweighed the benefits, and steps were taken to narrow the range of evidence considered relevant to the jury in an effort to enhance the predictability of verdicts.

In Chapter 7, I offer some suggestions about why the Athenians favored a contextual approach to justice. Athens' political structure as a direct, participatory democracy was paramount. The flexible approach benefited the poor citizens who formed the dominant political constituency of the democracy,[31] and promoted popular decision-making by granting juries maximum discretion in reaching their verdicts. The picture that I hope emerges from this study is that Athenian justice was no less purposefully democratic than its politics. That it can seem amateurish or alien to us is a measure of the degree to which modern "democracies" have abandoned popular decision-making with hardly a look back.

---

[31] As discussed in Chapter 2, the Athenian "poor" (*penêtes*) included not just the destitute but anyone who had to work for a living, a majority of Athenian citizens.

2
ATHENS AND ITS LEGAL SYSTEM

HISTORICAL BACKGROUND

Although we cannot trace the beginnings of Athenian democracy with any confidence in the details, the general trend is clear. Over time, ordinary men, neither well-born nor rich, acquired political power that culminated in a democracy more direct and more radical than any the world has known. Democratic rule was manifest throughout the city's governance, but nowhere did it carry greater weight than in its courts. What follows is a brief sketch of the historical development of this extraordinary democratic system from the late seventh century B.C.E. to the fourth century, the era in which the judicial system is most richly documented.[1]

In the earliest period for which we have some sort of historical evidence, a group of aristocratic families, the *eupatridai* (literally, those descended from good fathers) enjoyed a monopoly on the political offices known as archonships. Men who had served as archons became life members of the Council on Ares' Hill, or, to use the standard term, the Areopagus. We have only late and controversial evidence for the nature and extent of the Areopagus' powers in this period. It is also likely that there was some form in which popular will could find expression, an assembly, perhaps convened at moments of crisis, of those ordinary men who constituted the Athenian army. But it does seem that in the informal and decentralized politics of the nascent city, domination by the well born was the general rule until some time after the first half of the seventh century. As in other parts of archaic Greece, Athens saw the rise of groups outside the nobility now demanding a greater share in political power by virtue of their wealth and military contributions.

Athens' legal history might be said to begin with Draco's lawcode of 621/0 B.C.E., evidently a response to the violence that erupted after an aristocrat's attempt to make himself tyrant at Athens. Only fragments of the law on homicide survive, preserved verbatim on stone inscribed in the late fifth century. This law appears to mark the first step in the shift in emphasis from self-help to legal sanctions. It

---

[1] Important treatments of the topics discussed here in cursory form include Andrewes 1963; Osborne 1996; Murray 1993; Ober 1990:53–103; Wallace 1989; Gagarin 1981a, 1986; Carawan 1998; Hansen 1999; Anderson 2003; Ruschenbusch 1966.

has long been assumed that the Areopagus had jurisdiction in homicide cases, but even that is neither well attested nor beyond controversy. We can only guess about the venue for the adjudication of other legal disputes in this period – assuming that these disputes came before any judge or judges.

During the tenure of the lawgiver Solon, the center of political power began to shift from the well born to the well heeled. Although a fourth-century Athenian would probably not hesitate to refer to the body of Athenian law as "Solon's code," this would at best be a vast oversimplification. If we can trust the only surviving continuous narrative of the city's political development, the *Constitution of the Athenians*, Solon was appointed archon with extraordinary powers in 594/3 to resolve a severe economic and political crisis. His acts included the establishment of wealth qualifications, designated in bushels of grain, for holding various offices. By implication, membership in one of the *eupatrid* families was now irrelevant for political office. In the judicial sphere, Solon introduced two reforms of great significance: the provision for "appeal to the lawcourt," presumably from the decision of a magistrate, and the right of any man to bring a lawsuit on behalf of another, a reform likely designed to enhance access to justice for the less powerful. Many scholars believe that "the law court" referred to in the *Constitution of the Athenians* was the assembly of male citizens sitting as a judicial body.

Far from accepting the Solonian reforms, the *eupatridai* resisted with such vigor that no archon was elected in the year 590/89 and 586/5, "anarchy" in its literal sense. Peisistratus, a member of an aristocratic clan, succeeded in establishing himself and his family as tyrants, though he maintained the outward formality of the constitution already in place. His one known contribution to the legal system was the institution of a system of circuit judges who traveled to rural areas of Attica, the large territory outside the urban center of Athens, to decide disputes. This step not only expanded the role of the formal legal system in Athenian social life, but persisted in the form of "deme judges" empowered to decide minor disputes in the fourth century.

Without question, the single most important figure in the formation of the Athenian democracy was Cleisthenes. His reorganization of Attica in the last decade of the sixth century both consolidated the political entity known as Athens and made possible the wide scale and regular involvement of ordinary citizens in its governance. Under the reorganization, the "deme," the smallest political unit and roughly equivalent in rural areas to a village, supplied representatives chosen by lot for the Council of 500, the legislative body that prepared the agenda for the Assembly. Each deme was assigned to one of ten tribes. These tribes, each of which included demes from disparate geographical areas, in turn rotated in service as the executive committee of the Council. In this way, the reforms both insured widespread participation and weakened the political influence of local "big men." Remarkably enough, we have no specific evidence relating to the judicial system in this period of political upheaval and restructuring. Still, it is difficult to imagine that the popular court system of the classical period could have arisen before this profound shift toward democratic rule. It is not possible to assign a date to the creation of the popular courts as we find them in the classical period, but the Cleisthenic revolution must be considered a terminus post quem.

In 490 and again in 480, Athens led the Greek city-states in repelling the advance of the Persian empire. Land and sea victories in the Persian wars and their aftermath raised the stock of ordinary soldiers and sailors, who returned from their experiences with an enhanced sense of their importance to the city and hence their right to political power. Moreover, the vigor of democratic sentiment was likely increased by the pointed contrast between Greek freedom and the despotism of Persia, an empire in which all men were slaves save one, as Aeschylus puts it in his tragedy the *Persians*.

Despite these democratizing trends, the Areopagus, evidently still a conservative body, enjoyed a position of prominence, even acquiring some new powers (the sources provide no details) for some seventeen years after the conclusion of the Persian Wars. In 462/1 the radical politician Ephialtes conducted an attack on the Areopagus, stripping it of all powers other than the adjudication of homicide cases and supervision of some religious matters.

Athenian leadership in the Greek alliance against Persia, originally shared with Sparta, evolved into the Athenian empire in the mid-fifth century. This had two consequences especially important to the legal system. Some lawsuits originating in the subject cities were required to be heard in Athens, increasing the business of the courts. More important, the tribute received from subjects made it easier to introduce pay for jury service, a step attributed to Pericles, the city's leading politician and general. Although our sources provide no description of the legal system in the Periclean age, it seems likely that by this time the courts had taken on the forms and procedures seen in the surviving court speeches.

For my purposes here, Athens' subsequent history can be quickly summarized. In 404, Athens lost a decades-long struggle with Sparta, and with it its empire and economic supremacy. The city experienced two short-lived oligarchic revolutions in 411 and 404, after which the democracy was restored. These coups d'état provoked a revision of the lawcode of uncertain scope and enduring effect.[2] There was also a specific reform that introduced a distinction between decrees (*psêphismata*) enacted by the Assembly, and laws (*nomoi*) which required confirmation by a separate body drawn from the same pool as the jurors. Some scholars view this limitation on the legislative authority of the Assembly as evidence for a significant shift from the radical, direct democracy of the fifth century to a more moderate form of government. In any event, after these reforms, the city's legal and political institutions experienced only minor changes until Athens' capitulation to the Macedonians in 322/1 and the resulting dismantling of the democracy.

ATHENIAN SOCIETY

Although small by modern standards, Athens was the most populous of the classical Greek city-states, with a total population numbering in the hundreds of thousands. Athens' territory of approximately 900 square miles included rural villages, small towns, a cosmopolitan port known as the Piraeus, and, of course, the teeming city that served as the political, commercial, social, and religious center of the polis. What united this diverse collection of human settlements was citizenship, a hereditary status[3] that conferred (on men) the right to own land and to participate in the democracy as well as the duty of military service.

But citizens accounted for only a small portion of the total population of Athens. Metics were either manumitted slaves or freeborn foreigners living in Athens,[4] generally as craftsmen, traders, or businessmen. Athens relied on trade to bring in vital items such as grain and timber, and also to generate import and export taxes, yet the majority of those involved in trade were metics and

---

[2] These reforms are discussed in more detail in Chapter 5.

[3] Pericles' citizenship law of 451 B.C.E. limited citizenship to those with two citizen parents. In practice, entry into the citizenship rolls may have been more fluid and flexible (Scafuro 1994; E. Cohen 2000:79–103). In the fourth century, the Assembly could grant citizenship rights to particular individuals, though this seems to have been rare. We know of only 64 such grants of citizenship, and many were merely honorary statements of gratitude to foreign dignitaries who had no plans to exercise their newly granted citizenship rights (Hansen 1999:94–95).

[4] It seems likely that a foreigner was obliged to register as a metic (and pay the metic tax) once he had spent a short time – perhaps one month – living in Athens. For discussion of the evidence, see Whitehead 1977:7–10; Hansen 1999:117.

foreigners.[5] Despite their importance to the Athenian economy, metic status was not a privilege. Metics were required to have an Athenian citizen as a sponsor (*prostatês*), to pay a monthly tax, and to serve in the military, but were not permitted to exercise political rights, to own real property, or to marry a citizen, and had more limited legal rights than citizens.[6] Despite the legal and political liabilities of metics, not all these men were considered to be of a lower class or status than citizens.[7] One of the richest men in Athens was Pasion the banker, an ex-slave who spent much of his life as a metic before being granted citizenship.[8] Moreover, Athens' exclusive aristocratic clubs (*hetaireiai*) were known to admit metics.[9]

Slaves occupied the bottom rung of Athenian society. Regarded as the property of their masters, Athenian slaves were generally not bred locally but were captives of war or victims of piracy sold to Athenians by slave traders.[10] Prices were low enough that slaveholding was widespread even among citizens with small plots of land. Slaves' lifestyles could vary considerably. The majority worked the land or in their master's house or workshop. The least fortunate toiled in the silver mines and the most fortunate worked as skilled craftsmen or bankers and enjoyed de facto independence.

The numbers of citizens, metics, and slaves in classical Athens can only be guessed at from a census taken in 317 B.C.E., after the fall of the democracy, and from sporadic statements in our earlier sources providing estimates of troop strengths or the adult male citizen population. In the fourth century, the adult male

---

[5] Although metics and aliens comprised the majority of those involved in foreign trade, wealthy citizens did finance trade on occasion (e.g., Isoc. 7.32), and there are examples of citizen *emporoi* ("traders") and *nauklêroi* ("ship owners" or "ship captains") (e.g., Xen. *Mem.* 3.7.6; Lys. 6.19,49). For discussion, see Isager & Hansen 1975:70–74.

[6] The role of the *prostatês* is unclear (see, e.g., Whitehead 1977:90–91; Hansen 1999:117–118). On metic military service, see Thuc. 2.13.7; Whitehead 1977:82–86. Individual metics could be granted a special exemption from the ban on owning land through *enktêsis*, or could be relieved from the requirement of the monthly tax through *isotelia* (Hansen 1999:97, 118–119). The legal rights of metics are discussed later on in this chapter.

[7] Hansen 1999:86–87.

[8] Dem. 36.48; 59.2. On Pasion's banking career, see E. Cohen 1992:81–82; Isager & Hansen 1975:177–191.

[9] Pl. *Resp.*, 328b, discussed in Hansen 1999:87.

[10] On the import of slaves, see Isager & Hansen 1975:31–33; Garlan 1988:45–55; Hansen 1999:122–123. Alan Boegehold points out to me that a significant number of slaves may have been exposed (Athenian) babies.

citizen population was perhaps 30,000, the total citizen population approximately 100,000.[11] The numbers of metics and slaves are much less certain and are likely to have fluctuated at different times over the course of our period depending on the economic and political circumstances. Hansen's estimate of 40,000 metics, somewhere in the range of 150,000 slaves, and a total population of close to 300,000 seems reasonable.[12]

Farming was the occupation of choice for Athenian citizens. Other pursuits such as trade or manufacture were considered dishonorable, at least in the elite circles represented by our literary sources. For any citizen, however poor, to work for another man was distasteful, and far inferior to struggling to support oneself on a tiny plot of land. Perhaps for this reason, there were, in addition to large estates that produced olives, wine, and barley for sale, a significant number of small plots aimed primarily at feeding the owner's household.[13] Due to the dry climate, true self-sufficiency was rarely attainable, and it seems likely that even small farmers would often have to go to the city (or one of the smaller regional markets) to exchange their wine and olives for grain and other necessities. Of course, not all Athenians lived up to the agrarian ideal. Some citizens operated small craft workshops. Poor citizens without any land could eke out a living from a combination of seasonal farm work, off-season building projects in the city, wages for jury duty or attendance in the assembly, and wages for serving as a rower in the navy. Social security, in the form of a small daily payment, was available for the infirm and utterly destitute.[14]

Thus despite the political equality of all citizens, there were vast differences in economic wealth and social status. Ancient sources usually speak in terms of two economic classes: the rich (*plousioi* or, without the negative connotation often carried by that term, *hoi chrêmata echontes*, "those with [substantial] property"), which in most cases denoted men in the leisure class, and, second, the much larger class of "the poor" (*penêtes*), which had a broader meaning than the modern term and included anyone who had to work for a living.[15] Although any notion of

---

[11] Hansen 1999:90–93.

[12] Hansen 1999:90–94.

[13] On the prevalence of small farmers and their importance to the city as hoplite warriors, see Hanson 1998:206.

[14] Lys. 24.

[15] For a fuller discussion of these terms, see Ober 1990:194–196; Boegehold 1999:88–90. The wretchedly poor, those close to starvation, were termed *ptôchoi*. In most cases the *penês* was a self-employed farmer

class interest or solidarity was most probably limited to these two groups,[16] there were myriad finer distinctions in Athenian society. Particularly prominent was the division used to distinguish between citizens' roles in the military. The poorest citizens served in the navy or as light-armed troops, whereas men with enough money to buy a suit of heavy armor and a slave to accompany them into battle served as hoplite infantrymen. The wealthiest citizens rode in the cavalry. Within the upper class, additional distinction was reserved for those wealthy enough to be subject to the property tax and to be required to perform public services known as liturgies, such as personally paying for the upkeep of a naval ship or for the performance of a drama at a public festival. Although elite Athenian writers expressed concern that the non-elite majority would use its political power to effect a radical redistribution of wealth, these fears never came to fruition and the direct democracy remained remarkably stable despite the economic diversity among its voting citizens.[17]

Athenian life revolved around a complex network of overlapping relationships and obligations. The fundamental unit was the *oikos* ("household"). The oldest man in the family (or, in some cases, his adult son) acted as head of the household (*kurios*), controlling all the household property and serving as guardian for the women and minor males in the family.[18] Although the *kurios* had the power to dispose of the family wealth as he wished, there was a strong ideological preference for preserving the ancestral property intact for future generations,[19] and it seems that the *kurios* could even be prosecuted for dissipating his patrimony.[20] Male children, in turn, were obliged to support their elderly parents, give them a proper burial, and maintain the family cult.[21] In addition to members of one's *oikos* and larger kin group, neighbors played an important role in an Athenian's social life, particularly in rural areas. Because villages or small towns were far more common

---

or craftsman. For this reason, traditional Marxist categories cannot be easily applied to the Athenian situation.

[16] On the absence of a notion of a "middle class" in Athens, see Ober 1990:27–30.

[17] Aside from the two very brief oligarchic revolutions in 411 and 404 B.C.E., the democracy remained intact from the beginning of the fifth century until the city was defeated by the Macedonians. For discussion of how class tensions were mediated in the Athenian democracy, see Ober 1990:192–247.

[18] Hunter 1994:9–42; Foxhall 1989; MacDowell 1989a.

[19] E.g. Aesch. 1.95–105. For discussion, see Todd 1993:246.

[20] We know of no examples of cases where these procedures – the *graphê argias* and *graphê paranoias* – were used (Todd 1993:245).

[21] Aesch. 1.28–32; Andoc. 1.74.

than isolated farmsteads,[22] frequent interaction with neighbors was unavoidable. Reciprocal kindnesses and aid in times of shortage and emergencies were expected, and, indeed, neighbors often sought out and obtained no-interest friendly loans (*eranos* loans) from each other rather than approaching formal money lenders.[23]

Perhaps the most important site of political and social identity was the deme, the basic unit in the classical political system. Each of the 139 demes of Attica was a local community – often a village, though some were much larger than that – from which representatives for the Council, the executive body for the popular Assembly, were chosen.[24] Each deme had its own local assembly, magistrates, religious cults, and festivals, and handled the enrollment of local youths into citizenship. Isaeus *Against the Demesman* suggests that a special bond existed between demesmen:

> The most distressful thing of all has happened to me. I have been wronged
> by fellow demesmen, whose theft is not easy to overlook, but on the other
> hand it is unpleasant to hate them – men with whom I must sacrifice and
> share in social interactions.[25]

Indeed, an Athenian citizen's full name included not only his own name and the name of his father, but also the name of his deme. Because deme membership was hereditary, those who had moved away probably did not have quite the same level of deme identity and loyalty that those who lived in the close-knit deme community would have. Even for these citizens, however, polis-wide activities were arranged through their original deme: in addition to representation in the Council, military units were organized by deme,[26] as were the tickets and seating for city-wide religious festivals.[27]

---

[22] Osborne 1985b:190–195; cf. Roy 1988.

[23] For example, neighbors relied on each other for help in emergencies (Ar. *Nub.* 1322; *Thesm.* 241; Dem. 53.6–7), loans of household goods (Dem. 53.4; Theophr. *Char.*, passim), and testimony in legal cases (e.g., Dem. 47.60–1; Is. 3.13–15; Lyc. 1.19–20). For discussion of neighborly relations, including the practice of *eranos* loans, see Millett 1991:109–26, 139–148. On the complementary support functions served by kin and neighbors, see Osborne 1985b:127–153.

[24] On all aspects of deme life and identity, see Osborne, 1985b; Whitehead 1986.

[25] Is. fr. 4 (Thalheim). Deme loyalty is further suggested by the statement in the *Ath. Pol.* (27.3) that Cimon offered free meals not to all Athenian citizens but only to his fellow demesmen.

[26] E.g., Lys. 16.14; Theophr. *Char.* 25.

[27] Moreover, Osborne (1985b:147–153) points out that citizens who moved to the city or who owned property in demes other than their own usually also retained property in their original deme and thus some ties to that community.

Although residents (and perhaps even non-resident members) of rural demes likely identified first and foremost with the members of their local deme community, many Athenians probably also had regular contact with the city center. Athenians were accustomed to traveling long distances in a single day,[28] and even members of demes several miles away from Athens likely visited the city often to serve on a jury, attend the Assembly or theater, participate in religious festivals, or sell their produce and buy grain and other goods. In Theophrastus' sketch of a rural man (the *agroikos*) in the *Characters*, for example, the *agroikos* travels from his rural deme to the city on one occasion to attend the Assembly, and on another to get his hair cut, go to the baths, get his shoes fixed, and buy some fish.[29]

Athenian religion[30] differed from most modern religions in that it was not associated with a creed or fixed belief system. The gods demanded recognition through sacrifice and other ritual acts, but did not provide commandments or a moral code of conduct. Perhaps because Athenian religion focused on deeds rather than beliefs or morality, most priests were chosen by lot or through membership in certain aristocratic families and had no special vocation. The state, at the level of both the polis and the deme, sponsored regular sacrifices and large public festivals in honor of the gods. Major public festivals involved women, metics, and slaves as well as male citizens and included, over the course of several days, sacrifices, long processions, and musical and dramatic contests. Phratries, which were traditional kinship groups, also carried out religious functions and hosted festivals. Families had their own cults as well, and private sacrifice and ritual played an important role in everyday life.

In the classical period, Athenian moral values derived not from religious teachings per se but from tradition. The practices and moral beliefs of the ancestors were given deference and respect. The archonship of Solon in 594/3 B.C.E. stood out as a defining moment in the definition of Athenian values; Solon's laws and poetry were often used in the classical period as a source of moral and ethical precepts. This is not to say that Athenian moral values were completely static. Orators in the Assembly or law courts advancing new moral or policy arguments shamelessly cloaked their ideas in the mantle of the ancestors, Solon,

---

[28] Hansen 1999:60.
[29] Theophr. *Char.* 4.
[30] For a recent treatment see Parker 1996b.

the "ancestral constitution," or a fictional archaic lawgiver.[31] And, we will see below that the gradual shift from an emphasis on heroic values to cooperative values that accompanied the creation of the polis continued during the classical period.

How were society's values expressed and communicated? There was no state educational system, and boys who could afford private education typically received instruction limited to literacy,[32] music, and physical training. In the classical period, young men could take lessons more directly related to moral and political philosophy, most notoriously from the sophists, but these courses and their often iconoclastic teachings were limited to the elite and had little effect on popular morality.[33] Athenian popular values were communicated and reinforced primarily through political and cultural gatherings. When Athens was at war – which, in our period, was most of the time – a politician delivered an annual funeral oration in honor of the war dead. These orations normally incorporated references to Athenian cultural values, often contrasted with those of other city-states.[34] Some symbolic features of state festivals, public architecture, and dedications communicated important values. The honoring of war orphans as part of the introductory ceremony at the dramatic festival of Dionysia, for example, emphasized the city's gratitude for those who showed courage in war and sacrificed themselves for the state.[35] Tragic theater, of course, had much to say on the moral issues of the day, though gleaning a straightforward and consistent ethical message from these plays was probably just as difficult for the Athenian audience as it is for us. Finally, popular values were publicly contested and negotiated in debates before the Assembly and speeches before the law courts.[36]

---

[31] Thomas 1994:119–133; Hansen 1999:296–300.

[32] Reading was not without its moral teachings, of course, as advanced boys would memorize and recite Homer and other poetry.

[33] Absent popular misconceptions of sophistic teaching, the caricature of Socrates in Aristophanes' *Clouds* would not have worked as comedic material. In his *Apology* of Socrates, Plato argues that the stereotype of an intellectual was an important, perhaps crucial, element in the vote to convict.

[34] For discussion, see Loraux 1986.

[35] Goldhill 1990:97–129.

[36] For a discussion of how popular values were constructed and negotiated through public speech, see Ober 1990. Although the moral views expressed in surviving Assembly and law court speeches are designed to support the speaker's position, these self-serving arguments are nevertheless revealing because speakers presumably would not appeal to moral values not shared by the majority of the audience. For discussion of the use of oratory as a source for popular morality, see Dover 1974:13–14.

ATHENIAN MORAL VALUES

Popular court jurors did not reach a verdict by applying precise legal rules. Rather, they drew on commonly shared norms and values to reach a "just" decision in each case. In this section I briefly discuss some of the Athenian norms and values that were particularly important to legal argument and juror decision making. My aim is not to provide a comprehensive survey of Athenian popular moral values,[37] but rather to give a sketch of the "ethical baggage" Athenian jurors brought to their task.

Because much of our evidence for Athenian popular values comes from law court speeches, it is impossible to say with certainty whether the moral values expressed in court differed from, reflected, and/or helped shape the moral values that governed the Athenian street. However, the absence of a technical legal language or narrowly defined legal rules, the inclusive approach to relevance, and the participation of amateurs as speakers and jurors suggest that the values expressed in the courts were not substantially different from those held in society at large.[38] Nevertheless, the courts constituted a distinct institution, with their own procedures and social practices, and litigants certainly altered their arguments, rhetoric, and style somewhat to accommodate the expectations of the jurors.[39] Athenian litigation was, as one scholar points out, a "semiautonomous field,"[40] whose distinctive practices reflected, were influenced by and (most likely, also influenced) society at large.

For our purposes, what is important is that the moral values expressed in our sources − legal and otherwise − suggest that Athenian jurors' sense of justice and fairness reflected democratic cooperative values.[41] I first address the values of reciprocity, *philia* ("friendship") and fair dealing that animated Athenian society. I then discuss the scholarly debate over the relative importance of honor, revenge, and shame in classical Athenian culture, and argue that these values were moderated

---

[37] Dover's *Greek Popular Morality* (Dover 1974) does just that.

[38] For a discussion of the continuity between the legal system and Athenian society at large, see Carey 1994a.

[39] The most striking example of the different conventions of speech in and out of court is the avoidance of mentioning the names of respectable women in court to avoid dishonoring them (Schaps 1977). For discussion of stylistic differences between forensic and everyday speech, see Bers 1998. For a general discussion of the relationship between court and society, see Johnstone 1999:126–131.

[40] Johnstone 1999:126.

[41] Adkins 1975:172ff.

to a significant degree by norms of self-restraint, willingness to compromise, and obedience to individual conscience.

One of the basic values of Athenian social life was the principal of reciprocity. The notion of reciprocity was central to man's relationship with the gods: one offered prayers and sacrifices to the gods in the hope that they would requite these acts with suitable favors. When translated into the realm of human affairs, this idea of tit for tat could be mobilized in the service of both socially cooperative and socially disruptive ends; the value of reciprocity is sometimes expressed as giving each man his due or treating others as you would like to be treated,[42] sometimes as helping one's friends and harming one's enemies.[43] In the classical period, reciprocity, along with the concept of *philia*, resulted in social norms that encouraged cooperation in local Athenian communities. *Philia* does not correspond to modern ideas of friendship. It encompassed a variety of relationships, including (from strongest to weakest) immediate family, kin, friend, neighbor, demesman, and even fellow citizen, and included the reciprocal duties and obligations that accompanied each of these relations and differed according to the strength of the relational tie.[44] One was expected to offer assistance in times of emergency or shortage to those with whom one shared a bond of *philia*.[45] *Philia* relationships worked on a theory of generalized rather than specific reciprocity: because *philoi* generally interacted in a variety of spheres and had long-term relationships, it was understood that there was no need for immediate and exact repayment because any imbalance in services would eventually even itself out.[46]

At least, this was the ideal. In practice, relationships with kin, neighbors, and demesmen could at times deteriorate into enmity.[47] Reciprocity norms do not, however, seem to have resulted in the social disorder that one might expect from the slogan "harming one's enemies." Vendetta and feuds of the type familiar in other Mediterranean societies were unknown, and violence relatively rare.[48] This

---

[42] E.g., Pl. *Resp.* 331A; Ar. *Plut.* 1028f; Dem. 18.112; 23.106–107; Lyc. 1.88.

[43] E.g., Pl. *Resp.* 332A; Lys. 9.20.

[44] For a discussion of *philia*, see Arist. *Eth. Nic.* 1165a14–35; Millett 1991:110–114; Konstan 1997:53–59.

[45] E.g., Dem. 53.4; Din. 2.9; Ar. *Nub.* 1214, 1322; Xen. *Mem.* II.2.12.

[46] On the operation of "generalized reciprocity" in Athens, see Millett 1991:110–111.

[47] Such disputes are the subject of several law court speeches, including, for example, the inheritance speeches of Isaeus, and Demosthenes 53 and 57.

[48] Perhaps most notable is the fact that Athenians did not customarily arm themselves (Thuc. 1.5.3–6.3) or require private entourages of the sort familiar in Republican Rome (Herman 1994).

was due in part to the channeling of social conflict from the streets to the courts, and in part to cooperative values, discussed in more detail below, that encouraged self-restraint and compromise, even in the face of provocation by one's enemy.

Honesty and fair dealing were considered important components of *dikaiosynê* ("justice"), one of the primary Athenian virtues.[49] The discussion of *dikaiosynê* in the *Republic* makes clear that this concept is conventionally regarded as encompassing repayment of debts, payment according to a contract, promise, or obligation, safekeeping of money or property of another, and honesty in transactions.[50] Telling lies in the agora was proscribed by law,[51] and, in our surviving law court speeches, trickery and attempts to avoid making good on a business promise are represented as serious breaches of community values.[52]

To a modern, it may seem entirely natural that the Athenians had a notion that pursuit of one's personal advantage must be tempered by cooperative norms of fair dealing. But this was not always the case. In the Homeric poems (particularly in the figure of Odysseus), trickery, lying, and relentless pursuit of advantage were not necessarily to be deplored. As Adkins points out, the term *aischron* (disgraceful) began to be regularly associated with trickery and deception only in the late fifth century.[53] To cite one example of the new emphasis on fair dealing, in Sophocles' *Philoctetes*, Neoptolemus, coached by Odysseus, tricks Philoctetes into relinquishing his bow, the weapon needed to defeat Troy. But later, Neoptolemus insists on returning the bow on the grounds that it had been obtained unjustly. We would be very surprised to meet such a statement in Homer. The increasing emphasis on honesty and fair dealing apparent in fifth-century texts are but two examples of a cooperative ethics favored by the classical democratic polis.[54] The traditional explanation for this shift in moral values focuses on the development of

---

[49] The other principal virtues described by Plato in the *Republic* and the *Phaedo* are *sôphrosynê* (restraint), *andreia* (manliness), and *phronêsis* (practical widsom).

[50] Pl. *Resp.* 331C. For discussion, with further references, see Dover 1974:170–173.

[51] Hyp. 3.14.

[52] E.g., Hyp. 3; Dem. 35.17–25; 37.15; 49.1,2,4,27,54. For discussion of litigants' appeal to principles of trust and fair dealing, see Christ 1998b:180–191.

[53] Adkins 1975:172ff.

[54] To be sure, notions of community values are not entirely absent in Homer. The degree and quality of the difference cannot be comprehensively summarized in a few sentences, in part because the Homeric poems are no simple reflection of one time or place. The ethics of the *Dolôneia* represents one extreme; the society of the Phaetians, when prompted to adhere to a higher standard, represents the other. For an account that argues for an awareness of community values in Homer, see Raaflaub 1997.

hoplite warfare and the resulting dependence of the polis on men of what we might think of as a landed middle class.[55] Men who were not members of the aristocracy but had enough money to outfit themselves in hoplite armor became vital to the defense of the city and demanded enhanced political and social power and recognition. The tactics of hoplite warfare, which consisted of a close formation in which each man depended on his neighbor's shield for protection, left little opportunity for individual feats of valor. With power now dispersed among more men and the need for cooperation largely supplanting the traditional heroic values of honor, pursuit of individual advantage and loyalty to the local aristocratic clan became far less important than they once were.

Pertinent to an analysis of Greek moral sensibilities is the application of the shame/guilt dichotomy, borrowed from anthropology,[56] to Greek culture. Some scholars see classical Athenian culture as driven primarily by the linked considerations of honor, revenge, and shame.[57] Under this interpretation, Athenian social relations primarily involved competition for honor and status, which were defined purely in terms of how one was perceived by the outside world. Because honor was a zero-sum game, it often involved attempting to take advantage of the weakness of rivals to enhance one's own status. Any slight or provocation had to be met with swift revenge to avoid dishonor and shame. These normative expectations, so the theory goes, created an agonistic society prone to enmity and feuding, in which elites captured the law courts and used them as instruments to judge their rivalries for honor.

The suggestion that Greek society from Homer down through the classical period can be fruitfully interpreted as an honor/shame culture has been debated by classicists since the publication in 1951 of Dodds's *The Greeks and the Irrational*.[58] In this influential study, Dodds advanced the thesis that Greek culture evolved from what was predominantly a shame society to one that was predominantly a guilt society. In my view, although notions of honor and shame remained important in the classical Athenian value system, the notion of doing right according to

---

[55] Andrewes 1963. The evolution of the technique and the armor are controversial: some see the hoplite panoply and perhaps even "an embryonic hoplite phalanx" in the Homeric battle narratives (van Wees 1997:691). Yet, there is no suggestion that hoplite warfare was displacing the *aristeia* of the aristocratic heroes in the economy of military power in Homer (van Wees 1997:668–693).

[56] The most influential treatment: Benedict 1989.

[57] E.g., D. Cohen 1995:61–70.

[58] Dodds 2004 (originally published 1951).

individual conscience and norms of self-restraint and cooperation in the face of social conflict played an important role in Athenian popular morality. It is therefore unlikely that Athenian litigants and jurors viewed the popular courts as simply stages for elite competitions for honor.

To be sure, courage and attention to honor (*timê*) were rewarded in classical Athens, which is not surprising given the usefulness of these traits to an imperial city in a near-constant state of war.[59] Praise and public honor were often considered important incentives for virtuous behavior, and fear of shame strong deterrents.[60] The pursuit of honor through competition was ingrained in Athenian culture through ubiquitous athletic, musical, and dramatic competitions. Elite competitions for honor often took the form of public displays of beneficence and attempts to gain recognition as a successful general or political leader (*rhêtôr*).

But Athenian moral values were a good deal more complex than the pursuit of public honor and avoidance of shame. By the last quarter of the fifth century, an ordinary Athenian, a man with no direct exposure to the "New Learning" of the Sophists, could be expected to understand at least a primitive notion of conscience and guilt in moral agents. The matricide Orestes depicted in Aeschylus *Oresteia* (458 B.C.E.) is assailed by actual Furies and in need of ritual purification. By contrast, Euripides' character of the same name in the *Orestes*, produced exactly 50 years later, is by no means sure that the Furies he sees are any more than products of his own awareness that he has committed dreadful acts.[61] This is virtually a reference to conscience. Similar references to individual guilt and conscience are found in Sophocles, Aristophanes, Euripides, and Attic oratory, particularly in the speeches of Antiphon.[62]

Perhaps most important for our purposes are the cooperative values of self-restraint and willingness to compromise that preclude an interpretation of Athenian culture, and, in particular, the discourse of the law courts, as based entirely, or even predominantly, on an economy of honor. Because the evidence for an ethics of restraint comes from law court speeches, it is unclear how powerful such norms were in society at large and whether, as seems intuitively likely, the emphasis on moderation in the courts reinforced, or perhaps even partially gave rise to, a shift

---

[59] On the importance of military virtues in Athens, see W. V. Harris 2001:157–158.

[60] E.g., Dem. 4.10; 1.27; 22.76; Lyc. 1.46; Dover 1974:228–229.

[61] Eur. *Or.*396: ἡ ξύνεσις, ὅτι σύνοιδα δείν' ἐιργασμένος "my understanding, since I am conscious that I have committed dreadful acts."

[62] Cairns 1993:303–05, 343–351, 351–354.

away from an honor/revenge ethic in Athenian society. One scholar has recently observed that Athenian litigants often present themselves as abiding by a cooperative civic code of behavior, whereby one should exercise self-restraint and avoid retaliating when provoked, preferring to compromise or simply to ignore insults to end social conflict.[63] In addition, speakers almost never argue that violence of any sort is justified.[64] To cite a few examples of the ethics of restraint, the speakers in Demosthenes 21, 54, and Lysias 3 boast that they endured a long series of insults and violent injuries without retaliating in any way. As the speaker in Lysias *Against Simon* states, "I chose not to exact justice for these crimes rather than have the people think me to be unreasonable."[65] This type of self-presentation is precisely the opposite of what one would expect from litigants striving to gain honor under a traditional heroic code of values.

Moreover, law court speakers routinely claim that they were reluctant to litigate and would have preferred to settle the dispute amicably or through arbitration, and allege that the suit only reached the trial court because of their opponent's stubbornness and aggressiveness.[66] One was expected to settle a suit if at all possible, even if that meant accepting a resolution that was less than completely fair. The speaker in Demosthenes *Against Dionysodorus* states, "we agreed [to a settlement], not because we were ignorant of what was just in light of the contract, but because we thought that we should compromise a bit and yield so that we not be thought litigious (*philodikos*)."[67] Another litigant insists that settling a suit was a sign not of weakness, dishonor, or the lack of justice of one's case, but rather that a man was *metrios* ("moderate") and *apragmôn* ("one who minds his own business").[68] To be sure, traditional values do appear in forensic speeches on occasion, generally in the form of a prosecutor justifying his decision to bring suit and ignore the norms of self-restraint by arguing that the offense in question demanded

---

[63] See Herman 1993, 1995, 1996, 1998; cf. Fisher 1998. On classical texts questioning the traditional ethic of revenge, see W. V. Harris 2001:166ff.

[64] Gagarin 2002b. Lysias 1 is the sole counterexample. Gagarin points out that there is a noticeable difference between the approach to violence taken in the fourth-century law court speeches and Antiphon's Third Tetralogy, a fifth-century rhetorical exercise that reflects traditional Homeric values. This difference may suggest that there was a shift in values not only between the archaic and classical periods, but also between the fifth and fourth centuries.

[65] Lys. 3.9; Dem. 54.5–6. For discussion, see Herman 1995.

[66] E.g., Dem. 41.1; 54.24; 56.14; Lyc. 1.16; Lys. 9.7. For discussion, see Dover 1974:187–92.

[67] Dem. 56.14.

[68] Dem. 54.24.

revenge.[69] The law court speeches thus suggest that alongside the traditional pull of honor and revenge were strong norms of cooperation and moderation in the face of social conflict.

Given the complex attitudes toward competitive and cooperative values, it seems unlikely that the law courts served primarily as stages for elite competitions for honor. To win, litigants were encouraged to represent themselves in ways that decreased, rather than enhanced, their honor and status according to the traditional moral code. The focus on fair dealing and reasoned moderation in interacting with one's adversary and attempting to end the conflict peacefully is more consistent with the view that the jurors were attempting to reach a fair verdict in the case in light of the broad context of the dispute.

THE ATHENIAN LEGAL SYSTEM

Classical Athens was a participatory democracy run primarily by amateurs: with the exception of military generalships and a few other posts, state officials were selected by lot to serve one-year terms.[70] The Council, or executive body of the Assembly, was composed of men chosen by lot, and a new *epistatês* ("president") of the Council was chosen by lot daily. Adult male citizens voted in the Assembly on nearly every decision of the Athenian state, from the making of war and peace to honoring individuals with a free dinner. In the legal sphere, the Athenian hostility toward professionalism resulted in the expectation that private parties initiate lawsuits and, with some exceptions, represent themselves in court.[71] Though a small group of men became expert in the workings of the law courts, most players in the system – litigant, presiding magistrate, juror – were fundamentally laymen.

At nearly every stage in the legal process, the functioning of the system relied on private initiative. There was no police force to maintain public order or investigate crime. It was entirely up to the victim of damage or theft, for example, to seek

---

[69] E.g., Dem. 22.3, 49–51; 58.1–2. For discussion of vengeance (as opposed to private enmity) as a justification for prosecution, see D. Cohen 1995:82–85.

[70] Hansen 1999:233–237.

[71] In some high-profile political cases, the Assembly or Council could appoint a team of men to prosecute the case, and a board of magistrates selected by lot was responsible for prosecuting officials accused of financial mismanagement at their *euthyna* ("public accounting") (MacDowell 1978:61–62). A litigant could also donate some of his speaking time to a *sunêgoros* ("co-speaker"). The prevalence and role of co-speakers is a matter of some debate, but it is clear that they did not serve as legal representatives akin to modern lawyers. Compare Todd 1993:94–95 with Rubinstein 2000:58–65, 123–171.

out witnesses and act as his own private investigator. The law imposed reasonable limits on such investigations: a citizen was authorized to search another's house for stolen goods provided that the head of the household gave his consent and that the searcher left his cloak outside to make it more difficult to plant evidence.[72] A victim of physical violence or otherwise unlawful behavior typically called on bystanders to protect him and to serve as witnesses if the incident later resulted in a trial. For example, one litigant involved in a lover's quarrel over a boy describes how he and his boy companion were attacked by his opponent and assisted by passersby:

> The boy fled to the laundryman's shop, and these men violently fell on him
> all together and were dragging him out, and the boy yelled and screamed for
> witnesses. Many men ran up and expressed indignation at the scene, saying
> that what was happening was horrible, but the attackers gave no heed to
> what was said and beat up Molon the laundry man and some others who
> were trying to help.[73]

In most cases, such confrontations did not end in an arrest; if one party decided to bring legal action, he would be responsible for delivering the appropriate summons to his opponent at a later time to begin the formal court process.

However, summary arrest and execution without trial was possible in a limited set of circumstances, most notably in the case of *kakourgoi* ("wrongdoers").[74] This class seems to have included much of what we think of as street criminals: certain types of thieves, house burglars, clothes stealers, and pickpockets. If a man caught a thief *ep' autophôrôi* ("red-handed," which may mean "in the act" or merely that his guilt is manifest, as for example, if stolen goods are found on his person),[75] he could personally arrest him and hale him before a board of magistrates known as the Eleven.[76] Once before the Eleven, a man who admitted stealing was summarily executed, but if he refused to do so he was imprisoned pending a trial in the popular courts.

---

[72] For discussion, see Christ 1998a.

[73] Lys. 3.15–16.

[74] The definitive study of these procedures remains Hansen 1976.

[75] For a recent discussion of this question, see E. Harris 2001.

[76] In a rare exception to the reliance on private initiative at all stages of the legal process, if the man felt unable to arrest the thief on his own, he could ask a magistrate to make the arrest for him in a procedure known as *ephêgêsis*. For discussion, see Hansen 1976:24–35.

A man who had been wronged had a variety of options. He could, of course, ignore the legal system altogether and attempt to obtain redress through violence, or persuasion backed by threat of litigation. Alternatively, the parties involved could decide to submit their dispute to a mutually agreed upon third party for binding private arbitration.[77] Statements in our surviving speeches suggest that social norms favored private settlement rather than litigation, especially when a dispute arose between family members, friends, or neighbors; litigants commonly blame their opponent's obstinacy for the failure of private settlement.[78]

Despite this norm, there was a great deal of litigation in Athens. The courts were in session about 200 days a year, and could hear anywhere from four to upward of 40 cases in a day, depending on the type of case.[79] Thucydides tells us that foreigners called the Athenians *philodikoi* ("lovers of litigation"), and Athenian litigiousness is a common joke in Aristophanes' comedies.[80] One character jokes that Athenians are only good for serving as jurors,[81] and another looks at a map of Greece and does not recognize Athens because there are no sitting jurors visible.[82] The high frequency of Athenian litigation provides the premise for two of Aristophanes' plays: the characters in the *Birds* establish a new city in the sky to avoid the excessive litigation of Athens;[83] and the protagonist of the *Wasps* is an old man addicted to serving jury service. One suspects that the importance of personal honor (*timê*) in Athenian society had something to do with the high levels of litigation in Athens: despite social pressure to resolve disagreements amicably and informally, many Athenians may have found it difficult to back down, particularly once the possibility of litigation was introduced.[84] As Christ has pointed out, the format of the Athenian trial made it an attractive place for disputants who perceived their honor and reputation to be bound up in the disagreement.[85] Trials

---

[77] On private arbitration at Athens, see Scafuro 1997:131–140.

[78] On the importance of appearing eager to settle, see Hunter 1994:57.

[79] Hansen (1999:186–187) estimates that the court met between 175 and 225 days a year. *Dikai* worth less than 1000 drachma could be completed in under an hour, and up to four courts might be in session on any given day.

[80] Thuc. 1.77.

[81] Ar. *Pax* 505.: "you (Athenians) do nothing but bring lawsuits."

[82] Ar. *Nub.* 206–208.

[83] Ar. *Av.* 35–45.

[84] Frier (1985:31) notes that in republican Rome pretrial maneuvering often led to litigation, as neither party wanted to abandon the game without a victory.

[85] Christ 1998b:35.

took the form of a public contest (*agón*) before a jury, not unlike the dramatic, musical, and athletic competitions that permitted citizens to display their *aretê* ("excellence"). For many contemporary Americans, the process of litigation is distasteful, a disincentive to bringing suit or pressing criminal charges. Athenian court procedures, by contrast, were more attractive in some ways than other forms of resolution such as self-help.[86] Recognizing the importance of honor and reputation in many Athenians' decision to litigate is not tantamount to accepting the view that the formal legal charge was a mere pretext for a public competition for honor and prestige. Concerns for one's honor may have made disputants more likely to pursue litigation than other forms of dispute resolution, less likely to settle before trial, and more devastated in the face of an adverse verdict, but the focus of the trial was on finding a fair outcome to the specific dispute presented by the parties, rather than choosing which litigant deserved more honor.[87]

Who litigated in Athens? Athenian courts were largely, but not entirely, the province of male citizens. Foreigners and resident aliens, known as metics, were permitted to litigate in certain circumstances, most notably in commercial suits.[88] With a few exceptions, slaves could serve neither as plaintiffs nor defendants; when a slave was involved in a dispute, the case was brought by or against the slave's owner.[89] Similarly, women were forced to depend on their male legal guardians to act on their behalf in the legal sphere. Within the subset of male citizens the upper class elite accounted for a high proportion of trials. Wealthy men were more likely to be involved in disputes involving property and were better equipped to

---

[86] Of course, the prospect of speaking before hundreds of fellow citizens must have intimidated some Athenians. However, an Athenian would not find it as daunting to represent himself as one might at first imagine.

[87] Indeed, as Christ (1998b:36) points out, honor can be said to play an important role in contemporary American litigation.

[88] Aside from maritime cases, foreigners could bring suit only if they, or all members of their polis, had been given special dispensation to do so by the Athenian Assembly. For example, some states had bilateral agreements with Athens giving the citizens of each state access to the others' courts. Metics could litigate in private cases (*dikai*), but their ability to bring public suits (*graphai*) is unclear. For discussion, see Whitehead 1977:92–6; Patterson 2000.

[89] For example, a slave who acted without instructions from his owner might be sued directly, Dem. 55, and in a few special circumstances a slave could inform against his master without torture through a process known as *mênusis*. Slaves were probably able to litigate in maritime suits. Some scholars have recently argued that slaves had more access to Athenian courts than previously believed. For discussion, see Chapter 6.

pay for a speechwriter.[90] Our surviving forensic speeches were nearly all written for use by wealthy litigants, though this may simply reflect the fact that only speeches written by famous speechwriters were preserved for later study. Private suits involving small sums were resolved by a magistrate at a preliminary hearing,[91] which suggests that ordinary Athenians did avail themselves of the legal system, but that their cases often did not reach a popular court trial. Nevertheless, the small class of elites cannot account for *all* of the many trials that took place in Athens each year; it seems likely that the upper classes were over-represented among trial litigants but that ordinary Athenians did bring suits to court.

The typical process for ordinary cases in the Athenian popular courts is outlined in the following section. Once a man decided to go to law, he often had more than one type of procedure to choose from. There were two main categories of legal procedure: private cases (*dikai*), in which the victim (or his family in the case of murder) brought suit, and public cases (*graphai*) in which anyone was permitted to initiate a suit. According to Plutarch and Aristotle, the lawgiver Solon introduced this generalized standing rule in public cases to protect the weak,[92] but it is unclear how often disinterested parties brought cases for altruistic reasons. In our surviving *graphai* the prosecutor tends to be the primary party in interest, or at least a personal enemy of the defendant with something to gain by his conviction. Although volunteer prosecutors were vital to the functioning of the Athenian legal system, there was a real worry that some men would take advantage of the open standing rule by bringing frivolous and malicious suits (a practice known as sycophancy), perhaps in some cases with the hope of extorting a settlement from an innocent potential defendant. The practice of sycophancy was discouraged not only by a heavy social stigma, but also by a system of penalties for dropping a public case or failing to win one-fifth of the votes at trial.[93]

Although no ancient source explains why some charges were designated as *graphai* and others as *dikai*, *graphai* seem to have been cases that were thought to affect the community at large. This division does not map neatly onto the modern criminal-civil distinction; murder, for example, was a *dikē* because it was considered a crime against the family rather than the state. Bringing a *graphē* was a more serious affair

---

[90] For discussion, see Christ 1998b:32–34.
[91] Arist. *Ath. Pol.* 53.1.
[92] Arist. *Ath. Pol.* 9.1; Plut. *Sol.* 18; Osborne 1985a:40ff.
[93] On sycophancy, vexatious litigation, and attempts to deter this phenomenon in Athens, see Lofberg 1976; Osborne 1993; Christ 1998b:48–71; E. Harris 1999.

for both prosecutor and defendant: *graphai* were allotted more court time, involved greater penalties, and placed the prosecutor at risk of a 1000 drachma fine (perhaps 500 days' wages for a skilled workman) if he failed to receive at least one-fifth of the jurors' votes at trial.

The first step in bringing suit was to draw up and, accompanied by witnesses, personally deliver to his opponent a summons to appear before a magistrate to answer a particular charge. On the appointed day, the prosecutor presented his indictment to the magistrate, who collected court fees and arranged for a preliminary hearing.[94] We know very little about the purpose or procedures of the preliminary hearing, or *anakrisis*, but it seems that litigants gave sworn statements and presented at least some of the evidence that supported their assertions. These preliminary proceedings may have helped litigants prepare for trial by providing advance notice of their opponent's likely arguments, but there is no hint of the winnowing functions served by pretrial procedures in modern courts; the presiding magistrates, men without any formal legal expertise, did not dismiss suits on legal grounds or set out particular issues to be decided at trial.[95] In the fourth century, most private cases involving very small sums were decided directly by a magistrate following the *anakrisis*.[96] Public arbitration, a mandatory procedure that followed the *anakrisis* in most private cases in the fourth century, also reduced the volume of cases that came to trial by providing for referral to a public official for a non-binding decision.[97] The parties were required at this stage to place all documentary evidence such as contracts, wills, witness testimony, and laws they planned to use at trial in a sealed jar.

If either party rejected the arbitrator's ruling, the litigants proceeded to trial before a jury. Litigants were evidently expected to deliver their own speeches in court, though they could donate some of their speaking time to a co-speaker, or *sunégoros*.[98] Speakers could obtain the services of speech-writers, or *logographoi*, to

---

[94] It seems that indictments were orally presented in the fifth century, but were required to be in writing from about 380 B.C.E. (Calhoun 1919a).

[95] On the *anakrisis*, see Lämmli 1938:74–128; Harrison 1998:94–105; MacDowell 1978:240–42; Todd 1993:126–127; Boegehold 1995:79–80; E. Harris 2000:76–78. One confusing passage (Is. 10.2) does indicate that a litigant was pressured during the *anakrisis* into changing the wording of his plea, but the addition to the plea was factual rather than legal in nature.

[96] Arist. *Ath. Pol.* 53.1.

[97] On public arbitration, see Scafuro 1997:35–37, 383–391; Harrison 1998:66–68; Todd 1993:128–129.

[98] For discussion of the role of *sunégoroi*, see Rubinstein 2000; Todd 1993:94–95.

help them prepare their case, but orators never mention their *logographos* and generally pretend to be speaking extemporaneously in court.[99] In fact, speakers often boast of their inexperience in public speaking and ignorance of the law courts, perhaps to head off an accusation of sycophancy.[100] Specialized legal terminology never developed in Athens, and forensic speeches are dramatic recreations of the events told in laymen's terms. Presenting a case *pro se* was not as daunting in classical Athens as it may at first appear; most Athenians probably acquired some familiarity with the workings of the law courts, both from serving as jurors and by attending trials, which took place in or near the shopping district and served as a form of popular entertainment.[101]

Each litigant was allotted a fixed amount of time to present his case. Some private cases were completed in less than an hour, and no trial lasted longer than a day.[102] Unlike a modern trial, in which, after an opening statement summarizing the case, evidence is presented in a highly fragmented form, Athenian litigants provided a largely uninterrupted narrative of their case punctuated with the reading of evidence: in an Athenian court the evidence did not make the case but reinforced the claims and arguments presented in the litigant's speech. Although a magistrate chosen by lot from the citizen body for a one-year term presided over each popular court, he did not interrupt the speaker for introducing irrelevant material or permit anyone else to raise other legal objections, and did not even instruct the jury as to the laws.

The laws were inscribed on large stone blocks (*stêlai*) erected in various public areas of Athens. Beginning at the end of the fifth century copies were kept in a public building, but it is unclear whether this archive was sufficiently organized to serve as a "user-friendly" source of law for potential disputants.[103] Litigants were responsible for finding and quoting any laws that helped their case (presumably

---

[99] It is not clear whether the *logographos* generally wrote a complete text for the litigant to memorize or collaborated with his client in composing the speech. For discussion, see Dover 1968; Usher 1976. Logographers may also have assisted in other stages of the proceedings (e.g., Dem. 58.19: arranging a settlement).

[100] E.g., Ant. 5.1; Lys. 12.4; Dem. 27.2; Is. 8.5.

[101] Lanni 1997. On the other hand, the prospect of heckling jurors and spectators hardly made for a friendly environment (Bers 1985).

[102] A *graphê* was allotted an entire day. Private cases varied according to the seriousness of the charge and were timed by a water-clock (*klepsydra*). MacDowell (1978:249–50) estimates the length of various types of suit based on the one surviving Athenian judicial water-clock.

[103] Compare Thomas 1989:37 with Sickinger 1999:114–138, 160–169.

speech-writers assisted in this task), but there was no obligation to explain the relevant laws, and in fact some speeches do not cite any laws at all. There was no formal mechanism to prevent a speaker from misrepresenting the laws, though knowledgeable members of the jury and the crowd could heckle orators whose speeches were misleading.[104] In the fifth century, witnesses testified in person and could be cross-examined by the litigants, whereas beginning in the early fourth century litigants drafted a statement and the witness stepped forward during the trial simply to swear to the statement's veracity. Women were not permitted to serve as witnesses, and slave testimony could be introduced only if the evidence was obtained under torture.[105]

Cases were heard by juries, chosen by lot,[106] which generally ranged from 201 to 501 in size.[107] I have been using the term "jurors" as a translation for the Greek term *dikastai* to refer to the audience of these forensic speeches, but others prefer the translation "judges."[108] Neither English word is entirely satisfactory, because these men performed functions similar to those both of a modern judge and a modern jury. I refer to *dikastai* as jurors to avoid the connotations of professionalism that the word judges conjures up in the modern mind. Although all citizen men over 30 were eligible to serve as jurors, it seems likely that the poor, the elderly, and city-dwellers were disproportionately represented.[109] At least in Aristotle's time, an elaborate procedure of random selection was used to assign jurors to courtrooms.[110] This process was probably designed to prevent bribery of jurors, but a likely side effect may have been to turn this step into a ceremony that would impress litigants, jurors, and bystanders with the seriousness of the occasion.[111]

---

[104] On jury heckling, see Bers 1985. The penalty for citing a non-existent law was death (Dem. 26.24), although there are no attested examples of cases brought under this law.

[105] Whether this practice was actually employed in the courts or was rather a "legal fiction" has been the subject of recent scholarly dispute (Mirhady 1996, 2000; Gagarin 1996, 1997a; Thür 1996).

[106] Each year, a panel of 6000 potential jurors was given the dicastic oath. It is unclear how this panel was chosen. On court days, anyone in the panel who wished to serve on a jury could present himself at the court and enter the lot that, at least by the time of Aristotle, randomly assigned jurors to courtrooms.

[107] There are occasional examples of panels of 1001, 1501, 2001, and even 2501 (Hansen 1999:187).

[108] E.g., E. Harris 1994a:136.

[109] Hansen 1999:183–186; Ober 1990:122–124; Sinclair 1988:124–127; Markle 1985:277–281; Todd 1990a:146; Boegehold 1999:88–90. For the minority view that juries were selected primarily from the middle and upper classes, see Jones 1977:36–37.

[110] Arist. *Ath. Pol.* 63.1.

[111] Bers 2000.

There was no process like our *voir dire*, meant to exclude from the jury those with some knowledge of the litigants or the case. On the contrary, Athenian litigants at times encouraged jurors to base their decision on preexisting knowledge. In his prosecution of Timarchus, Aeschines tells the jurors:

> First, let nothing be more persuasive for you than what you yourselves know and believe concerning Timarchus here. Examine the issue not from the present but from the past. For the statements made in the past about Timarchus and about what this man is accustomed to doing were made with a view toward the truth, while those that are going to be spoken today are for the purpose of deceiving you in order to get a decision. Cast your ballot according to the longer time and the truth and the facts you yourselves know.[112]

Although the jury might know something of a party's reputation or of the facts of the case, especially in high profile cases, the *dikastai* were nothing like the self-informing juries of medieval England. Jurors did not bring the local knowledge of a small community into court with them; they were randomly chosen from a city with a population in the hundreds of thousands.[113]

A simple majority vote of the jury, taken without deliberation, determined the outcome of the trial. No reasons for the verdict were given, and there was no provision for appeal from the judgment of the people.[114] Though the punishment for some offenses was set by statute, in others the jury was required to choose between the penalties suggested by each party in a second speech. It was not permitted to give a compromise punishment. It is through this practice, known as *timêsis*,[115] that Socrates virtually signed his own death warrant. After suggesting that the state reward him with meals at the public expense, he finally agreed to propose a very small fine as a penalty. The jury, which only narrowly voted

---

[112] Aesch. 1.93.

[113] On the Athenian population, see Hansen 1999:90–94.

[114] A dissatisfied litigant might, however, indirectly attack the judgment by means of a suit for false witness or a new case, ostensibly involving a different incident and/or using a different procedure. Some of the surviving speeches point explicitly to a protracted series of connected legal confrontations (Osborne 1985a:52).

[115] On the process of *timêsis*, see Todd 1993:133–135; Scafuro 1997:54–55.

for conviction, was thereby induced to vote overwhelmingly for the prosecutors' proposal of execution.[116]

Imprisonment was rarely used as a punishment. The most common types of penalties in public suits were monetary fines, loss of citizen status (*atimia*), exile, and execution, which involved either poisoning by hemlock or, more gruesomely, being shackled to wooden planks and left to die.[117] Magistrates known as "the Eleven" supervised executions. Whereas public officials were involved in the enforcement of state fines in public suits, victorious litigants in private suits were responsible for personally collecting on the judgment.[118]

Although most cases in the Athenian system adhered to the procedures outlined above, there were a handful of extraordinary proceedings that did not follow this general pattern. In certain major political trials, a team of prosecutors was appointed to represent the state. Some cases were heard by the entire Assembly sitting in judgment whereas others came before a special jury of soldiers. In the case of homicide, special procedures obtained from the initiation of charges through trial, which took place in one of five special courts depending on the nature of the accusations. Beginning in the middle of the fourth century, an expedited and modified procedure within the popular courts was employed in maritime suits. I examine the special homicide and maritime procedures in Chapters 4 and 6, respectively. But first, we turn in the next chapter to a discussion of the ordinary popular courts. We will see that the popular court system exemplified the radical democratic spirit of classical Athens not only in the composition of the jury but also in its unique approach to legal decision making.

---

[116] Pl. *Ap.* 36a. Todd (1993:134 n. 12) estimates from a passage of Diogenes Laertius that Socrates was convicted by a vote of approximately 280 to 220, but sentenced to death by a vote of 360 to 140.

[117] On capital punishment in Athens, see Barkan 1935; Gernet 1981:252–276; Todd 2000. On imprisonment, see Hunter 1997. On penalties generally, see Todd 1993:139–144; Debrunner Hall 1996; Allen 2000:197–242.

[118] Successful litigants who were unable to gain satisfaction could return to court to obtain a possession order through the *dikê exoulês*, but, even armed with such an order, it was ultimately up to the private party to collect on the judgment. For discussion, see Todd 1993:144–145.

3 RELEVANCE IN THE POPULAR COURTS

THE MODERN READER OF A SPEECH INTENDED FOR DELIVERY IN THE ATHENIAN popular courts is immediately struck by a bizarre amalgam of the familiar and the foreign. Alongside a narrative of the events in question, bolstered by witness testimony and the discussion and citation of laws, one finds a variety of material that would be considered irrelevant or inadmissible in a modern courtroom. Launching personal attacks unrelated to the charges in the case, for example alleging that one's opponent is sexually profligate,[1] or that he is descended from slaves,[2] was commonplace. The character and reputation not only of the litigants but of their ancestors and family members were regular topics of discussion.[3] Defendants shamelessly appealed to the jurors for pity, going so far as to bring their weeping children up to the dais as they spoke.[4]

The presence of extra-legal information and argumentation[5] in the popular courts is an important clue to understanding the nature of Athenian legal process. Did the Athenian courts serve, as some scholars have argued,[6] primarily as a forum for litigants to publicly contest their relative honor and prestige before the jury? On this view, it is the seemingly irrelevant arguments that were most important to litigants and jurors, whereas the law under which the suit was brought mattered little.[7] Or are extra-legal arguments simply stray comments to be chalked up to the amateurism and informality of the Athenian system, the attempts of individual litigants to divert the jury from its task of applying the law?[8]

[1] E.g., Andoc. 1.100; Lys. 14.25–26.
[2] Lys. 30.2.
[3] E.g., Lys. 14.24; 18.24–27; 20.28; Is. 5.46.
[4] Lys. 20.34.
[5] For a definition of "extra-legal" argumentation, see Chapter 1.
[6] D. Cohen 1995:87–90; Osborne 1985a:53. D. Cohen (1995:87–88) argues that Athenian judges and litigants acknowledged that litigation was primarily a form of feuding behavior.
[7] D. Cohen 1995:90; Osborne 1985a:53. Under this view, the choice of legal charge, in particular whether to bring a public or private suit, did, however, have important consequences in the game of honor (Osborne 1985a:53).
[8] E. Harris 1994a:137; 2000:78 &n.85; Rhodes 2004.

This chapter examines the Athenians' collectively held assumptions of what types of information and arguments should be presented in the popular courts, the broadest jurisdiction in the Athenian legal system. I suggest that both extra-legal and legal information were considered relevant and important to the jury's decision because Athenian juries aimed at reaching a just verdict taking into account the particular circumstances of the individual case rather than applying abstract rules and principles provided by statutes to the case at hand. It was up to the jury to decide on a case-by-case basis which of the variety of legal and extra-legal arguments presented at trial should be determinative, and, indeed, the relative importance of legal and contextual evidence was often explicitly disputed by the parties. The Athenian popular courts thus did not exhibit "autonomous" legal argument, that is, the logical application of a self-contained body of rules to a specific case independent of its social, political, or economic context.[9] The unusual aspects of Athenian popular court presentation stem from their different sense of what constituted justice – one that emphasized discretionary and equitable assessments rather than the regular and predictable application of abstract, standardized rules. We will see in later chapters that the Athenians recognized that their discretionary approach to judicial process was not without its tradeoffs. Nevertheless, it was this unique approach that the Athenians chose to use in the vast majority of cases.

EXTRA-LEGAL ARGUMENTATION

Philocleon, the inveterate juror of Aristophanes' comedy *The Wasps*, provides what must be a recognizable though exaggerated account of the ploys litigants use to win over the jury:

> I listen to them saying everything to promote their acquittal. Come, let me
> see, what wheedling isn't there for a juryman to hear there? Some bewail
> their poverty and exaggerate their actual troubles until they make their
> troubles equal to my own. Some tell us stories, others some funny piece of
> Aesop. Others make jokes to get me to laugh and lay aside my anger. And if
> we are not won over by these devices, right away he drags in his kids by the
> hand, boys and girls, and I hear them as they bow their heads and bleat in a
> chorus . . .[10]

---

[9] For a discussion of notions of legal autonomy at Rome, see Frier 1985:184–191.

[10] Ar. *Vesp.* 562–570.

There appears to have been no rule establishing the range and types of information and argument appropriate for popular court speeches. *The Constitution of the Athenians*, a partial history and description of Athenian institutions probably written by Aristotle or his students, states that litigants in private cases took an oath to speak to the point, but this oath is never mentioned in our surviving popular court speeches and appears to have had no effect on litigants' arguments.[11] Speakers were limited only by the time limit and their own sense of what arguments were likely to persuade the jury. Although anything was fair game in the popular courts — Lycurgus' extended quotations from the poets Euripides, Homer, and Tyrtaeus on the honor and glory of battle in his prosecution of a citizen who left Athens when the city was threatened with attack[12] are perhaps the most creative use of speaking time in our surviving speeches — there are discernible categories of extra-legal evidence that appear again and again in the corpus.[13] Experienced speechwriters undoubtedly could predict the types of arguments and information likely to appeal to the jury and constructed their speeches accordingly. Indeed, there is evidence that juries at times expressed their displeasure at a litigant's choice of arguments: one speaker tries to head off such criticism, pleading, "And let none of you challenge me while I am in the middle of my speech with shouts of 'why are you telling us this?'"[14]

It is, therefore, possible to discuss Athenian notions of the types of information and arguments that were particularly relevant to popular court decisions in the absence of a stricture on the presentation of evidence in these courts. Because we rarely know the outcome of an ancient case and generally do not have the opposing litigant's speech that would allow a comparison, it is impossible to know which strategies were most persuasive to an Athenian jury. In fact, as we will see, the categories of relevant evidence were fluid and contestable. Nevertheless, the surviving speeches clearly show the popular court juries' receptivity to three

---

[11] Arist. *Ath. Pol.* 67.1. For further discussion of this passage and a comparison to the relevancy rule of the homicide courts, see Chapter 4.

[12] Lyc. 1.100, 103, 107. For discussion, see Dorjahn 1927; Perlman 1964; Hall 1995.

[13] Rhodes (2004) argues that court speeches focus mostly on the issue in dispute. My own view is that most popular court speeches contain a mixture of legal and extra-legal information, and it was left to the jury to determine which sort of evidence was most important in any individual suit. In any case, the repeated use of a particular type of extra-legal information in our surviving speeches suggests that this sort of evidence was considered relevant to a popular court jury's verdict, even if, as Rhodes argues, it accounts for only a small portion of litigants' arguments.

[14] Hyp. 1col.43. In his defense of Euxenippus, Hyperides (4.10) suggests that speakers sometimes encourage jurors to heckle their opponents if they try to make particular arguments.

sorts of argument: (1) the expansion of the litigant's plea beyond the strict limits of the event in question to encompass the broader background of the dispute; (2) defense appeals for the jury's pity based on the potential harmful effects of an adverse verdict; and (3) arguments based on the character of the parties. These three categories of evidence overlap – character evidence, for example, can be used to show that the defendant does or does not deserve pity – but for the sake of clarity I will discuss them separately.

In this section, I take up the three types of extra-legal argumentation in turn, showing that the Athenians viewed them as relevant to reaching a just resolution to the dispute rather than as evidence in a public competition for prestige unrelated to the triggering event and legal charge. Of course, some litigants were undoubtedly motivated by a desire to gain honor on a public stage. Moreover, I do not doubt that the courts at times functioned in a manner far from the ideal, or that popular court trials may have also served a variety of social or ideological functions in Athenian society. However, I am concerned with the *primary* aim of the popular lawcourts, as it was understood by the majority of the participants. My contention is that litigants and jurors by and large viewed extra-legal argumentation as intended to assist the jury in its legal task of reaching a just resolution to the specific dispute that gave rise to the suit. The final two sections of this chapter discuss the role of statutes in Athenian popular court litigation, and how jurors evaluated the mass of legal and extra-legal argumentation presented to them.

Before I examine in detail each of the three types of extra-legal information considered relevant in the Athenian popular courts, a few general comments may help to clarify my approach. I discuss types of information and argument that are common enough in our surviving speeches to indicate that speechwriters and jurors thought them relevant to popular court decision making. In any individual case, however, litigants might dispute the relevance and relative importance of different types of argument. The corpus of forensic speeches contains, for example, impassioned arguments both for and against the relevance of character evidence.[15] Indeed, speakers sometimes contend that the jury should ignore extra-legal evidence and focus solely on the legal arguments made in the case.[16] Such arguments were themselves part of the remarkably individualized and case-specific approach

---

[15] Compare, for example, Dem. 36.55 and Dem. 52.1. Character evidence is both the most common form of extra-legal argumentation in our surviving speeches, and the most controversial.

[16] E.g., Isoc. 18.34–35; Dem. 52.1–2; Hyp. 4.32. These statements may draw on ambivalence about the decision making process of the popular courts and the appeal of alternative approaches to relevance, such as that employed in the homicide courts. For discussion, see Chapter 4.

to justice employed in the popular courts: we will see that most speeches included a mixture of extra-legal and legal argument, and it was left to the jurors to decide which sorts of evidence were most important given the particular circumstances of the case.

In what follows, there is an implicit, and, in a few instances, explicit, comparison between the Athenians' broad notion of relevance and the stricter approach of the modern American system. In practice, of course, modern trial lawyers are often able to communicate to a jury a good deal of information that is not strictly related to proving the elements of the charge or claim.[17] Nevertheless, there is a crucial distinction between ancient and modern legal practice. In modern courts the law is set apart as the valid, authoritative rule of decision, and extra-legal norms can only trump legal ones surreptitiously.[18] In Athenian courts, by contrast, we will see that there was no authoritative rule of decision.

I focus in this section on the content of the extra-legal material in our surviving speeches because I argue that this material provided information vital to the jury's verdict. This is not to deny the importance of the format of extra-legal argumentation. We will see that litigants often provide extensive background information about the dispute and the parties by presenting their case in the form of a story. In the hands of a talented logographer these accounts could be literary and entertaining pieces of prose. Artful narratives allowed speakers to hold the jurors' attention, assisted the jurors in processing and remembering complex material that was presented orally, and gave the speaker an opportunity to display an appealing and sympathetic persona.

Appeals for pity and some forms of character arguments, such as the recitation of a litigant's public services, were common *topoi* that served to orient the audience by placing a litigant's presentation squarely in the familiar genre of forensic oratory. Although the format, placement, and type of extra-legal argumentation used by a litigant were influenced to some degree by the requirements of the genre and jurors' expectations,[19] extra-legal argumentation did not consist of presenting

---

[17] Burns (1999:29–30, 36, 201), for example, argues that the American rules of evidence are flexible enough to permit an attorney to argue for a verdict based on extra-legal norms, and that, in practice, the trial jury's task is to decide between a variety of competing norms – legal, economic, moral, political, and professional. For further discussion of modern notions of relevance, see Chapter 1.

[18] Burns 1999:36.

[19] Rhetorical handbooks called for forensic speeches to be divided into four main parts: *prooimion* (introduction); *diêgêsis* (narrative); *pistis* (proof); and *epilogos* (conclusion). Topoi tend to be associated with a particular part; appeals to emotion, for example, were thought to be appropriate in *epilogoi* and *prooimia*. For further discussion, see Usher 1999:22–26; Kennedy 1991:8–9.

generalized "stock" arguments. Rather, we will see that speakers presented highly individualized arguments based on the specific character and interactions of the parties, and, in the case of appeals to pity, the effects an adverse verdict would have on the litigant and his family given his particular circumstances.

BACKGROUND INFORMATION AND FAIRNESS IN LIGHT OF THE PARTICULAR CIRCUMSTANCES OF THE CASE

Modern lawyers translate a client's story into legal form largely by winnowing down the client's experience to a limited set of facts that correspond to claims and arguments recognized by the applicable law.[20] Athenian litigants, by contrast, provide a "wide-angle"[21] view of the case, one that includes not only a complete account of the event in question, but also information regarding the social context of the dispute, including discussion of the long-term relationship and interactions of the parties. As Humphreys points out, litigants sought to recreate the "social milieu" and portray the background of the case "in such a way that the jury will feel that, in the circumstances, he has the right on his side."[22] We will see that this often involved demonstrating one's respect for the reciprocal obligations owed to relatives, friends, and neighbors, and one's adherence to cooperative norms of fair dealing and a moderate approach to conflict.

Demosthenes *Against Nicostratus* illustrates the tendency of litigants to provide a highly contextualized account of a dispute. The suit is an *apographê*, a procedure through which any Athenian could proclaim articles of property belonging to a state debtor subject to seizure and public sale.[23] The legal issue in this case seems quite simple: Apollodorus is challenging the defendants' claim of ownership

---

[20] For a discussion of the process of translating lived experience into a legal discourse, see White 1990:179–201, 257–269; see also Alfieri 1991:2107; Sarat 1996:354; Cunningham 1992; Gilkerson 1992:922; Sherwin 1994:39. This is far from a straightforward process. For further discussion, see Chapter 1.

[21] Scheppele 1989:2096.

[22] Humphreys 1983:248; 1985b:350–356. For a discussion of the creation of the litigant's social milieu that focuses on *êthopoiia*, or dramatic characterization, see Scafuro 1997:50–66. The Barotse of Africa provide an example of a society that had a similarly broad notion of relevance in their courts, but used contextual information in a very different way than did the Athenians. According to Gluckman (1973:21), Barotse judges consider the relations of the parties and the background of the dispute in order to seek out a compromise that will not break up the relationships of those involved. Athenian jurors, by contrast, used context to help them evaluate the justice of the parties' actions and to arrive at a "fair" result, one that generally involved choosing between the litigants' accounts rather than reaching a compromise solution.

[23] On the *apographê* procedure, see Osborne 1985a:40–58; Harrison 1998:211–217; Lipsius 1905–1915: 302ff.

over two slaves, arguing that they actually belong to the defendants' brother Arethusius, a state debtor, and should therefore be confiscated. Apollodorus offers witness testimony of Arethusius' debt and ownership of the slaves, arguing that the defendants, Nicostratus and Deinon, are asserting that they own the slaves to protect their brother's property from confiscation.[24]

From the perspective of modern notions of legal relevance, one might expect the speech to begin and end with this apparently quite damning evidence. Apollodorus does not, however, discuss the slaves until the last quarter of his speech, but instead devotes the bulk of his time to a detailed narrative of how his past friendship with the defendant Nicostratus soured and eventually led to his filing suit against Nicostratus' brother Arethusius, thereby securing the public fine that rendered Arethusius a debtor to the state. He begins by recounting the close bond of friendship (*philia*) and trust he and Nicostratus had shared as neighbors: Nicostratus managed Apollodorus' affairs whenever he was away, and, when Nicostratus was taken captive and sold as a slave, Apollodorus gave his brother money to rescue him and later mortgaged his property to help Nicostratus pay the ransom debt.[25] Far from expressing gratitude for this generosity, Nicostratus conspired against him, perhaps, as Apollodorus suggests, in order to avoid having to pay off the mortgage on Apollodorus' property.[26] Nicostratus caused Apollodorus to be fined for non-appearance in response to a citation, enlisting his brother Arethusius to testify falsely that he had been properly served when he in fact had no knowledge of the suit. He also secured a default judgment against him in this case and forcibly seized all the furniture in his house. When Apollodorus learned of this, he filed an action for false citation against Arethusius. Nicostratus and his brothers did not back down, but tried to dissuade him from pursuing the case by vandalizing his farm and physically assaulting him.[27] Undeterred, Apollodorus pressed on with his suit and secured a one-talent fine against Arethusius. Only after providing this background information does Apollodorus turn to arguing that the slaves at issue belong to Arethusius and are therefore subject to forfeiture. Apollodorus thus gives the jury a full picture of the social context of the dispute, one that emphasizes his mistreatment by the defendants and suggests that

[24] Dem. 53.18–25.
[25] Dem. 53. 4–14.
[26] Dem. 53.14.
[27] Dem. 14–17.

Arethusius, due to his dishonest dealings and breach of the obligations of friend-ship, fully deserves his status as a state debtor and the confiscation of property that Apollodorus seeks.[28]

Contextual information such as that found in *Against Nicostratus* is a common feature of Athenian court speeches. In cases that are part of a series of suits between the parties, speakers do not confine their argument to the immediate issue in question but rather recount the past litigation in some detail.[29] One speaker announces in his opening his intention to provide extensive contextual information:

> Because there have previously been lawsuits, gentlemen of the jury, between
> us and these same men concerning the estate of Hagnias, and they will not
> stop acting lawlessly and violently, using any means available to acquire
> things that do not belong to them, it is perhaps necessary to explain what
> has happened from the beginning. For in this way, gentlemen of the jury,
> you will more easily follow all the arguments in my speech, and these men
> will be revealed for the sort of men they are, in particular that they started
> on their mischief a long time ago now and are continuing in it, thinking that
> they should do whatever occurs to them.[30]

This practice is particularly prominent in speeches for suits charging false testi-mony, which generally include an attempt to re-argue the previous case as well as evidence that a statement made by one of the opponent's witnesses was false. For instance, in one false testimony suit the plaintiff states, "I now present to you a just request, that you both determine whether the testimony is false or true, and, at the same time, examine the entire matter from the beginning."[31]

Litigants also commonly discuss the manner in which each of the parties has conducted himself in the course of litigation, appealing to cooperative values and norms of moderation. They emphasize their own reasonableness and willingness to settle or arbitrate the claim, and portray their opponents as litigious, dishonest,

---

[28] As Christ (1998b:177) points out, Apollodorus' account of a trusting friendship betrayed may well
be more fiction than fact: Nicostratus worked for Apollodorus and they may have shared economic
relations rather than bonds of intimate *philia*. What matters for our purposes is that Apollodorus chose
to present the case in its broader context, however misleading his account may be.

[29] E.g., Dem. 21.78ff; 29.6, 27; 43.1–2; 47.46; Andoc. 1.117ff; Is. 2.27–37; 5.5ff.

[30] Dem. 43.1–2.

[31] Dem. 47.46; see also Dem. 29.9,27; 45.1–2; Is. 2.27–37. For discussion, see Bonner 1905:18.

and even violent.[32] The speaker in Demosthenes *Against Evergus*, for example, contrasts his own restraint in pursuing his claim with his opponent's[33] violent and inappropriate use of self-help.[34] The dispute in this case arose out of the litigants' service as trierarchs, wealthy citizens who were called on to finance the operation of an Athenian warship during their one-year terms. One of the speaker's duties as trierarch was to collect state-owned naval equipment which Theophemus, a former trierarch, had failed to return. The speaker explains that he repeatedly tried to persuade Theophemus to return or replace the equipment before securing a court order and, when even that had no effect, he obtained a decree from the Council authorizing him to recover the debt through self-help. The speaker emphasizes that he carried out the Boule's instructions in a reasonable manner: he waited for Theophemus to return before seizing any property, he was careful to ascertain that there were no women in the house before entering, and he gave Theophemus the option of appealing to the Boule before he began the confiscation.[35] The parties' roles were later reversed when the speaker was delinquent in paying out a judgment won by Theophemus. The speaker tells us that although Theophemus granted him an extension on the payment, he nevertheless appeared when the speaker was absent and proceeded to seize property worth more than the outstanding debt. In the process, he caused the death of the speaker's old nurse by beating her mercilessly while prying a cup from her hands. Even after the speaker had paid the debt, Theophemus refused to return the property and carried out another forcible seizure. The prevalence of these types of arguments in our surviving popular court speeches suggests that the Athenians considered evidence of the conduct of the parties in the course of litigation relevant to the jury's decision.

---

[32] E.g. Dem 44.31:

> I think it is necessary to speak also of the things they have done in the time since the case regarding the estate was brought, and the way they have dealt with us, for I think that no one else has been as unlawfully treated in connection with an inheritance lawsuit as we have been.

See also Dem. 21.78ff; 27.1; 29.58; 30.2; 41.1–2; 42.11–12; 47.81; 48.2, 40; Is. 5.28–30. For discussion of the importance of appearing eager to settle, see Hunter 1994:57.

[33] In this suit for false testimony his opponents are technically Evergus and Mnesibulus, though he directs much of his argument against Theophemus, his opponent in the original action.

[34] For discussion of the contrast in methods of self-help in this and other cases, see Christ 1998a:534–541; Hunter 1994:122–124.

[35] Dem. 47.34–38.

When relatives or friends face each other in court, speakers describe the long-term relationship and interaction of the parties and seek to represent themselves as honoring the obligations traditionally associated with bonds of *philia* ("friendship"),[36] and to portray their opponents as having violated these norms.[37] Law-court speakers do not discuss why information about the relationship between the parties was considered relevant to the jury's decision, but it is common sense that such relationships are relevant to a moral assessment of the situation. The Athenians recognized this. In the *Nichomachean Ethics*[38] Aristotle explains that just as the duties and obligations one owes to family, friends, fellow citizens, and other types of relations differ, "Wrongs are also of a different quality in the case of each of these [relationships], and are more serious the more intimate the friendship." He continues, "For example, it is worse to deprive a friend of money than a citizen, and to fail to help a brother than a stranger, and to hit a father than anyone else."[39] Information about the relationship between the parties helped the jury evaluate the severity of the allegations and the extent of moral blame borne by each side.[40]

In addition to presenting evidence about relationships and interactions prior to the event at issue, litigants at times provide a highly contextualized account of the dispute itself. They often include arguments that are not explicitly recognized by law but that contribute to the jury's overall sense of the fair result of the dispute. For example, speakers at times discuss the extenuating (and, less commonly, aggravating) circumstances surrounding the incident – such as the absence of intent, the offender's youth, or his intoxication[41] – even though the laws enforced

---

[36] *Philia* encompassed relatives as well as friends, and, at least in Aristotle's formulation, extended even to fellow citizens. Arist. *Eth. Nic.*1165a14–35. The duties associated with *philia* depended on the degree of closeness between the parties. For discussion, see Chapter 1. For more extensive discussions of *philia*, see Millett 1991:110–114, Konstan 1997:56ff.

[37] Christ 1998b:167–180. Christ discusses the emphasis on the breach of *philia* in cases involving relatives, friends, neighbors, and demesmen. Christ (1998b:167) points out that litigants at times even exaggerate the intimacy of their past relationship in order to present their cases in terms of a breach of *philia*.

[38] Aristotle's theoretical works must be used with great care as a source for the ideals or practice of the Athenian lawcourts. For example, although Aristotle suggests in the *Rhetoric* (1375a) that litigants should use arguments from fairness (*epieikeia*) when the written laws are unfavorable to their case, Athenian litigants generally do not explicitly appeal to *epieikeia* (Carey 1996:42). However, as Millett (1991:112) points out, the *Ethics* does seem to be a reliable source of Athenian popular values; Aristotle sets out to examine beliefs that are "especially prevalent or appear to have some rationale" (τὰς μάλιστα ἐπιπολαζούσας ἢ δοκούσας ἔχειν τινὰ λόγον: Arist. *Eth. Nic.* 1095a28).

[39] Arist. *Eth. Nic.* 1160a3ff.

[40] This evaluation might also be of use in deciding whether the defendant deserves the prescribed penalty.

[41] Although intoxication is most often referred to as a mitigating factor in our surviving speeches, it is occasionally also cited for the purposes of aggravation. For discussion, see Saunders 1991b:111. That a

by the popular courts did not formally recognize such defenses,[42] and did not provide for degrees of offenses based on their severity.[43] This practice did not go entirely unchallenged, however: The speaker in Demosthenes 54 argues that his opponent's attempt to characterize the assault in question as a harmless scuffle typical among boisterous young men could support mitigation at the penalty phase of the case,[44] but was not relevant to the jury's verdict on guilt.[45]

Discussion of the circumstances and context of the contested event is most prominent in suits involving a challenge to a will.[46] Litigants often appeal to a variety of arguments rooted in notions of fairness and justice unrelated to the issue of the formal validity of the will. Speakers compare their relationship to the deceased with that of their opponents in an effort to argue that they have the better claim to the estate: they present evidence that they were closer in affection to the deceased, performed his burial rites, or nursed him when he was ill, and suggest that their opponents were detested by the dead man and took no interest in his affairs until it was time to claim his estate.[47] One litigant goes so far as to suggest that equitable arguments trump a will or any other sort of legal claim, asserting that "when it comes to all those engaged in inheritance disputes, whenever they can demonstrate that they themselves (just as we are) are closer to the deceased both in blood and friendship, it seems to me that other arguments are superfluous."[48]

---

circumstance such as intoxication could be argued both as a mitigating and an aggravating factor is indicative of the ad hoc nature of popular court decision making. Litigants drew on commonly held beliefs and social norms in making their arguments, but there were no unwritten legal rules regarding how a jury should interpret such evidence.

[42] The homicide laws, which were enforced not in the popular courts but in special homicide tribunals, *did* make distinctions based on the offenders' intent. For discussion, see Chapter 4.

[43] These topoi have been catalogued and discussed in detail in Saunders 1991b:109–118, Dorjahn 1930:162–172, and Scafuro 1997:248–256.

[44] The process of determining penalties in *agónes timêtoi* is discussed later in this chapter.

[45] Dem. 54.21–22; see also Aesch. 3.198. Scafuro (1997:248) points out that as a practical matter, arguments for mitigation and exculpation are used interchangeably at the guilt phase of Athenian trials. The relationship between the argumentation at the guilt and penalty phases is discussed later in this chapter.

[46] For further discussion of the use of arguments from fairness in the popular courts as compared to the more restrictive view of relevance in the special maritime procedures, see Chapter 6. Other recent discussions of the use of arguments from "fairness" or "equity" include Scafuro 1997:50–66; Christ 1998b:194ff; Biscardi 1970:219–232. For a contrary view, see E. Harris 2000.

[47] E.g., Is. 1.4,17, 19, 20, 30, 33, 37, 42; 4.19; 6.51; 7.8, 11, 12, 33–37; 9.4, 27–32. For discussion, see Hardcastle 1980:11–22; Avramović 1997:54–8. For an argument that equity argumentation in Isaeus is a response to obscurities and gaps in the inheritance laws rather than an attempt to appeal to fairness, see Lawless 1991:110–134.

[48] Is. 1.17.

Another suggests that an airtight "legal" case is insufficient if justice (*to dikaion*) is on the opponent's side:

> Concerning the issue itself I think that I have sufficiently proved my case. But, so that no one may think either that I possess the estate for no good reason, or that this woman [my opponent], is being deprived of the money after having treated Thrasylochus [the deceased] in a kindhearted way, I would like to talk also about these matters. For I would be ashamed for the deceased unless all of you were persuaded that what he did [bequeath his fortune to me in his will] comported not only with the law, but also with justice.[49]

The speaker concludes with a summary of his arguments that places equitable considerations on an equal footing with the will and the law: "First, my friendship with the men who have bequeathed the estate . . . then the many good deeds I did for them when they were down on their luck . . . in addition the will, . . . further, the law . . ."[50]

The frequency and centrality of discussion of the background and interaction of the parties in our surviving speeches indicate that this type of information was considered relevant to the jury's decision. It has been suggested that the prevalence of such extra-legal arguments suggests that Athenian litigants and jurors regarded the court process as serving primarily a social role – the assertion of competitive advantage in a narrow stratum of society. One scholar, for example, explains the tendency to discuss the broader conflict between the parties as evidence that litigants were engaged in a competition for prestige unrelated to the "ostensible subject of the suit": "rather than thinking in terms of a 'just resolution' of the dispute one should think instead of how the game of honor is being played."[51]

There may be a simpler explanation, however, one rooted in the pervasive amateurism of the Athenian courts. Human beings naturally tend to think about social interaction in story form.[52] The restrictive evidence regimes of contemporary

---

[49] Isoc. 19.16. Although this speech was delivered in a court in Aegina rather than Athens, it was written by the Athenian logographer and rhetorician, Isocrates, and appears to follow the conventions of Athenian legal discourse. Speakers in Athenian courts similarly assume the relevance of arguments from fairness.

[50] Isoc. 19.50.

[51] D. Cohen 1995:90.

[52] E.g., Bennett & Feldman 1981:7. Empirical data shows that, despite the fragmented form of the modern trial, juries deliberate in a narrative mode (Hastie, et al. 1983:22–23). For this reason, modern trial

jury-based legal systems are, from a layperson's perspective, counterintuitive. Amateurs left to their own devices in contemporary small claims courts, for example, often set their dispute in a broader context and use a variety of everyday storytelling techniques forbidden in formal court settings.[53] It is not surprising that amateur Athenian litigants would consider evidence concerning the background of the dispute, the parties' conduct in the course of litigation, and arguments from fairness relevant in reaching a just outcome to the issue at hand. There is no need to resort to a theory of the Athenian court system as a forum primarily concerned with social competition to explain the contextual information included in our surviving popular court speeches. Indeed, the substantive norms to which litigants appeal – the ethics of fair dealing, honoring reciprocal obligations, and favoring settlement and moderation over violence and litigation – are inconsistent with a model of lawcourt interaction as a form of feuding behavior or competition for honor. We will see that this explanation for the prevalence of extra-legal material becomes even more attractive when we consider that Athenian law court speeches generally include what a modern would consider relevant legal argument as well as such extra-legal argumentation.

Defense Appeals Based on the Harsh Effects of an Adverse Verdict

The second major category of extra-legal argumentation in the popular courts is the appeal for the jurors' pity based on the misfortune that will befall the defendant and his family if he is found guilty.[54] From a modern perspective, this information is relevant, if at all, to sentencing rather than the determination of guilt. Indeed, in modern criminal law there is some dispute over whether evidence about the harm a conviction and sentence will cause to third parties, such as the defendant's dependent children, should be considered even at sentencing.[55] The frequency of this topos in Athenian defense speeches and its anticipation by prosecutors

lawyers attempt to present their case in the form of a coherent story. For discussion see Bennett & Feldman 1981:7; Ferguson 1996:85; Lempert 1991:561.

[53] O'Barr & Conley 1985:661–701. Storytelling may have also eased the burden on litigants and jurors by making it easier to remember a prepared text and easier to follow a complex and lengthy oral presentation.

[54] Two recent treatments of this topos are Johnstone 1999:109–125; Konstan 2000. I discuss here only verbal appeals to pity; for a treatment of dramatized appeals such as weeping and parading one's children before the jury, see Johnstone 1999:114–122.

[55] For discussion see Brown 2002.

suggest that appeals to pity were for the most part considered appropriate in the popular courts.[56] Indeed, it has been demonstrated that prosecutors are more likely to argue that their particular opponent's character or actions have rendered him undeserving of pity rather than to challenge the legitimacy of the practice itself.[57]

The surviving Athenian verbal appeals to "pity" (*eleos*) and "pardon" (*sungnômê*) in the courts did not take the same form as their modern counterparts, in large part because they appear in speeches at the guilt rather than the sentencing phase.[58] In a recent article on the use of pity in Athenian law, Konstan points out that Athenian litigants who appeal to the jurors' pity do not concede guilt, and therefore express no remorse. There is no Athenian equivalent of the "abuse excuse" or arguments for reduced punishment based on the defendant's disadvantaged upbringing or sincere regret. Instead, Athenians provide information about the severe effects an adverse verdict will have on themselves and their families.[59] In Konstan's view, speakers who appeal to pity proceed on the assumption that they are innocent of the charge and use the topos "as another means by which a defendant insisted on his innocence"[60] and as "a way of charging the jury to take seriously the power at their disposal, and be certain that they do not do grave harm, as they can, on the basis of insufficient evidence."[61] It is true that appeals to pity are always made in a manner consistent with innocence, and litigants do at times complain that if convicted their suffering will be all the worse for being undeserved.[62] Nevertheless, discussion of the effects a serious penalty will have on the defendant likely served the additional purpose of assisting the jury in determining whether a conviction was a fair result given all of the circumstances, including the severity of the likely

---

[56] E.g., Lys. 9.22; 18.27; 19.33, 53; 20.34–35; 21.25; Hyp. 1.19–20; Isoc. 16.47; Dem. 27.66–69; 45.85; 55.35; 57.70; Johnstone (1999:111) shows that nearly half of defense speeches include a verbal appeal to the jurors' pity.

[57] Johnstone 1999:113.

[58] Appeals to pity may well have played a more central role in *timêsis*, the process of assessing the penalty that occurred in those cases where the law did not specify the punishment. Unfortunately, the only such speech that survives is Plato's account of Socrates' defense speeches. Socrates refuses to stoop to asking for the jury's pity even at the penalty phase, but his trial strategy can hardly be considered typical.

[59] Konstan 2000:133ff.

[60] Konstan 2000:136.

[61] Konstan 2000:138.

[62] E.g., Dem. 28.18–19; Lys. 19.45.

penalty. The trial verdict encompassed much more than a decision regarding factual guilt. The effects of an adverse verdict were thought relevant to the jury's highly particularized and discretionary calculation of moral desert at the guilt phase.

As a practical matter, Athenian jurors had little control over the specific penalty imposed after a conviction. For some offenses (*atimêtoi*), the penalty was fixed by statute. For others (*timêtoi*), the jury chose between the penalties proposed by the opposing parties during a second round of speeches.[63] Even in these cases, it seems that juries were not always given a choice at the penalty phase: once a verdict of guilty was entered, the litigants could reach an agreement on the proposed penalty.[64] Whereas modern jurors in non-capital cases are generally not informed of the penalty faced by the defendant precisely to prevent sentencing information from influencing their decision on guilt,[65] Athenian litigants regularly inform the jury of the penalty at issue. Even in cases without fixed penalties, jurors would often have a fair idea during trial of the range of penalties likely to be proposed. Prosecutors at times discussed their proposed penalty during the guilt phase,[66] and in some suits – particularly those which called for restitution, such as theft or breach of contract – the prosecutor included the value of his claim in the indictment.[67] A juror who believed that the defendant was guilty of the charge but did not deserve to suffer the fixed or probable penalty was more likely to vote to acquit than (in the case of an *agôn timêtos*) to assume in the absence of deliberation that his fellow jurors shared his desire for a lenient sentence and that the defendant would propose a more acceptable penalty. The attempt of the prosecutor in Lysias 15 vigorously to dissuade jurors from considering the severity of the penalty in

---

[63] For a list of actions that had fixed penalties and those that were determined in a sentencing hearing see Harrison 1998:80–82.

[64] Is. 5.18; Dem. 47.42–43; see also Dem. 58.70. Scafuro (1997:393–394) suggests that there may have been a regular procedure for compromise in trials without fixed penalties after a verdict on the offense was given.

[65] Some modern legal commentators (e.g., Heumann & Cassack 1983; Sauer 1995) have argued that where the sentence is largely determined at the trial stage, as is the case when mandatory minimum penalties, three strikes laws, or sentencing guidelines apply, jurors should be informed of the sentencing consequences of finding the defendant guilty.

[66] Isoc. 20.19; Dem. 56.43–44; 58.19. For discussion, see Todd 1993:134–135.

[67] E.g., Dem. 45.46; Ar. *Vesp.* 897; Dion. Hal. *Dein.* 3. For discussion see Harrison 1998:80–81; Boegehold 1995:24 & n.15. Although a defendant could submit a lower proposal at the penalty phase, it would be very risky for a convicted defendant to propose a sum that was vastly lower than the value of the contract or the goods in question.

their determination of guilt suggests that this practice may have been frequent in Athens:

> And so, gentlemen of the jury, if it seems to you that the penalty is too great and the law excessively harsh, you must remember that you are here not to make laws regarding these matters, but to cast your ballot according to the laws as they exist, and not to show pity for the wrongdoers, but rather to express your anger at them and to help the entire city.[68]

It is important to note that appeals to pity in the Athenian courts were firmly rooted in the defendant's particular circumstances; litigants generally do not criticize the penalty itself as disproportionate to the charges, but rather bemoan the tragic effects that penalty will have on them given their specific situation. These arguments are thus examples of the weakest form of what is known in modern parlance as "jury nullification." A taxonomy of jury nullification includes three varieties, from strongest to weakest: (1) acquittal contrary to law because the jury believes that the defendant's act should not be proscribed; (2) acquittal because the jury believes that the act, though criminal, does not deserve the punishment prescribed for it; and (3) acquittal because the jury believes not that the law or its punishment is unjust in the abstract, but that such punishment is inappropriate given the particular circumstances of the case.[69] It is the third form of nullification that we meet in the Athenian speeches.

The particular circumstances that could render punishment inappropriate in the eyes of an Athenian jury included not only the circumstances surrounding the act itself, but also the tragic effects the penalty would have on the defendant and his family. Particularly common are appeals that an adverse verdict will leave the defendant's family without support or the means to dower its unmarried women,[70] and that failure to pay a fine will lead to the defendant's loss of citizen rights.[71] Alcibiades the Younger, for example, explains that the five-talent penalty carries more serious consequences for him than for other defendants: "For even though

---

[68] Lys. 15.9.

[69] Green 1985:xviii. On modern debates over jury nullification, see Noah 2001; Pettys 2001; Liepold 1996; Butler 1995.

[70] Lys. 19.33; 21.24–25; Dem. 28.19.

[71] Lys. 18.1; 9.21; 20.34; Isoc. 16.45–46. Failure to pay a debt to the state could lead to *atimia*, or loss of citizen rights, until the debt was repaid. Arguments that the proscribed penalty would have tragic effects are by no means limited to capital cases; defendants argue for acquittal on the basis of heavy fines that might drag one's family into poverty or result in *atimia*.

the same legal punishments apply to all, the risk is not the same for everyone; rather, those who have money suffer a fine, but those who are impoverished, as I am, are in danger of losing their civic rights [i.e., *atimia*], which is, I think, a greater misfortune than exile.... Therefore I beg you to help me and not allow me to be abused by my enemies, to be stripped of my country, or to become a curiosity because of my rotten luck."[72] Athenian notions of relevance in the popular courts thus extended to information regarding the concrete effects of the laws and legal decisions on the lives of individuals. Unlike modern jurors and judges, Athenian jurors were constantly made aware of the violence inherent in their judicial decisions.[73] Although Athenian defendants do not explicitly discuss what role their appeals to pity should play in the jury's decision, it seems likely that these arguments were thought not only to remind the jury of the seriousness of their task but also to assist in its determination of whether a conviction was a just result in the particular circumstances of the case.

The role of the Athenian popular court jury in judging whether a defendant who had committed the acts charged might nevertheless not merit conviction and penalty is more explicit in the special procedure known as *apophasis*.[74] *Apophasis* was used most commonly in charges of corruption, official misconduct, and treason. Under this procedure, the Areopagus, a council comprised of former magistrates,[75] conducted an investigation and published a preliminary, non-binding report. The case was then passed to a popular court for a final decision. The most famous example of this procedure occurred in the context of the Harpalus affair in 323 B.C.E., in which a number of prominent politicians, including Demosthenes, were prosecuted for corruption. Four prosecution speeches connected to this affair survive. These four speeches are remarkable in that they do not discuss the evidence against the politicians at all; only two witnesses are called in all of the speeches, and the speakers repeatedly insist that the jury should blindly

---

[72] Isoc. 16.47–48. In describing the consequences he would face if convicted as a greater misfortune than exile, Alcibiades the Younger probably refers to the exile suffered by his famous father for treason.

[73] In a seminal article, Robert Cover (1986) discussed the concept of "law's violence" – the threat of violence that makes possible seemingly peaceful legal acts such as the sentencing of a criminal defendant, and the violence perpetrated on legal subjects by judicial decisions – and how the process of modern legal interpretation tends to push the reality of law's violence into the background of legal officials' minds.

[74] *Apophasis*, introduced in the 340s, was one of the new powers granted to the Areopagus in the middle of the fourth century. For discussion of this procedure, see Hansen 1975:39–40; 1991:292–294; Worthington 1992:357–362; Carawan 1985; Wallace 1989:113–119; Rubinstein 2000:112ff.; de Bruyn 1995:117–146.

[75] For discussion of the composition of the Areopagus, see Chapter 4.

accept the report of the Areopagus. For example, in one speech Dinarchus states "the [Areopagus] Council has found Demonsthenes guilty. What more need we say?"[76] It is understandable that the prosecutors in this case would emphasize the Areopagus' favorable verdict, and presumably the defense speeches that do not survive did not show so much deference to the Areopagus' decision. Nevertheless, it is striking that the prosecutors in the Harpalus affair do not seem to consider discussing the evidence for the defendants' corruption as their primary task.[77] This trial strategy is even more surprising when we consider that the report of the Areopagus upon which the prosecutors rely did not include the evidence or reasoning for their verdict; Hyperides indicates that the council simply published a list of names and the amount of money taken as a bribe.[78]

Thus in the Harpalus affair the jurors were expected to render a verdict upholding or overturning the Areopagus' report even though they were not presented with any evidence regarding the facts of the case. A passage in the first speech of Dinarchus explains this paradox by suggesting that the popular court jury's task may have included more than reaching a decision on the factual question of guilt. He notes that the Areopagus' inquiry is limited to establishing the facts:

> Unlike you [popular court jurors], who (now don't get angry at me for saying this) sometimes are accustomed when rendering a verdict to privilege mercy over justice, the [Areopagus] Council simply seeks to report anyone who is liable to the charge and has committed crimes contrary to your ancestral ways.[79]

Dinarchus goes on to list cases in which the popular court jury acquitted men found guilty by the Areopagus in *apophasis*, adding this (doubtless at least partially self-serving) explanation:

---

[76]   Din. 1.84. See also Din. 2.6.

[77]   The first prosecution speaker, Stratocles, apparently briefly summarized the charges, but there is no indication that he presented evidence or extended argument on the corruption charge. Din. 1.1. As Carawan (1985:134) points out, although it is possible that the speeches that do not survive presented evidence on the charges, the absence of any reference to evidence and the focus on the report of the Areopagus in the speeches we do have suggest that "the report of the Areopagus represented the sum of the evidence, and the jurors were asked to accept the judgment of the Areopagus on the facts of the case."

[78]   Hyp. 5.6. De Bruyn (1995:143–144) suggests that the Areopagus' report would generally include more information than was given in the Harpalus case.

[79]   Din. 1.55.

Judging the case, you [the popular court jurors] acquitted them. It was not that you were charging the Areopagus Council with being incorrect, but that you placed mercy rather than justice first, believing the penalty to be too harsh given the crime committed by the defendants. . . . The report of the Areopagus Council was not shown to be false. Rather, even though the report was true, it seemed best to the jurors to acquit Polyeuctus. For the Areopagus Council was assigned to seek out the truth; but the court, I say, judged him worthy of pardon.[80]

The surviving prosecution speeches in the Harpalus affair support this account of the jury's role: The prosecutors devote much of their time to broad attacks on the character of the defendants and other arguments suggesting that severe punishment is merited and pity inappropriate.[81] Thus, the two-staged *apophasis* procedure highlights what must have been one of the elements of popular-court decision making in ordinary cases as well: The determination of whether the allegations, even if true, merit punishment in light of the particular circumstances of the case and the defendant.

ARGUMENTS CONCERNING THE CHARACTER OF THE LITIGANTS

The most common type of extra-legal argumentation in our surviving speeches is the liberal use of character evidence. Litigants present themselves as upstanding citizens by describing their military exploits or the public services they (and their families) have done for the state, such as equipping a warship or paying for a dramatic festival;[82] and they criticize their opponents, for example, for failing to pay taxes and shirking military duty and public services,[83] committing other crimes in the past,[84] and being of low birth.[85] Some form of discussion of character occurs

---

[80] Din. 1.57–59.

[81] E.g., Din. 1.47, 71ff, 82, 94ff, 109–111; 2.1–2, 11ff; 3.11,15,18, 20; Hyp. 5.26, 40.

[82] E.g., Lys. 16.18; Is. 4.27; 7.37–41; Isoc. 18.58–61; Dem. 54.44. Such public services ("liturgies") were imposed on wealthy individuals. For discussion of references to liturgies in court speeches, see Johnstone 1999:93–100.

[83] E.g., Is. 5.45–6; Dem. 21.154; 54.44; 42.22.

[84] E.g., Lys. 14.21; 30.6, 9ff; Is. 8.40; Dem. 40.38; 57.58–60; Hyp 2.10; Din. 2.1–2, 11ff.

[85] E.g., Dem. 18.129–30; Lys. 30.2. For discussion of the topoi relating to character, see Carey 1994b; Lateiner 1981.

in 70 out of 87 popular court speeches.[86] Despite the frequency of arguments from character, there was clearly some ambivalence about the wisdom of this practice: litigants sometimes charge that they have resorted to a discussion of character only because their opponents' slander has forced them to respond,[87] and speakers sometimes urge the jury to ignore questions of reputation and character when reaching their decision.[88] Perhaps because of the contestability of character evidence and a worry that its use might lead to verdicts based solely on the prejudices of the jury,[89] in several cases litigants preface their character evidence with an explanation of why it is relevant to the jury's decision. These passages, along with other aspects of the way in which character evidence is used in our surviving speeches, suggest that discussion of character was considered relevant both to discovering the truth and to determining whether the defendant deserved the prescribed or likely penalty. Of course, it is difficult to pinpoint the intended effect of any particular piece of evidence; discussions of character likely operated on more than one level of meaning.[90] Nevertheless, the liberal use of character evidence in our surviving speeches is most plausibly explained as part of the attempt to reach a just resolution that took into account the unique circumstances of each case.

The first justification for character evidence we meet in the speeches is that it assists the jury in finding facts through an argument from *eikos*, or probability.[91] The Athenians tended to view character as stable and unchanging.[92] That a defendant had committed crimes in the past or otherwise exhibited bad morals or character

---

[86] Speeches in maritime suits (*dikai emporikai*) are not included in this calculation. For a discussion of relevance in maritime cases, see Chapter 6.

[87] E.g., Lys. 9.3; 30.15; Hyp. 1.8–9; Dem. 52.1. Litigants also at times apologize and suggest that they recognize discussion of character as a digression. E.g., Dem. 57.63; Is. 5.12.

[88] E.g., Dem. 52.1–2; Hyp.4.32.

[89] The defendant in Hyp. 4.32, for example, expresses the fear that his opponent has emphasized the speaker's wealth in the hope that the jury will convict him out of spite.

[90] Carey 1996:42–43.

[91] For discussion, see Saunders 1991b:113; Johnstone 1999:95–97.

[92] The speaker in Demosthenes 58, for example, recounts his opponent's past bad acts and asserts, "remembering these things, you should suppose that this man is the same now as he was then." Dem. 58.28. See also Dem. 25.15; 36.55; Hyp. 1.14ff; Eur. *fr.* 810; Men. *Epit.* 1094–1101; Soph. *fr.* 739. Although passages assuming a stable character predominate in our sources, speakers and dramatists do at times argue that one's character can change over time or be affected by the environment when this position is helpful to the argument or the dramatic situation. For a detailed discussion of passages on either side, see Dover 1974:88–95.

was considered highly probative of whether he was guilty of the offense charged
and whether he was telling the truth in his present speech. Thus, for example, one
speaker states, "If you knew the shamelessness of Diocles and what sort of man
he was in other matters, you would not doubt any of the things I have said."[93]
Another explains his decision to discuss the prosecutor's history of bringing false
accusations and the defendant's good character at some length:

> Now I think, men of Athens, that presenting witnesses on these matters is
> more to the point than anything. For if a man is always acting as a sycophant
> [i.e., one who is excessively litigious], what must you think he is doing in this
> case? And by Zeus, men of Athens, I think it is also to the point to present
> to you all signs of Phormio's character and his righteousness and generosity.
> The man who is unjust in all his dealings might, if it happens, have wronged
> this man too. On the other hand, he who has never done wrong to anyone,
> but rather has voluntarily done good deeds for many people, on what basis
> would he, in any probability, have done wrong to this man alone?[94]

Character was all the more relevant to fact finding in a world without modern
techniques of forensic investigation and evidence gathering: in the absence of hard
evidence, character was a proxy for guilt or innocence. Speakers at times argue
that evidence of a man's character over the course of his entire life is more reliable
than the rhetoric and misleading statements made by litigants during the trial.
One defendant tells the jury, "I think you should judge me not from the slanders
of the prosecutor, but rather by examining how I have lived my entire life. You
see, it's impossible for anyone in the city, whether wicked or decent, to escape
the notice of the citizen body."[95] He then cites his clean record and meritorious
service to the city before arguing, "You ought to take these things as proof for
the purpose of this case that the charges against me are false."[96]

---

[93] Is. 8.40.

[94] Dem. 36.54–55.

[95] Hyp. 1.14.

[96] Hyp. 1.18. In a similar vein, the speaker in Lysias 19 argues,

> Bear in mind that while someone might be able for a short time to fake his character, there is not
> one man who could conceal his wickedness for seventy years. . . . Therefore it is not right to
> trust the words of the prosecutors more than the deeds which they have done during their whole
> life, and also time, which you must consider the clearest means of ascertaining the truth.

Lys. 19.60–61. See also Dem 58.27; cf. Aesch. 1.93.

The second reason given for the citation of character evidence is that it is relevant to the jury's assessment of whether the defendant deserves the penalty for the charge or should be given pardon.[97] To cite just one example, the prosecutor in Dinarchus *Against Aristogeiton* engages in an extended character attack on Aristogeiton, noting that he failed to support or properly bury his father, had been convicted on several charges in the past, and was even so base that his fellow criminals in prison voted to shun him.[98] The speaker then asserts that Aritogeiton has forfeited any right to a lenient penalty, stating that he deserves to suffer execution "on the basis of both his whole life and the things he has done now."[99]

Litigants generally do not challenge the idea that one's character should be factored into the jury's calculation of moral desert, even though character is normally regarded in classical Greek culture as stable and unchanging, with the implicit assumption that it is a natural attribute over which the defendant has no control.[100] Athenian litigants do not argue that they should not be held responsible for immutable character traits, though we have seen that litigants sometimes argue that the lack of intent to commit the act is an extenuating circumstance. Philocleon's defense in the trial scene of Aristophanes' comedy the *Wasps* illustrates the typical view we find in the law courts that actions taken in keeping with one's immutable character do not render them involuntary (*akôn*): he states, "Forgive me, since I did this *akôn* and not from (i.e. not consistent with) my character."[101] The tragic poets, by contrast, express a more complicated approach to the relationship between character and moral blame. In some notable instances, tragedians wrestled with questions of the justice of punishment for inherited guilt, immutable characteristics, and actions beyond one's control. In Sophocles' Oedipus plays, to take the most familiar example, we meet statements on both sides of the question:

---

[97] On the use of the defendant's record for this purpose, see Saunders 1991b:113–118. Saunders points out that litigants sometimes use a defendant's record not only to argue about what the defendant deserves based on his past, but also what is in the best interests of the *dêmos*, for example that a wealthy defendant will continue to perform public services if acquitted. Arguments such as this contemplating a direct quid pro quo are rare, however.

[98] Din. 2.8–13.

[99] Din. 2.11. For other examples, see Isoc. 18.47; Lys. 20.34; 30.6; Din. 3.5, Dem. 45.63ff.

[100] Saunders (1991b:116–17) points out that Demosthenes sometimes implicitly distinguishes between "offenders who are evil by nature and those whose depravity has been acquired." Whereas acquired depravity may be more serious (at least for Demosthenes), litigants do not suggest that the presence of immutable bad character traits are an excuse for wrongdoing.

[101] Ar. *Vesp.* 1001–1002.

in *Oedipus the King*, Oedipus, once exposed as guilty of parricide and incest, not only accepts his responsibility but even consigns himself to the unexpected self-inflicted punishment of blinding, whereas in *Oedipus at Colonus* he argues that he should not be blamed for acts committed in ignorance.[102]

It has been pointed out that character evidence in the court speeches focuses most commonly on the defendant rather than the prosecutor.[103] The emphasis on the defendant supports the view that the frequent citations to character in Athenian litigation are designed to assist the jury in reaching a fair verdict rather than to provide ammunition in a contest for honor between the litigants:[104] the defendant's reputation and record is part of the contextual information considered by the jury in determining whether a conviction and the resulting penalty are warranted.[105] Although there are a handful of passages that suggest a non-legal purpose for the citation of character evidence – most notably, statements that the jury should acquit a defendant because he has performed expensive public services in the past and, if victorious, will continue to do so in the future[106] – the bulk of the evidence suggests that the liberal use of arguments from character reflect the Athenian popular court's highly discretionary and equitable mode of decision making.[107] In sum, the prevalence of extra-legal argumentation such as information regarding the background and context of the dispute, appeals to pity, and character evidence indicates not that the courts functioned primarily as a form of social drama but

[102] Soph. *OC* 971–982.

[103] Johnstone 1999:94; Rubinstein 2000:195.

[104] Johnstone (1999:96) expresses this idea in terms of the defendant using character evidence to attack the plausibility of the prosecutor's narrative, whereas Rubinstein (2000:218) states, "the measurement of the defendant's *timê* was not relative to the personal record of his prosecutor(s), but, rather, relative to the accusations levelled against him."

[105] In fact, the instances where prosecutors do cite their public services tend to be cases involving inheritance and cases – such as assault – where the prosecutor argues that the defendant's honor has been violated (Johnstone 1999:98–100). The prosecutor's character is relevant to the resolution of the dispute in these types of suit because in inheritance cases it addresses whether the prosecutor deserves to own the property under the circumstances, and in assault cases it is relevant to the seriousness of the crime.

[106] Is. 6.61; 7.38–42; Lys.18.20–21; 19.61; 21.25; Dem. 28.24. For discussion, see Johnstone 1999:101. Generalized requests for *charis* on the basis of prior service and good character seem to be part of the calculation of moral desert (cf. Johnstone 1999:100–108).

[107] Though, as noted above, it is difficult to pinpoint the intended effect of extra-legal argumentation such as the use of character evidence and these devices most likely operated on more than one level of meaning (Carey 1996:42–43).

that the Athenians had, by modern standards, an extremely broad notion of what information was relevant to reaching a just legal verdict.

THE USE OF LAW IN POPULAR COURT SPEECHES

The Athenians' broad view of relevance extended to the discussion of law in popular court speeches. Rather than focus on the elements of the particular charge at issue and apply them to the facts of the case, Athenian litigants at times cite an array of laws that do not govern the charges in the case,[108] and at other times do not deem it relevant to discuss – or even mention – the law under which the suit was brought.[109] A brief examination of the peculiar treatment of statutes in the popular courts suggests that statutes and legal argument served to assist the jury in obtaining a broad view of the individual case before it rather than focusing the dispute on one or a few points of disagreement concerning the relevant law.

Ariston's prosecution of Conon in Demosthenes 54 illustrates popular court litigants' lax approach to the statute under which a suit is brought. While walking through the agora one evening, Ariston was jumped, beaten, and stripped by a group of drunken men. Adding insult to injury, Ariston reports, one of his attackers yelled epithets at him and stood over him crowing and flapping his arms at his sides like a victorious fighting cock.[110] Ariston explains that because of his youth and inexperience he settled on bringing a private suit (*dikê*) for assault even though Conon's actions made him liable to the more serious charges of clothes stealing (a capital offense when brought through the summary arrest procedure) or *hubris*, a public charge (*graphê*) that was not clearly defined but seems to have involved an affront to one's honor.[111] Perhaps because the formal charge was considered as much a means to get one's grievance heard as a precise legal basis for

---

[108] For example, speakers sometimes cite laws to bolster their portrayal of the character of the parties (De Brauw 2001–2002), or to give the general impression that their position is supported by the laws (Carey 1996:44–45). Ford (1999) provides a case study of the use of law in Aeschines *Against Timarchus*. He notes that the discussion of the law at issue, which accounts for only one-sixth of the speech (1.28–32), is surrounded by a number of laws irrelevant to the charge but useful in constructing an image of the education and moral character of a proper orator that can be contrasted with the record and character of the speaker's opponent (Ford 1999:241).

[109] E.g., Lys. 30, Hyp. 3.

[110] Dem. 54.9.

[111] Dem. 54.1. For various theories on the meaning of *hubris*, see Millett 1998; D. L. Cairns 1996; Fisher 1992:36–85; MacDowell 1976.

the suit, Ariston does not restrict his legal arguments to the charge under which the case was brought. As has often been pointed out, he argues throughout his speech that Conon is guilty of *hubris* as well as simple assault: from the first word (ὑβρισθείς) to the penultimate sentence (ὑβριστέοι) he characterizes Conon's actions as *hubris*,[112] and he notes Conon's humiliating display over him as "proof" of *hubris*, and thus of guilt.[113] Most surprising to a modern reader is Ariston's decision to have the laws prohibiting clothestealing and *hubris* read to the jury, but *not* the law of assault.[114] Ariston apparently believed that evidence that Conon was also guilty of the greater crime of *hubris* was relevant to the jury's decision.

The speaker in Demosthenes *Against Phaenippus* demonstrates a similar tendency. This case involved an *antidosis* ("exchange"), one of the more peculiar procedures in Athenian law. In the absence of universal taxation, wealthy Athenians were appointed to perform expensive public services such as outfitting a warship or paying for a dramatic festival. Under the *antidosis* procedure, a man could seek to avoid an assigned liturgy by proposing a richer man to perform the service in his stead.[115] By doing so, he challenged the allegedly wealthier man to choose between carrying out the liturgy or exchanging all of his property with the challenger. If he chose to make the exchange, the parties were required by law to produce an inventory of their property within three days, and each was permitted to inspect the other's estate and seal the doors of storage rooms and the like to prevent his opponent from concealing or removing any of his property. It seems unlikely that exchanges took place very often, if at all; more commonly, the second man would refuse both options and the case would be brought before a jury to determine which party should perform the liturgy.[116] If a challenge to an exchange was accepted, but the challenger believed that the exchange was not being properly or honestly carried out, he had the right to abandon the exchange and demand a trial.[117] In such a case, the jury was to decide simply which party was required to

---

[112] D. Cohen 1995:120ff.

[113] Dem. 54.9.

[114] Dem. 54.24.

[115] For discussion of this procedure, see, e.g., MacDowell 1978:161–164; Harrison 1998:236–238.

[116] It seemed that exchange was always a possibility, however. For discussion, see Harrison 1998:237 n.2.

[117] It is possible that the man challenged could also terminate the exchange agreement and call for a trial. In Demosthenes 42, the speaker, who originally made the challenge to exchange, tells us that his opponent brought a counter-suit against him for failing to include his mining assets in his inventory. Dem. 42.17–19.

perform the public service; by bringing the suit to trial the parties had terminated the agreement to exchange property, and any violations of the *antidosis* procedure were not formally before the court.[118]

The speaker *in Against Phaenippus* initiates such a suit after his opponent Phaenippus initially agreed to an exchange but failed to produce the required inventory on time and allegedly attempted to conceal the true value of his property by removing grain, timber, and wine from his estate and claiming various debts on the farm that did not exist when the speaker first inspected the property for mortgage stones.[119] Although the relevant law calls for the jury simply to determine which party is wealthier and therefore liable to perform the liturgy, the speaker focuses on his opponent's violation of the law requiring the presentation of an inventory within three days: his opening suggests that it is the violation of this law that is the basis for his suit;[120] he has the statute read out in the course of his speech;[121] and he expects the jurors to consider this violation along with the relative wealth of the parties in reaching their decision:

> I beg all of you, gentlemen of the jury, that if I demonstrate that this man here, Phaenippus, has both violated the just regulations in the law [requiring the production of the inventory] and is richer than I am, to help me and put this man instead of me on the list of Three Hundred [liable to liturgies and the *proeisphora*].[122]

The loose approach of the speakers in these two cases to the formal charge is in keeping with the general Athenian reluctance to rely on arguments that might be perceived to be based on procedural or legal technicalities.[123] For example, litigants note when their opponent has violated the relevant statute of limitations, but do not argue that the case should be decided on these grounds.[124] The speaker in Demosthenes *Against Apaturius* emphasizes that he is quoting the one-year statute

---

[118] Dem. 28.17; Isoc. 15.5. For discussion, see MacDowell 1978:163–164.

[119] Dem. 42.5–10. Mortgage stones (*horoi*) were large inscribed pillars set up on a piece of property to give notice of a mortgage. For discussion, see Fine 1951; Finley 1985; Millett 1982; E. Harris 1988.

[120] Dem. 42.1–2.

[121] Dem. 42.16.

[122] Dem. 42.4. The speaker also emphasizes Phaenippus' failure to produce an inventory at a later date agreed upon by the parties.

[123] This reluctance was due in part to the fact that technical issues were raised at trial rather than in preliminary procedures as they are in modern legal systems.

[124] Millett 1993; for discussion of statutes of limitations in Athens, see Charles 1938.

of limitation for sureties merely as circumstantial evidence to support his version of the facts:

> I do not rely heavily on the law [i.e., the statute of limitations], arguing that
> I do not have to pay the penalty if I did act as a surety, but rather I am
> saying that the law serves as a witness that I did not act as a surety, as does
> this man himself, for in that case he would have initiated a suit against me as
> a surety within the time limit set forth in the law.[125]

Of all our surviving speeches, one would expect those brought through the *paragraphê* procedure to contain the most focused legal argumentation. The *paragraphê* was a plea challenging an allegedly illegal lawsuit. If this counter-suit was successful, the original case was dropped, but if the jury rejected the *paragraphê*, the original suit proceeded as normal and was heard by a new jury.[126] *Paragraphai* could be brought on a number of theories, including the execution of a discharge or release, or that the plaintiff had chosen the wrong legal procedure. One would expect *paragraphai* speeches to concentrate exclusively on the legal issues of the counter-suit, yet all except one of our nine surviving cases include detailed discussions of the original dispute.[127] The speaker *in Against Callimachus* states, "I will demonstrate that Callimachus is not only suing in violation of the agreements [i.e., the Amnesty], but also that he is bringing these charges falsely,"[128] and the speaker in another case implies that his opponent brought a *paragraphê* merely to have the advantage of being the first speaker when the case was brought before a jury.[129] Juries thus appear to have considered the merits of the case as a whole in addition to the specific question raised in the counter-suit when deciding whether to dismiss the suit through the *paragraphê* procedure.

Even discussions of the specific charge at issue left much to the discretion of the jury because Athenian laws were so vague. Generally, as is often pointed out, Athenian laws simply state the name of the offense, the procedure for bringing suit under the law, and in some cases the prescribed penalty; our surviving laws

---

[125] Dem. 33.27. See also Dem. 36.26–27; 38.17.

[126] For the *paragraphê* procedure, see Isager & Hansen 1975:123–131; Harrison 1998:106–24; Todd 1993:135–138; Wolff 1966.

[127] For a detailed analysis, see Harrison 1998:109–119. The one exception is Lysias 23, which, as Todd (1993:138 n.19) points out, may be a special case.

[128] Isoc. 18.4.

[129] Dem. 45.6.

and decrees do not define the crime or describe the essential characteristics of behavior governed by the law. The decree of Cannonus is characteristically vague about the definition of the offense even though it provides detailed instructions for the method of trial and penalty:

> If anyone wrongs the people of Athens, then that man, while chained up, is to be tried before the people, and if he is found guilty, he is to be killed by being thrown into a pit and his money confiscated and a tithe given to the goddess.[130]

Similarly, the law against *hubris* does not define this elusive offense: "If anyone commits *hubris* against anyone, whether a child, a woman, or a man, free or slave, or commits any unlawful act against any of these, any Athenian who wishes may bring a public indictment. . . . "[131] The lack of precise legal definitions was by no means limited to extraordinary procedures or offenses that by their nature involve a high degree of subjectivity. Indeed, Aristotle notes the need for precise definitions of theft (*klopê*) and adultery (*moicheia*), offenses not obviously problematic, as well as *hubris*.[132] There is evidence that some viewed the vagueness of the laws as a merit: *The Constitution of the Athenians* reports that "some men think that he [Solon] deliberately made the laws unclear in order that the demos would have power over the verdict."[133] The absence of carefully defined laws specifying the required elements of each charge invited litigants to bring a wide range of arguments to bear on the case. In many cases, the primary purpose of the relevant law may have been to set out a procedure for obtaining redress for a broad class of offenses. Once the case came to court, the jury attempted to arrive at a just verdict looking at the individual case as a whole without focusing exclusively on determining whether the defendant's behavior satisfied the formal criteria of the specific charge at hand.

---

[130] Xen. *Hell.* 1.7.20. Prosecution under the Cannonus decree appears to have been short lived. For discussion, see Lavelle 1988.

[131] Dem. 21.47.

[132] Arist. *Rhet.* 1374a8. For the vagueness of the laws, see D. Cohen 1983:6–7; D. Cohen 1995:189; see also E. Harris 1988. Carey (1998) has shown that laws relating to family and religion are unusual in that they are often more substantive than procedural in character.

[133] Arist. *Ath.Pol.* 9.2. The author of the *Rhetorica ad Alexandrum* viewed the ambiguity of the laws as a strategic opportunity, instructing speakers to use ambiguous laws (*amphiboloi nomoi*) to his advantage. *Rhet. ad Alex.*1443a30.

This is not to say that Athenian litigants could not or did not use legal reasoning to argue for a particular interpretation of a vague or ambiguous law.[134] A common litigation strategy was to rely on the legal fiction that the laws were created by a single lawgiver and thus formed a coherent whole, making it possible to use principles from unrelated laws to interpret a particular law.[135] For example, Isaeus' speech *On the Estate of Ciron* includes an argument that attempts to resolve a gap in the law which states that in the absence of a male heir a female child can inherit as an *epiklêros* ("heiress") ahead of collateral relatives such as the deceased's brother or nephew,[136] but does not specify whether such a woman's child may also inherit ahead of a collateral.[137] The speaker attempts to establish that a daughter's son takes precedence before a brother's son by discussing two related laws and arguing from the apparent logic of the inheritance system as a whole. The speaker argues first that because a daughter inherits before a brother, a daughter's child therefore should inherit before a brother's child.[138] He bolsters his argument by quoting the law under which descendants are obliged to support their indigent and infirm parents and grandparents, whereas collaterals have no such obligation.[139] By arguing that if a man is legally bound to support his grandfather he therefore has a corresponding right to inherit his estate, the speaker presupposes a coherent system underlying the inheritance laws that can be used to interpret an ambiguous law.[140]

As ingenious and potentially persuasive as these types of arguments are, it is striking that legal reasoning was not considered an authoritative guide to a verdict;

---

[134] For recent discussions of legal argumentation in Attic oratory, see, e.g., Johnstone 1999:21–45; E. Harris 2000; Hillgruber 1988:105–120.

[135] Johnstone 1999:25–33.

[136] A female child of a man who died without a male heir did not directly inherit, but possession of his estate went with her when she married.

[137] The law is quoted in Demosthenes 43.51.

[138] Is. 8.31.

[139] Is. 8.34.

[140] Another example, discussed by both Johnstone (1999:28) and E. Harris (2000:47–54) occurs in Hyperides 3. The speaker bought two slaves and was fooled into signing a sales contract that made him responsible for the (quite substantial) debts previously incurred by the slaves. The law of contract stated simply that agreements are binding, and the speaker attempts to read a provision voiding unjust contracts into the law by citing a variety of laws that cast doubt on the validity of contracts in other contexts: he cites a statute permitting a man who unknowingly buys a slave with physical disabilities to return him, a law invalidating wills made under the influence of old age, insanity, or coercion, a statute prohibiting telling lies in the agora, and a law stating that children are legitimate only if the marriage was lawful (Hyp. 3.15–18).

interpretation and application of the law at issue was certainly considered relevant to the jury's decision, but there is no indication that a litigant was expected to limit himself to or even focus on such questions.[141] In fact, discussion of the relevant laws was only one weapon in an Athenian litigant's arsenal. The speaker in *On the Estate of Ciron* follows his legal argument that descendants take precedence over collaterals with an extended character attack on his opponent Diocles:[142] he details his past plots to defraud, deprive of citizen rights, and even murder various family members, and, in a surprising crescendo, he ends his speech with a deposition showing that Diocles was caught as an adulterer.[143]

In modern legal systems, one of the primary functions of law is to provide a means to focus a dispute on one or a few aspects of disagreement recognized by the relevant law; as White notes, law "compel[s] those who disagree about one thing to speak a language which expresses their actual or pretended agreement about everything else."[144] In Athens, law served no such purpose; the legal charge provided a means to get a dispute before a jury and an important source for litigants' arguments, but did not serve to narrow the range of information and argument that was considered relevant to the jury's decision.

THE JURY'S EVALUATION OF EXTRA-LEGAL AND LEGAL ARGUMENTATION

We have seen that both extra-legal and legal argumentation were considered relevant in the popular courts. Although modern accounts of the Athenian legal system tend to emphasize one or the other of these types of material, neither is dominant in our surviving sources. There is, however, some variation in the distribution of contextual and legal material between various types of speech.[145]

---

[141] On the persuasive but non-binding nature of statute law in Athens, see Todd 1993:59–60 and Sealey 1994:54.

[142] Although Diocles was not a litigant in this suit, the speaker presents him as his true opponent in the dispute.

[143] Is. 8.36–44.

[144] White 1990:179.

[145] Rubinstein (2000:194–198) has pointed out that there are some important differences in the argumentation found in *graphai* and *dikai*. Although speeches in public cases (particularly those delivered by prosecutors) include fewer discussions of public services and character evidence, speeches in *graphai* are not noticeably more focused on the specific legal charge than those in *dikai*. Thus, for example,

Most notably, defendants focus more on extra-legal information and argumentation than prosecutors, who tend to rely more heavily on the law in constructing their arguments.[146] This is only to be expected. As Nussbaum points out, there is a natural link between particularized justice and leniency.[147] Because justice starts from the premise that a wrong must be righted and that the offender must suffer sufficiently to balance out a deliberate wrong, and because "the circumstances of human life throw up many and various obstacles to meeting the tough standards of justice," a close examination of the particular context of a dispute will more commonly suggest mitigating than aggravating factors.[148]

Despite these variations between different types of speeches, most popular court orations include a mixture of contextual and legal argumentation. Speeches that contain only information that would be irrelevant by modern standards are rare, those focusing solely on the relevant facts and law even rarer.[149] Isaeus *On the Estate of Ciron* (discussed in a previous section) illustrates the balance of legal and extra-legal argumentation found in many popular court speeches: the speaker devotes roughly the same amount of effort to explaining that the law favors descendants over collaterals as he does to arguing that his opponent Diocles does not deserve to enjoy the fruits of the estate.[150]

How did an Athenian jury go about evaluating the mass of information and argument, both contextual and legal, presented in a popular court case? Athenian juries offered no reasons for their verdicts, and we rarely know the outcome of the cases for which speeches are preserved. One clue is an enigmatic and controversial

Yunis (1988) has demonstrated that in *graphê paranomón* cases political arguments were as relevant and important as the legal argument that the defendant's proposed decree was in conflict with an existing law. Both ancient and modern writers have also noted that extra-legal argumentation was particularly prevalent in inheritance disputes (Arist. [Pr.] 29.3; see also D. Cohen 1995:163–180).

[146] For discussion, see Johnstone 1999:49–60. Of course, Athenian prosecutors did regularly use contextual information (e.g., Dem. 53; 54; Aesch. 1; Lys. 10; 14; 15; Din. 1; 2; 3).

[147] Nussbaum 1993.

[148] Nussbaum 1993.

[149] The two most egregious examples in the former category are the prosecution speeches delivered by *sunêgoroi* (co-speakers) against the younger Alcibiades preserved in Lysias 14 and 15, and even in these cases the speech of the primary prosecutor, now lost, may have included more legal argumentation. In the latter category may be placed Demosthenes 41 and 44, Isocrates 21, and Lysias 17. Scafuro (1997:56) also notes the mixture of legal and extra-legal information in most lawcourt speeches.

[150] Is. 8. The speaker also includes a brief discussion of the effects an adverse verdict would have on him (Is. 8.43–45).

phrase in the dikastic oath which was sworn each year by the panel of potential jurors. According to the standard reconstruction, the oath stated in part, "I shall vote according to the laws and decrees of the Athenian people and the Council of the Five Hundred, but concerning things about which there are no laws, I shall decide to the best of my judgment, neither with favor nor enmity."[151] Although some scholars have viewed the jurors' oath as evidence that the jury was limited to strictly applying the laws in all but the unusual case where there was no applicable statute, others have argued convincingly that the jurors' "best judgment" (*dikaiotatê gnômê*) necessarily played a much greater role in legal verdicts, noting particularly the broad discretion given to juries to interpret and apply often vague and ambiguous laws.[152]

We cannot know for certain how the average Athenian juror conceived of his task, but our surviving speeches suggest that even the relative importance of legal and contextual evidence in any individual case was open to dispute. Some speakers attempt to focus the jury's attention on their legal arguments by reminding them of their oath to vote according to the laws,[153] or by arguing that the jury should not be affected by the social standing of the litigants.[154] We have seen that others insist on the relevance of contextual information such as the defendant's behavior throughout his life and the likely effects of a verdict on the parties. As has often been pointed out, the treatment of legal and extra-legal arguments

[151] This reconstruction, quoted from Scafuro (1997:50), does not correspond precisely to any passage in the Attic orators. The clause relating to the jury's *dikaiotatê gnômê* appears in most, but not all citations of the oath, and the further limitation that *dikaiotatê gnômê* was to be used "concerning things about which there are no laws" appears in two of these passages. See Dem. 20.118; 23.96; 24.149–151; 39.40. On the reconstruction of the oath, see Biscardi 1970:222 n.20; Scafuro 1997:50; Johnstone 1999:41 & nn. 101–103.

[152] For a recent account of the scholarly controversy over the meaning of the dikastic oath, see Scafuro 1997:50–51. Biscardi (1970:226–228) offers a compromise view between those who argue that *dikaiotatê gnômê* came into play only to fill gaps in the law, and those who argue that it was also used to resolve conflicts between law and equity. He argues that the *dikaiotatê gnômê* played a central role in assisting jurors in carrying out their task of interpreting and applying the law; if a law appeared to be contrary to substantive justice, this was a sure sign that the law had been wrongly interpreted and should be reinterpreted with the assistance of the *dikaiotatê gnômê*. Thus, for Biscardi a statute was never disregarded in favor of equity, but reinterpreted in light of it; the law was preeminent, but the *dikaiotatê gnômê* served as the "soupape de sureté" for the system (Biscardi 1970:232).

[153] For a discussion of the use of the dikastic oath in Athenian court speeches, see Johnstone 1999:35–42. Johnstone notes that speakers also sometimes referred to the oath to claim authority for their particular interpretation of the law.

[154] Isoc. 18.34–35; 20.19; Dem. 52.1–2; Hyp. 4.32.

was not, however, entirely symmetrical: law court speakers do not explicitly urge jurors to ignore the law in favor of fairness and other extra-legal considerations. Rather, they typically argue that both law and justice support their claim.[155] This is hardly surprising. The general notion of the supremacy of law was central to Athenian democratic ideology, which held that adherence to law was one of the distinctions, perhaps the most important, that separated democracy from tyranny.[156] To suggest explicitly that the law was in some way inadequate would, at worst, raise suspicion of antidemocratic sentiment, and, at best, result rhetorically in a serious self-inflicted wound. Even though litigants do not urge the jurors to disregard the law, the explicit insistence on the relevance and importance of extra-legal argumentation in many of our speeches suggests that it was accepted that extra-legal arguments could take precedence over the dictates of the written law.

Even when the litigants in a particular case did not explicitly argue about the relative importance of legal and contextual evidence, they could make very different choices about what types of evidence to include and emphasize in their speeches. The dispute over Demosthenes' crown, one of the few cases in which the speeches of both speakers survive, illustrates the lack of consensus on the relative importance of legal and extra-legal argumentation. Aeschines, who failed to win even one-fifth of the jurors' votes, opens his speech with a long discussion of the relevant laws,[157] whereas Demosthenes responds to these legal arguments in a mere nine sections, shunted off to an inconspicuous part of his speech.[158] Such a situation, in which the jurors are presented with two contrasting views of "the case," each of which employs a radically different balance between legal and extra-legal argumentation, suggests that neither form of argumentation was considered ex ante decisive or even superior to the other. It seems that there simply was no authoritative rule of decision in Athenian courts; the jury panel was typically presented with a highly particularized and contextualized account

---

[155] E.g., Carey 1996:41; Christ 1998b:195.

[156] Aeschines' remark is typical:

> It is agreed that there are three types of government among all men: tyranny, oligarchy, and democracy. Tyrannies and oligarchies are administered according to the character of their leaders, while democratic cities according to the established laws.

Aesch. 1.4.

[157] Aesch. 3.8–48.

[158] Dem. 18.111–120. For discussion of which orator had the better legal case, compare Gwatkin 1957:129 with E. Harris 1994a:141.

of the facts and law relating to a dispute and left to its own devices to arrive at a just resolution to the individual case.

***

From a modern perspective, the Athenians employed a remarkably broad approach to relevance in their popular courts. Types of evidence that moderns generally consider inadmissible and even unfairly prejudicial were deemed relevant and important to the Athenian popular court jury's verdict. The effect a conviction will have on the defendant's children, how the parties conducted themselves in the course of litigation, the character and deeds of the parties' ancestors, the character of the victim, and whether the parties were relatives, friends, or strangers were all considered relevant to the question of guilt. But the most striking feature of Athenian popular court practice is not that the Athenians made different judgments than moderns as to the relevance and admissibility of specific types of evidence. More extraordinary is the process by which relevance and the relative weight of evidence were determined. It was up to the litigants to choose the types of information and arguments, both legal and extra-legal, to present, and to argue for the importance of these arguments to the jury's verdict. It was up to the jury to determine in each individual case what sorts of arguments to credit in reaching a just resolution to the dispute. The popular courts' ad hoc, discretionary approach was the dominant, but not the only, mode of legal decision making in the Athenian system. In the remaining chapters, we will explore the alternative Athenian approaches to law, the costs and benefits of popular-court style discretionary justice, and why the Athenians chose to adopt this approach in their largest jurisdiction.

4 THE HOMICIDE COURTS

DISCUSSIONS OF ATHENIAN NOTIONS OF LAW AND THE ROLE OF THE COURTS IN Athenian society have so far focused on speeches delivered in the popular courts. As we have seen, in the popular courts the laws were largely undefined and the litigants observed no rule of relevance. But there were also special homicide courts – highly respected, seldom used,[1] and largely omitted from modern discussions of the aims of the law courts. These courts – which almost certainly developed earlier than the popular courts – reportedly employed a rule prohibiting irrelevant statements. Additionally, they applied laws that exhibited greater legal definition and substantive content than those used in the popular courts. The unusual composition and procedures of the homicide courts made these courts (at least in theory) far more congenial than the popular courts to legal argument, and so less vulnerable to influences based on the character and social standing of the litigants. This chapter explores these differences, their place in the Athenian concept of justice, and the possible reasons for the different treatment of homicide and related offenses. The homicide procedures reveal that the Athenians could conceive of a system that encouraged the regular application of abstract rules without regard to the broader social context of the dispute, but rejected this model in favor of a more discretionary approach in the popular courts.

The Five Homicide Courts

In the classical period, five special courts shared jurisdiction over most cases involving homicide. The Areopagus Council was the most celebrated of these courts. The Areopagus is most widely known from Aeschylus' dramatic account in the *Eumenides*, where Athena inaugurates the court to judge Orestes for the murder of his mother. In the play, the Furies, the spirits of retribution who pursue Orestes following his matricide and prosecute the case against him, are forced to accept this new court's judgment in favor of the defendant. The creation of the

---

[1] There are only fifteen confirmed or possible court cases of homicide from 507–322 B.C.E. (Herman 1994: 101). There are only three surviving speeches in homicide cases before the special homicide tribunals (Lys. 1; Ant. 1; Ant. 6).

Areopagus is represented as paradigmatic of a wider revolution: the abandonment of blood-feud and vendetta in favor of legal justice. As we will see, Aeschylus' complex presentation of the Areopagus – both as a superior, and thus unusual, law court, and as a symbol for the entire legal system – mirrors the Areopagus' role in historical Athens.

The Areopagus tried cases involving intentional killing and wounding, arson, and poisoning by the defendant's own hand resulting in death.[2] Conviction on these charges resulted in execution, though those accused of intentional homicide could voluntarily go into permanent exile after the first set of trial speeches[3] if they did not like their chances with the jury.[4] The court at the Palladion had competence over cases of unintentional homicide and the killing of a slave, metic, or foreigner.[5] The penalty for unintentional homicide was exile, with the provision that the victim's family had the option of granting a pardon.[6] In its description of the Palladion's jurisdiction, *The Constitution of the Athenians* also refers to *bouleusis*, which means literally "planning," and appears to connote indirect responsibility for a death, as opposed to carrying out a homicide with one's own hand.[7] Although some scholars contend that *bouleusis* was a separate offense tried only in the Palladion, it has been argued convincingly that those accused of indirect responsibility for a killing were prosecuted for homicide (*dikê phonou*)

---

[2] Arist. *Ath. Pol.* 57.3; Dem. 23.22. Thür (1991) offers a different account, arguing that the Areopagus had jurisdiction over cases of homicide committed by one's own hand (*autocheir*), and that the issue of premeditation was pertinent to sentencing in both the Areopagus and the Palladion courts, but was not relevant to jurisdiction. For a convincing critique of Thür's thesis, see Wallace 1991. I discuss the meaning of *ek pronoias*, generally translated "with premeditation" or "with intent" later in this chapter. Until sometime in the fourth century, the Areopagus also had jurisdiction over the destruction of sacred olive trees (Arist. *Ath. Pol.* 60.2; Lys. 7), and it may have had supervision over other religious matters at various times. For discussion, see Wallace 1989:106–112.

[3] In homicide trials there were two sets of speeches on guilt (Ant. 5.13; 6.14).

[4] Ant. 5.13; Dem. 23.69. For discussion, see MacDowell 1963:113–116. Such a choice between a certain, lesser penalty and the uncertainty of the jury's verdict is similar to the modern practice of plea bargaining. There is, however, an important difference: plea bargaining stems from a desire to reduce the state's costs by avoiding trial; In Athens, even in cases where the defendant chooses exile, the court has to be assembled and half of the trial conducted.

[5] Arist. *Ath. Pol.* 57.3:

> Suits for involuntary homicide, and planning [*bouleusis*], and if someone kills a slave, a metic or a foreigner, are held at the court of the Palladion.

[6] The penalty for killing a metic or foreigner appears to have been exile as well. For discussion of the evidence, see MacDowell 1963:126–127.

[7] MacDowell (1963:62) has pointed out that our surviving legal texts often contrast *bouleusis* with *cheiri* or *autocheir*, "with one's own hand" (Ant. 6.16; And. 1.94; Pl. *Leg.* 871e–872b).

and received the same legal treatment as the actual killer (i.e., trial before the Areopagus in cases of intentional homicide and the Palladion in the somewhat less common case of *bouleusis* of unintentional homicide).[8] The Delphinion heard cases in which the defendant admitted that he had killed the victim, but pleaded that he had done so lawfully, and was therefore exempt from punishment.[9] Examples of lawful homicide included killing a man caught lying with one's wife, self-defense, and accidentally killing a fellow soldier in war.[10] In cases within the Areopagus' jurisdiction, the entire Council, which was composed of all the former archons[11] in the city, sat to hear the case. Cases before the Palladion and Delphinion were tried before a body of 51 men known as the *ephetai*. As I discuss in more detail below, to the best of our knowledge the *ephetai* were drawn from members of the Areopagus Council.

The Prytaneion court appears to have been concerned primarily with matters of religion and ritual, hearing cases in which an animal or an inanimate object had caused a death, or where the identity of the killer was unknown.[12] The court proclaimed the unknown killer an exile, and objects and perhaps also animals found responsible for a death were cast beyond the borders of Attica.[13] Finally, the court "in Phreatto"[14] was charged with judging a somewhat unlikely scenario: if a defendant in exile for a prior offense was charged with homicide or wounding, he was not permitted to enter Attica but was obliged to deliver his defense to the court from a ship anchored off shore.[15] Aristotle notes that trials in the court in Phreatto were extremely rare, and in fact we know of no case tried there.[16]

I focus on the Areopagus, the Palladion, and the Delphinion, and do not address the court in Phreatto or the Prytaneion, about which we know very

---

[8] Gagarin 1990b; cf. Sealey 1983: 277; MacDowell 1963:58–69.

[9] Dem. 23.74 (*ennomôs*); Arist. *Ath. Pol.* 57.3 (*kata tous nomous*). On the authenticity of the laws cited in Demosthenes 23, see Carawan 1998:88–98.

[10] For discussion of the specific requirements of each of these excuses from liability, see MacDowell 1963:73–79.

[11] Archons were magistrates whose duties included presiding over popular court trials. In the classical period, nine archons were selected by lot each year.

[12] Arist. *Ath. Pol.* 57.4; Dem. 23.76. The composition of the Prytaneion may have differed from the other homicide courts. See Arist. *Pol.* 1300b24–30; Arist. *Ath. Pol.* 57.3–4; Plut. *Sol.* 19.4; for discussion, see MacDowell 1963:88.

[13] For discussion, see MacDowell 1963:85–89.

[14] It is unclear whether Phreatto refers to a place or the name of a man after whom the court was named. For discussion of the evidence, see MacDowell 1963:82–83.

[15] Arist. *Ath. Pol.* 57.3; Dem. 23.77.

[16] Arist. *Pol.* 1300b29–30; Boegehold 1995:49–50; MacDowell 1963:84.

little. Following the standard convention, I refer to these courts as "the homicide courts," though their jurisdiction was not limited exclusively to homicide and not all cases of homicide were tried in them. As noted above a few other offenses, such as wounding and arson, were also heard in these courts. And beginning at the end of the fifth century, at least some types of homicide could be tried in the ordinary popular courts through a special procedure known as *apagôgê*. The homicide courts observed a number of distinctive procedures suggesting a particularly rigorous approach to the charge and the evidence. The most interesting for our purposes is the rule against irrelevant statements, which we will explore in detail in the following section. Other unusual features include a lengthy preliminary process involving three "pre-trials" (*prodikasiai*) held a month apart before the magistrate,[17] and the use of special oaths. Witnesses in the homicide courts were required to swear not just to the truth of their testimony, but to whether the accused had or had not committed the homicide.[18] After the verdict the victorious litigant was obliged to swear that the verdict was correct.[19]

A MODEL COURT

Throughout the classical period, the Areopagus and, by association, the other homicide courts,[20] had a reputation for being the finest law courts in Athens. In Xenophon's *Memorabilia*, Socrates asserts that there are no jurors "who decide cases and do all other things more nobly, more lawfully, with more solemnity, or more justly,"[21] than the Areopagus. Demosthenes speaks of the Areopagus as uniquely immune from extreme political swings:

> With regard to this court alone, no tyrant, no oligarchy, and no democracy
> has dared to take away jurisdiction over homicide suits, but all think the

[17] Ant. 6.42.
[18] Ant. 1.28; 5.12; Isoc. 18.56.
[19] Aesch. 2.87. The litigant also swore to that he had spoken truthfully.
[20] There are surprisingly few references to the Palladion and Delphinion in our sources, though it seems highly probable that praise of the Areopagus must often refer to these courts as well. Demosthenes 23 treats these three courts as a group, linking the Palladion and the Areopagus as "two courts of such a [great] age and [lofty] character and practices handed down from remote antiquity" and describing the Delphinion as "a third court in addition to these [the Areopagus and Palladion], which is the most holy and awe-inducing of all" (Dem. 23. 73–74). The Areopagus evidently came to serve *pars pro toto* as a symbol of the other homicide courts.
[21] Xen. *Mem.* 3.5.20.

justice they themselves would devise to deal with these matters inferior to the justice found in that court [i.e. the Areopagus]. Besides these considerations, only here no one – neither convicted defendants nor unsuccessful prosecutors – has ever proved that the judgment was made unjustly.[22]

Lycurgus calls the Areopagus the "the most noble example of the Greeks," going so far as to make the incredible statement: "even those who have been convicted agree that the verdict is just."[23] In accordance with the democratic reforms of Ephialtes in the middle of the fifth century, the functions of the Areopagus had been reduced primarily to trying homicide cases, but about a century later the powers of the Council were expanded and the Areopagus once again became a political force.[24] One might at first be tempted to dismiss the praise of the Areopagus' competence as a law court as a reflection of its enhanced political powers at the time. But even earlier writers like Lysias and Antiphon refer to trials in the Areopagus as taking place "in the most holy and august court,"[25] and to its members "the most pious and fairest judges of the Greeks."[26]

What set the homicide courts apart in the minds of Athenians was their unique procedures. Antiphon states:

> On account of these things, the laws, the oaths, the sacrifices, the public announcements, and all the other things that happen in a homicide suit, are very different from other procedures because the facts themselves, concerning which the stakes are the greatest, must be known correctly.[27]

This passage and others like it suggest that the rules of these courts encouraged the homicide judges to base their decisions primarily on the factual and legal issues of the case and minimize some of the features that we have seen are characteristic of the popular law courts, such as the use of extra-legal argumentation.[28] A brief examination of two speeches, one written by Antiphon sometime around 420 B.C.E.,

---

[22] Dem. 23.65–6.

[23] Lyc. 1.12.

[24] See, e.g., Wallace 1989:1–22; Rhodes 1980:305.

[25] Lys. 6.14.

[26] Ant. 6.51. The extraordinary reputation of the Areopagus extended into the Roman period; in a letter of A.D. 165, Marcus Aurelius refers to this council as "the most respected court" and a decade later laments that the Areopagus no longer requires the *trigonia* of its members (Oliver 1989: Doc. 173; 184)

[27] Ant. 6.6.

[28] Passages comparing notions of relevance in the homicide and popular courts are discussed later in this chapter.

the other by Lycurgus in 330, illustrates that the Areopagus was thought to arrive at decisions in a manner very different from that of the popular courts. In both cases, a speaker in a popular law court expresses regret that the jury will not be following the rules and procedures of the Areopagus and the special homicide courts. We can postpone detailed discussion of the various procedural differences between the popular and homicide courts alluded to in these speeches until later in the chapter. For the moment, what is important is that in both cases the speaker holds up the more narrowly focused legal approach taken by the homicide courts as a model of legal decision making.

Although Antiphon *On the Murder of Herodes* concerns a murder, the prosecutors used the special *apagôgê* procedure[29] to bring the defendant before an ordinary popular court rather than a homicide court. The defendant takes care at the beginning of his speech not to alienate the popular jury when he protests that his motivation is not to evade the popular court: "It's not that I would flee trial before you, the people, because even if you were not under oath and were deciding not according to any law I would entrust my life to your vote. . . ."[30] Nevertheless, much of his defense is devoted to arguing that it is illegal to deprive him of the special homicide procedures.[31] He pines after the rule prohibiting irrelevant statements used in homicide cases, telling the prosecutor:

> You had to swear the greatest and most powerful oath, calling destruction
> down upon yourself, and your family and household, in very truth that you
> would accuse me only concerning the homicide itself, [arguing] that I killed,
> with the result that, had I done many bad acts, I would not be convicted for
> any reason other than the charge itself, and, had I done many good deeds, I
> would not be saved because of this good conduct.[32]

The defendant also expresses resentment at the disadvantage to which an inexperienced defendant is exposed in the popular courts. He states, "it is inevitable, whenever someone is inexperienced in court debate, that he is more at the mercy of the words of the prosecutors rather than the deeds themselves and the truth of

---

[29] The *apagôgê* procedure is discussed later in this chapter. For a general discussion of Antiphon 5, see Gagarin 1989.

[30] Ant. 5.8.

[31] Ant. 5.8–14.

[32] Ant. 5.11.

what happened."[33] The defendant's anxiety that his inability to speak will prejudice the jury comports with his desire for his case to be heard in the homicide courts, which were thought to have placed more emphasis on the dispute itself than on the social standing or speaking ability of the litigants.[34] Finally, the speaker warns the jury of the dangers of allowing emotion to influence verdicts. He relates a story of a case in which a group of magistrates were wrongly accused and urges the jury to avoid making a similar mistake. He notes, "Once the Hellenotamiae were falsely accused of corruption just as I am now, and all these men, except for one, were executed through anger rather than reason. Later the true facts became clear. . . ."[35] Thus, the speaker in *On the Murder of Herodes* objects to the character-istics of the popular courts that distract the jury from forming a judgment based solely on legal and factual issues in dispute, and pleads, remarkably enough, not to be acquitted permanently, but merely to be turned over to a proper homicide court where, presumably, he hopes to find impartial justice.[36]

There is no murder in Lycurgus *Against Leocrates*, but the speaker objects to the manner in which popular courts generally arrive at verdicts, and urges the jurors to be more like the Areopagites:

> I will make a just accusation, neither lying nor discussing irrelevant matters.
> You see that most of those who come before you make the oddest speeches,
> either giving advice here on public matters, or making accusations and
> slanders about all things except the subject matter of the vote you are about
> to cast . . . And you are the cause of this state of affairs, gentlemen, for you
> have given this authority to those who come before you here, even though

---

[33] Ant. 5.3.

[34] Contrast the faith in the Areopagus professed by the speaker in Lysias 3.2:

> Now if some other men were about to render judgment about me, I would be extremely
> frightened by the danger, seeing that between rigging [by one's opponents] and chance many
> cases turn out contrary to the expectation of the defendants, but since, however, I have come
> before you [the Areopagus], I hope to receive justice.

[35] Ant. 5.69. The speaker also states:

> In this way it is good to test the facts with the help of time. . . . For the passing of one day into
> another is a great way, gentlemen, to turn the verdict away from anger and to discover the truth
> of what happened (5.69–72).

The speaker may be referring to the delay imposed by the unique requirement that three *prodikasiai*, each a month apart, be held prior to the hearing-in-chief in homicide cases.

[36] Ant. 5.90.

you have in the Areopagus court the most noble example of the Greeks. . . .
Looking to [the Areopagus] you should not allow them to speak outside the
point.[37]

At the end of his speech, Lycurgus claims that he at least has lived up to a higher
standard, recognizable as that attributed to the Areopagus: "I have concluded
the trial rightly and justly, without slandering the whole life of this man [my
opponent] or making accusations that are not to the point."[38]

In both these cases, the speaker appears to be drawing on a widely held belief
that the Areopagus and other homicide courts were superior tribunals because
they operated on a narrower legal plane than did the popular courts. Three special
features of the homicide courts contributed to their reputation for legalism: (1) the
use of a council of ex-archons who served for life rather than a large popular court
jury; (2) a greater emphasis on substantive law and therefore legal argumentation;
and (3) a rule prohibiting irrelevant statements. In the following sections I examine
each of these characteristics in some detail to map the contours of the perceived
and real differences between the approach to law and legal process used in these
two types of court.

Whereas it is clear that the Athenians believed that the homicide courts judged
in an entirely different manner from the popular courts, we will see that in practice
the differences between these two types of tribunal were more modest, though
nevertheless palpable and important. I refer to the "legalism" of the homicide
courts not in an absolute sense, but only relative to the popular courts; even
on the broadest view of the differentiae, the homicide courts remain strikingly
different from contemporary western courts. For our purposes, the perceived
differences in the decision making processes of these courts are as interesting
as any real differences. In the Athenian imagination, the homicide courts served
as an antithesis to the popular courts, and the comparison offers insight into
unresolved tensions in the Athenian concept of justice.

LEGALISM IN THE HOMICIDE COURTS: COMPOSITION

The differences in age and legal experience between the panels judging homicide
and popular court cases helped foster the impression that the homicide courts

[37] Lyc. 1.11–13.
[38] Lyc. 1.149.

employed a more formal legal approach in reaching their verdicts than did the popular courts. The composition of the Areopagus Council differed from the mass juries of the popular courts in important respects: membership was limited to ex-archons,[39] and Areopagites served for life.[40] Demographic models suggest that the Council probably comprised between 145 and 175 men.[41] By comparison, popular court panels were never smaller than 201, and many panels were considerably larger. The median age of the Areopagus has been calculated as lying between 52 and 57 years,[42] a good deal older than the average popular court juror. The estimated age distribution of the Areopagus is thus roughly consistent with the parallel Isocrates draws between this body and the Spartan council of elders, the *Gerousia*.[43]

A priori, the composition of the Areopagus is likely to have affected – or, more importantly, have been perceived to have affected – the decision making process of the homicide courts. Somewhat smaller and more cohesive by virtue of a stable membership than a popular court jury, the Areopagus probably achieved a degree of uniformity in the way it went about its business. In Athenian culture older men were generally regarded as less impetuous and therefore less likely to be swayed by emotional appeals.[44] This stereotype may in turn have influenced the strategy of speakers before this tribunal. It also seems probable that the Areopagites developed a close familiarity with Athenian laws and procedures. Life tenure offered the possibility of repeated service as homicide judges, though it is possible that, at least in the fourth century, homicide trials were rare. But at a minimum, all members of the Areopagus had spent one year as an archon, conducting preliminary legal hearings and presiding at trials before the popular courts. As a result, they probably were – and were regarded as – more sophisticated, and thus less likely to be misled on matters of law than the members of the mass jury panels of the popular courts. Of course, the Areopagites' legal knowledge was

---

[39] Dem. 24.22; Arist. *Ath. Pol.* 60.3.
[40] Lys. 26.11; Arist. *Ath. Pol.* 3.6.
[41] Hansen & Pedersen 1990.
[42] Hansen & Pedersen 1990:76.
[43] Isoc. 12.154. This 30-member Spartan senate consisted of two Spartan kings who served ex officio plus 28 men over age 60 who served for life and tried cases in which the penalty was death, exile, or disfranchisement (Plut. *Lyc.* 26.2; Arist. *Pol.* 1294b 33–34). Unlike the Areopagites, the Spartan *gerontes* were elected in the Assembly (Arist. *Pol.* 1271a 9–18).
[44] The *locus classicus* for the characteristics of the young and old and how they can be best accommodated by speakers is Aristotle's *Rhetoric* (1388b31–1390a27). For discussion of popular stereotypes regarding age, with references, see Dover 1974:102–105.

practical rather than theoretical; there is no evidence that the Areopagus developed a collective sense of jurisprudence over time. It would be going too far to call them "legal experts." To borrow the words Plato uses in the *Gorgias* to describe the practice of rhetoric, the Areopagites might not have possessed *epistêmê* ("exact knowledge"), but there is no denying their *tribê* ("experience," literally "rubbing," the tactile sense that comes from repeated handling of material).

The impression that the Areopagus dispensed a different brand of justice was fueled by the Council's reputation for enforcing strict rules of behavior and decorum. According to tradition, the Areopagites were expected to be particularly upright and respectable citizens: several sources report that the smallest of infractions could lead to expulsion.[45] For instance, Plutarch states that members were not permitted to write comedies,[46] and a fragment of Hyperides preserved in Athenaeus claims that the Areopagus did not accept men who ate in a pub.[47] Aeschines also relates a story in which the demos is censured for laughing in the presence of the Areopagites.[48] In the *Areopagiticus*, Isocrates offers an idealized view of the moral transformation that accompanies admission to the Areopagus: "We would see that those who are intolerable with respect to all other matters, whenever they go up to the Areopagus, they shrink from acting according to their nature, abiding rather by the customs there than by their own wickedness."[49] The Areopagus was not a particularly selective institution in the classical period – by the mid-fifth century archons were chosen by lot from all but the lowest class of citizens and by the mid-fourth century all citizens were eligible.[50] Nevertheless, it is clear that the aura surrounding its members and presumably their judicial decisions was very different from the Athenians' attitude toward the popular courts.

The legal experience and high moral character associated with the Areopagus may also have applied to the homicide courts at the Palladion, which tried cases of unintentional homicide and the killing of non-citizens, and the Delphinion, which had jurisdiction over lawful homicide cases. In the fifth century, cases in these special courts operated under the same procedures as the Areopagus but

---

[45] Din. 1.55–56.
[46] Plut. *Mor.* 348b.
[47] Ath. *Deipno.* 566–568.
[48] Aesch. 1.81–5.
[49] Isoc.7.38.
[50] Hansen 1999:288–289.

were tried before fifty-one men known as *ephetai*.[51] We cannot know for certain how the *ephetai* were chosen, but the most likely possibility, based on our limited evidence, is that they were selected from the Areopagites. A fragment of Androtion appears to identify the *ephetai* as Areopagite judges, but the meaning of the passage is too obscure to draw any firm conclusions.[52] In the course of a discussion of the homicide courts, *The Constitution of the Athenians* states, "Men chosen by lot try these cases, except those that are held on the Areopagus."[53] Carawan has argued that in the context of a passage discussing the special homicide courts "the men chosen by lot" most likely refers to men chosen by lot from the Areopagus, pointing out that all other references in *The Constitution of the Athenians* to dicastic jurors selected by lot specifically mention *dikastai* or *dikastêria*.[54] Although these passages are far from conclusive, it is probable that the 51 *ephetai* judging cases in the homicide tribunals were members of the Areopagus. Whereas our sources make clear that

---

[51] IG i² 115; Dem. 43.57; 23.37–8; Poll. 8.125.

[52] *FGRHist* 324 F4:

> ἐκ γὰρ τῶν ἐννέα καθισταμένων ἀρχόντων Ἀθήνησι τοὺς Ἀρεοπαγίτας ἔδει
> συνεστάναι δικαστάς, ὡς φησιν Ἀνδροτίων ἐν δευτέρᾳ τῶν Ἀτθίδων· ὕστερον δὲ
> πλειόνων γέγονεν ἡ ἐξ Ἀρείου πάγου βουλή, τουτέστιν ἡ ἐξ ἀνδρῶν περιφανεστέρων
> πεντήκοντα καὶ ἑνός, πλὴν ἐξ εὐπατριδῶν, ὡς ἔφημεν, καὶ πλούτῳ καὶ βίῳ σώφρονι
> διαφερόντων, ὡς ἱστορεῖ φιλόχορος διὰ τῆς τρίτης τῶν αὐτοῦ Ἀτθίδων.

> The judges of the Areopagus had to be assembled from the nine elected archons at Athens, as Androtion says in Book Two of the *Atthides*. Later the Council of the Areopagus was comprised of more members, i.e., from the fifty-one men of the more illustrious, but only from Eupatrids [roughly, the Athenian blueblood families], as we said, and those who excel in wealth and a restrained lifestyle, as Philochorus records in the third book of his *Atthides*. This passage thus associates the "fifty-one" (a number linked to the *ephetai* in a number of ancient passages, e.g., Dem. 43.57) with the Areopagus, and seems to state that the Areopagus was formed from the *ephetai*, though the word πλειόνων is puzzling if that is the case. It has further been suggested that this passage indicates a distinction between Ἀρεοπαγῖται δικασταί, "Areopagite judges," which has been interpreted to mean the fifty-one *ephetai*, and ἡ ἐξ Ἀρείου πάγου βουλή, the Council of the Areopagus, though this conclusion is hardly required by the text. For discussion of this difficult passage, see Bonner & Smith 1930:99–100; MacDowell 1963:51–52; Carawan 1998:14–15; cf. Wallace, 1989:14–16.

[53] Arist. *Ath. Pol.* 57.4: δικάζουσι δ' οἱ λαχόντες ταῦ[τ' ἄνδρες], πλὴν τῶν ἐν Ἀρείῳ πάγῳ γιγ-νομένων. The crucial words of the papyrus are unclear. The passage could also read οἱ λαχόντες ταῦ[τα να' ἄνδρες] suggested as a possibility by Stroud (1968b), and favored by Rhodes (1993:646–8). The reading οἱ λαχόντες ταῦ[τ'ἐφέται] has now been widely rejected. For discussion of the various possible readings, see Rhodes 1993:646–648.

[54] Carawan 1991:15. If this hypothesis is correct, the use of the lot to select the *ephetai*, a democratic feature one would not expect to see in the time of Draco, was probably introduced in conjunction with democratic reforms and was not the original mode of selection.

the *ephetai* judged cases in the Palladion and Delphinion in the early fifth century, some scholars contend that ordinary jurors replaced the *ephetai* in these special homicide courts at some point under the democracy.[55] The evidence for this view is quite weak, however, and it is far more likely that the *ephetai* continued to judge cases brought in the Palladion and Delphinion throughout the classical period.[56]

If the hypothesis that members of the Areopagus judged cases in the Palladion and Delphinion in panels of 51 known as *ephetai* throughout the fifth and fourth centuries is correct, the composition of these homicide courts would have set them apart from the popular courts. Like the Areopagus, these panels of older men with life tenure had more legal experience and may have been thought to be more familiar with the laws and less likely to be swayed by emotional appeals or rhetorical flourishes than ordinary juries. But what is most important for our purposes is that the procedures used in these homicide courts more closely resembled those of the Areopagus than those of the popular courts and that the Athenians considered the Areopagus and the *ephetic* courts special, related tribunals distinct from the popular courts. For example, the speaker in Antiphon *On the Chorus Boy* discusses the unique procedures of the homicide courts as a group[57]

---

[55] A variety of periods for the proposed changeover have been suggested, including the time of Solon (Sealey 1983:294–295), Pericles' reform of the Areopagus (Smith 1924), and the reforms of 403/2 (Philippi 1874:320).

[56] The primary support for the view that the homicide courts were manned by ordinary jurors by the fourth century comes from two passages in which a law court speaker who appears to be describing a previous trial at the Palladion mentions a jury panel of 700 or 500 rather than the *ephetai*. MacDowell (1963:53–54) and Carawan (1991:3–5) have argued convincingly that the speaker in the first passage (Isoc. 18.52–54) refers to a 700-member dicastic court trying Callimachus for perjury committed during the homicide trial, rather than the homicide trial itself. In the second passage (Dem. 59.10), the speaker describes a false homicide charge brought by Stephanus in the Palladion. The speaker suggests that it became clear during the trial that Stephanus had been bribed to bring the false charges, and that he therefore managed to get only a few votes. The crucial phrase is ὀλίγας ψήφους μεταλαβὼν ἐκ πεντακοσίων δραχμῶν, "he got a few votes out of [i.e., for the expenditure of] five hundred drachmas." Although this text follows most of the manuscripts, many editors have deleted δραχμῶν, leaving the phrase "a few votes out of a total of five hundred," which suggests that a jury of five hundred decided the case. But there is no need to delete the reference to drachmai from the manuscripts to make sense of the passage. The five hundred drachmai must represent the amount Stephanus was paid to bring the false prosecution, not the number of jurors (Rhodes 1993:647; Kapparis 1999:189). For arguments supporting the view that the *ephetai* continued to judge in the homicide courts throughout the classical period, see MacDowell 1963:52–57; Carawan 1998:155–160; Harrison, 1998:40–42; Kapparis 1999:188–189.

[57] Ant. 6.6.

and in Demosthenes *Against Aristocrates* the speaker praises the Areopagus and other homicide courts together as ancient and well-respected tribunals.[58] As we will see, the Palladion and Delphinion were, like the Areopagus, more conducive to legal reasoning and less receptive to evidence irrelevant to the charge before it.

LEGALISM IN THE HOMICIDE COURTS: LEGAL ARGUMENTATION

One of the most distinctive features of the Athenian legal system is its focus on procedural rather than substantive law. We saw in the previous chapter that many of our surviving laws do not list the elements of the offense or offer any guidance as to how the law should be interpreted, but merely prescribe the legal procedures to be followed in the case of an offense that is named but not further described.[59] Although the laws enforced by the homicide courts display a similar procedural orientation,[60] they are unusual in that they include significant substantive content. The homicide statutes exhibit greater precision in describing the circumstances (or "elements") that must be present for a violation of the law to occur than most of the statutes at issue in popular court cases.[61] These statutes thus appear to encourage a greater emphasis on relevant legal argumentation, that is, arguments that are focused on satisfying the specific criteria of the offense under which the charge was brought, than the mode of argumentation typical of the popular courts.[62]

In contrast to the vagueness characteristic of Athenian laws, the lawful homicide statute quoted by Demosthenes lists specific situations in which homicide is *not* punishable:

> If someone kills involuntarily in an athletic competition, or overpowering someone on the road [i.e. defending oneself from a highway robber], or

---

[58] Dem. 23.73–74.

[59] See Chapter 3. There are exceptions to this generalization, particularly in laws relating to the family and religion (Carey 1998).

[60] Indeed, the laws we have are concerned with jurisdiction rather than substance (Dem. 23.22, 74).

[61] The homicide statutes do, however, still leave some crucial terms undefined (for example, the elements of *bouleusis*, "planning" a homicide).

[62] We saw in the preceding chapter that even where popular court litigants engage in legal argumentation by discussing laws, they often cite and discuss a variety of laws in addition to, or instead of, the statute under which the case was brought; popular court speakers generally do not focus on showing that the criteria of the specific offense at issue were or were not satisfied.

unknowingly in war [i.e. "friendly fire"], or taking a man with his wife,
sister, daughter, or concubine whom he has for begetting free children,
because of these things he is not to go into exile as a homicide.[63]

This list is not exclusive; there are other laws that provided for further types of
lawful homicide, but in each case the law describes a specific form of killing that is
permitted.[64] There was no general provision exempting just or morally defensible
killings from punishment, and it appears that defendants pleading lawful homicide
were obliged to argue that their case was covered by an existing statute.[65] Thus
the lawful homicide statute would tend to focus the litigants' arguments at trial
on whether the killing met the legal criteria for lawful homicide.[66]

Homicide and wounding – both charges within the purview of the special
homicide courts – are the only cases in which the Athenians distinguished between
different mental states of the offender. Cases alleging intentional killing and
wounding were heard in the Areopagus, whereas the Palladion had competence
over cases of unintentional homicide. We know very little about the preliminary
procedures in a homicide case, but it seems that the nature of the plaintiff's charge
determined whether the accused was tried for intentional homicide, a capital
charge,[67] or for unintentional homicide, a crime punished by exile.[68] As is typical of

---

[63] Dem. 23.53.

[64] E.g., Dem. 23.60: "If someone acting in self-defense immediately kills a man who is unjustly seizing
him and leading him away by force, then the killing is without penalty"; Dem. 24.113 (killing a burglar
at night); Dem. 23.28 (killing a convicted killer who was present illegally in Athens).

[65] Carawan notes that both Demosthenes and Aristotle (*Ath.Pol.* 57.3) state that the defendant must argue
that he acted in accordance with the law (ἐννόμως, ἐν νόμῳ). Carawan 1998: 282 n. 1; cf. Gagarin 1978:
112 n.7 (noting that the later sources use *dikaios* when referring to lawful homicide).

[66] Carawan (1998: 283) suggests that the basileus, the magistrate who handled homicide charges, determined
whether the defense put forward by the accused qualified as lawful homicide under the statutes, taking
this issue off the table at the trial in the Delphinion. It is extremely unlikely that the basileus, an official
chosen by lot for a one-year term, would make such a determination rather than leave the issue to the
more experienced *ephetai* at trial. In any case, Carawan's suggestion is at odds with our only surviving lawful
homicide trial, Lysias *On the Death of Eratosthenes*, in which the question of whether the speaker legitimately caught Eratosthenes *in flagrante delicto* rather than merely setting him up is central to the dispute.

[67] A defendant in the Areopagus could voluntarily withdraw into exile at the close of his first speech to
avoid execution (Ant. 5.15; Dem. 23.69). In making his decision, a defendant might have relied on the
vocal responses of the judges (Bers 1985:14–15).

[68] Exiled killers might later be pardoned by the victim's relatives (Dem. 23.72). A homicide prosecution
began when the victim's relatives brought a charge against the accused to the basileus, who then held
three pre-trials, or *prodikasiai*, before bringing the case to trial in one of the homicide courts (Ant. 6.42).
The basileus assigned the case on the basis of the arguments made at these pre-trials. In a case of

Athenian statutes, the homicide laws do not seem to have defined what constitutes intentional or unintentional homicide. The statutes simply refer to homicide or wounding committed with or without *pronoia* ("intent").[69] Even though the homicide laws did not define *pronoia*, by distinguishing between intentional and unintentional homicide in setting out the jurisdiction of the Areopagus and the Palladion, the laws offered substantive guidance by encouraging litigants in the Areopagus to focus on the issue of intent. These apparently jurisdictional laws established that *pronoia* was an essential element of intentional homicide. A story recounted in the corpus of Aristotle suggests that the Areopagus acquitted defendants who killed unintentionally:

> For example, they say that at one time a woman gave a love-potion to someone to drink, and then the man died because of the potion, and she was acquitted in the Areopagus. Where, letting her off, they acquitted her for no other reason than that the deed was not done with intent (*ouk ek pronoias*). She gave it for love, but failed in this objective. Therefore it seemed to them to be not intentional (*ouk hekousion*), because she gave him the dose of the potion not with the intention of him dying.[70]

We would expect that the requirement that the prosecutor prove *pronoia* to gain a conviction would have helped to focus the litigants' arguments on the nature of the crime and the mental state of the alleged offender and would have given the Areopagites some guidance in how to reach their verdict.

intentional or unintentional homicide, the determination was based on the nature of the plaintiff's accusation. If the defendant pleaded lawful homicide, however, the case was assigned to the Delphinion (Arist. *Ath. Pol.* 57.3). Presumably the different penalties as well as the nature of the killing and the strength of the case would influence the plaintiff's choice of charges.

[69] Dem. 23.22; IG i² 115.11. Loomis (1972) has argued convincingly that the Athenians made no legal distinction between ἐκ προνοίας *and* ἐκούσιος *or* μὴ ἐκ προνοίας *and* ἀκούσιος, and that *pronoia* is best interpreted as having the legal force of "intent." See also Gagarin 1981a:30–36; Sealey 1983:277–278; cf. Cantarella 1976:95–106; Carawan 1998:39–41. The law at Dem. 23.22 similarly does not define *trauma* ("wounding"). For the hypothesis that *trauma* requires a wound inflicted by a weapon, see Phillips 2000:177.

[70] Arist. [*Mag. Mor.*] 1188b30–38. We must be cautious in drawing conclusions from this passage, which is part of a discussion of philosophical aspects of intentionality and may reflect the author's purpose as much as historical reality. However, the emphasis on *pronoia* in our surviving speeches does support the interpretation that the Areopagus acquitted defendants who killed unintentionally. Further support is provided by the fact that if the Areopagus found the defendant guilty only of lawful homicide, it was obliged to acquit (Lys. 1.30).

Did the unusual aspects of the homicide statutes result in a notably different mode of argumentation in the homicide courts? Because the surviving homicide speeches are few and significantly older than most of the surviving popular court speeches, it is hazardous to compare the nature of legal argumentation in the two types of court. Any differences may simply reflect the development of court rhetoric over time.[71] Nevertheless, an examination of our three surviving intentional wounding or homicide cases (Lys.3, 4; Ant. 1); our one involuntary homicide case (Ant. 6); and our one lawful homicide speech (Lys. 1) may shed some light on whether speeches in the homicide courts were more focused on discussing the elements of the offense under which the case was brought.[72] For this purpose, I do not include the three *Tetralogies* of Antiphon, rhetorical showpieces apparently written for hypothetical cases.[73] Each *Tetralogy* includes model speeches for the prosecution and defense in a homicide case and appears to be designed to explore how to argue a particular issue (respectively, identity, causation, and responsibility). The *Tetralogies'* focus on the specific issue in dispute cannot safely be taken as representative of Athenian homicide trials. It is perhaps telling, however, that the author of the *Tetralogies*[74] chose the homicide courts as the setting to explore argumentation of complex factual and legal issues; it may be that he thought the focused arguments of the *Tetralogies* were more in keeping with the reputation and practices of the homicide courts than that of the popular courts.

Lysias *Against Simon* and Lysias *On a Premeditated Wounding* are both speeches delivered in the Areopagus by defendants charged with intentional wounding

---

[71] Indeed, the surviving homicide speeches were traditionally interpreted, following Solmsen, as examples of pre-rational, formalistic argumentation. For two different critiques of Solmsen's theory, see Carawan 1998:22ff; Gagarin 1990a:22–32.

[72] Although Lysias 7 was delivered in the Areopagus, I do not discuss the legal argumentation of this speech because it concerns the destruction of sacred olives rather than the homicide statutes. In this section, I am concerned with the extent to which litigants in the homicide courts addressed the requirements of the governing statute in their speeches; I do not address the question of relevance (i.e., the presence or absence of extra-legal argumentation) until the following section of this chapter. Thus for purposes of this section, a homicide speech exhibits "relevant legal argumentation" if the speaker presents the case in terms of the required elements of the underlying charge, even if the speech also contains extra-legal argumentation as well.

[73] For a recent review of the extensive bibliography on the authorship, dating, and context of the *Tetralogies*, see Carawan: 1998: 171–177.

[74] Whether the author of the *Tetralogies* is the same as the author of Antiphon's court speeches and the philosophical works attributed to Antiphon is a notoriously difficult question in classical scholarship. For a recent discussion of this problem and an argument for single authorship of these works, see Gagarin 2002a: 37–52.

(*trauma ek pronoias*). In the context of wounding (*trauma*), *pronoia* appears to have meant intent to kill, making intentional wounding roughly equivalent to the modern charge of battery with intent to commit murder.[75] Both suits involve fights that arose out of a quarrel over a lover (in *Against Simon* a Plataean boy; in *On a Premeditated Wounding* a female slave). In both cases the speaker argues that the injuries were inflicted during an impromptu scuffle, anchoring his defense in the absence of the required element of *pronoia*. The speaker in *Against Simon* devotes nearly his entire proof section to discussing the absence of *pronoia*.[76] The prosecutor apparently attempted to prove intent to kill *a fortiori* by showing the presence of premeditation, arguing that the defendant came to his house carrying a weapon and intending to kill him: "He says that we went to his house carrying a piece of broken pottery, and that I threatened to kill him, and that this constitutes *pronoia*."[77] The speaker refutes this argument by noting that it is improbable that he would plan to kill Simon by going to his house in broad daylight without any friends or other support.[78] He then argues that the nature of the fight itself – a fracas in which Simon and his supporters rather than the speaker were the primary aggressors and did the most damage – indicates that there was no intent to kill.[79] The speaker concludes his proof by stating that the charge of intentional wounding requires intent to kill,[80] and reiterating that one who inflicts a wound during a confused melee does not have sufficient intent to merit conviction.[81] The speaker in *On a Premeditated Wounding* also repeatedly emphasizes the absence of *pronoia* in his speech. He refutes a similar attempt by the prosecutor to show premeditation based on the presence of a weapon (again a piece of broken pottery),[82] and twice refers to the presence or absence of *pronoia* as the crux of the case.[83]

---

[75] Carey 1989:109; Cantarella 1976:98–101; cf. Phillips 2000:160–161.

[76] Lys. 3.28–42. Some form of the word *pronoia* appears eight times in this passage.

[77] Lys. 3.28.

[78] Lys. 3.29–34. Perhaps implied is also the improbability that an *ostrakon* would be his murder weapon of choice. For an argument along these lines, see Lys. 4.6.

[79] Lys. 3.35–39.

[80] Lys. 3.41: "In addition I did not think that there was any *pronoia* where a man wounds without intending to kill."

[81] Lys. 3.41–43.

[82] Lys. 4.6.

[83] Lys. 4.12: "That there was no *pronoia* and that I did not wrong this man, O Council, I have demonstrated from so many proofs and witnesses."; Lys. 4.18: "I would not be able to produce any other [proofs] apart from these [challenges] to show that I did not premeditate anything against him."

In Antiphon *Against the Stepmother*, our only surviving case of intentional homicide, the speaker is prosecuting his stepmother for poisoning his father. According to the speaker, the defendant persuaded the mistress of Philoneus, a friend of the speaker's father, to give the poison to both Philoneus and the speaker's father. The speaker asserts that although Philoneus' mistress mistakenly believed that the potion was an aphrodisiac, the defendant was fully aware of the lethal content of the mixture. Throughout this oration, the speaker offers very little proof or probability to support his assertions, and his discussion of the decisive issue of intent is no exception. It is clear, however, that the prosecutor is aware that a showing of intent is required for a conviction. He states at the outset that he will prove that the defendant murdered his father "intentionally and with premeditation,"[84] by showing that she had been caught attempting to kill him on several previous occasions; he notes that the Areopagites are charged with assisting victims who have been murdered intentionally;[85] and he emphatically repeats that the defendant killed her husband intentionally.[86]

The arguments of these three speeches thus suggest that speakers in intentional wounding and homicide cases before the Areopagus were aware that *pronoia* was an essential element of the offense. This requirement appears to have focused homicide speeches on the legal requirements of the relevant statute: although the speeches sometimes contain other, often forceful and lengthy, arguments, the speeches always remain tethered to the central task of proving or disproving the charge of intentional homicide. By contrast, speeches in the popular courts are rarely so narrowly focused on the specific charge at issue. Demosthenes *Against Conon*, a popular court speech in an assault case not dissimilar to the intentional wounding scenarios of *Against Simon* and *On a Premeditated Wounding*, offers a useful comparison. Ariston prosecutes Conon for *aikeia* ("assault") after the defendant and a group of his drinking buddies attacked him one night while he was walking through the agora and beat him nearly to death. We saw in Chapter 3 that although the formal charge was *aikeia*, Ariston argues in the speech that Conon was guilty of clothes-stealing and the more serious charge of *hubris* ("outrage").[87] Indeed, he

---

[84] Ant. 1.3: ἐξ ἐπιβουλῆς καὶ προβουλῆς.

[85] Ant. 1.22.

[86] Ant. 1.25, 26, 27. The speaker is also careful to note that his father died violently to insure that the killing was considered a homicide rather than a case of poisoning because under the statute the Areopagus had jurisdiction only over poisoning carried out by the defendant's own hand (Gagarin 1998b:15 n.11).

[87] Dem. 54.24.

calls for the laws relating to these two offenses, but *not* the law relating to *aikeia*, to be read to the jury.[88] Another popular court speech involving violence, Isocrates *Against Lochites*, is similarly unfocused on the requirements of the charged offense: we are not certain whether the formal charge was *aikeia* or *hubris*.[89]

In sum, it seems that the mode of legal argumentation in intentional homicide and wounding cases before the Areopagus was significantly different from the approach to law taken in popular court suits. Speakers (and presumably judges) in the Areopagus were aware that intent was a crucial issue under the governing statute that demanded their attention, whereas popular court speeches do not display the same attention to showing that the requirements of the law under which the case was brought have or have not been met.

We turn now to the two surviving speeches delivered before the Palladion and Delphinion. In both cases, the speaker makes sure to argue that the elements of the governing statute were or were not met, but the arguments in the speeches are not as clearly different from popular court discourse as those delivered in the Areopagus. Antiphon *On the Chorus Boy*, involves what must have been an unusual charge: *bouleusis* ("planning") of an unintentional homicide. The speaker was assigned the task of training a chorus of boys for a dramatic festival, and delegated this task to his son-in-law and three other trusted men. During the training, one of the boys was given a potion to drink, probably to alleviate a sore throat, and died from the mixture. The boy's brother prosecuted the speaker in the Palladion, arguing that he was indirectly responsible for the accidental death. The speaker offers two main arguments regarding the death: first, that he took all due care in arranging for the training of the chorus,[90] and, second, that he was not involved in any way in the decision to give the boy the drug.[91]

At first blush these arguments appear to reveal a rather sloppy approach to the legal issue in dispute. If *bouleusis* of unintentional homicide required that the

---

[88] D. Cohen 1995:120ff. Arguing that Conon is guilty of *hubris* is not entirely irrelevant; *aikeia* was presumably a lesser-included offense of *hubris*, though, of course, the Athenians would not have articulated it in this way. However, Ariston's focus on making out a case of *hubris* while failing to even cite or refer to the assault statute under which the case was brought (to say nothing of his citation of the unrelated statute for clothes-stealing) reveals a lack of attention to the elements of the specific charge at issue that appears to be characteristic of popular court speakers and, I suggest, uncharacteristic of litigants in intentional homicide cases before the Areopagus.

[89] For discussion of the evidence, see Phillips 2000:184–185.

[90] Ant. 6.11–13.

[91] Ant. 6.15–18.

defendant ordered or was at least aware that the boy was given the drug, the first argument is otiose. If, on the other hand, a chorus master can be held liable for actions that are taken by his delegates in the course of training the chorus, the argument that the defendant took no part in the giving of the drug would do him little good. It seems likely that cases of "planning" an accidental death were unusual, and that the level of involvement necessary for a conviction in such a case was not defined by the laws and was contested in this suit. The prosecutor probably admitted the defendant's lack of involvement and knowledge, but argued that he was nevertheless responsible for the acts of his subordinates, and perhaps criticized specific aspects of the training arrangements.[92] The speaker thus first attempts to refute the prosecutor's case by showing that he discharged his duty as choregus "as best and justly as I was able." He describes the care he took in making arrangements for the training and appointing four trustworthy men to run the operation. He then argues for a more limited interpretation of *bouleusis*, one that requires some involvement in or knowledge of the giving of the drug before liability can attach.[93] Thus even though the uncertainty in the law regarding *bouleusis* of unintentional homicide causes this speech to be less focused on the specific elements of the offense than speakers in intentional homicide and wounding cases, the speaker does home in on the contested legal issue and offer arguments to support his acquittal under both potential interpretations of the law.[94]

The final speech in our survey of legal argumentation before the homicide courts is one of the best-known pieces of Attic oratory: Lysias *On the Death of Eratosthenes*. This case is something of an exception: the arguments in this speech are not significantly different from those likely to be made by a popular court speaker. The speaker, Euphiletus, allegedly discovered Eratosthenes committing adultery with his wife in his home and killed him immediately. He is now pleading lawful homicide before the Delphinion. After a long narrative detailing how he slowly came to discover his wife's infidelities, the speaker turns to demonstrating that his actions fall within the ambit of the lawful homicide statute, which provides that a man who kills another upon catching him in intercourse with his wife shall not be

---

[92]   Gagarin 1998b:74.

[93]   E.g. Ant. 6.15: "I will demonstrate to you that I did not order the boy to drink the drug, nor did I force him to drink, give it to him to drink, nor was I even present when he drank it."

[94]   The speaker also devotes a substantial portion of his defense to criticism of his accusers' motives. What is important for our purposes here is that the speaker attempts to argue that his actions did not give rise to liability for *bouleusis* of homicide, rather than making arguments based on a number of laws in addition to the specific charge at issue, or neglecting the governing law altogether.

punished. He has this law read out to the jury,[95] and he argues at length that he did not entrap Eratosthenes. Rather, he asserts, he was unprepared when Eratosthenes came to his home, hastily gathered some neighbors as witnesses and supporters, and properly seized him while he was still lying with his wife.[96] Euphiletus thus offers a detailed argument that the killing meets the requirements of the lawful homicide statute.[97] The speaker doesn't stop there, however. Euphiletus' excursus on the laws relating to rape and adultery[98] in an attempt to emphasize the seriousness of Eratosthenes' act and the justice of his response is clearly unrelated to the issue of whether the killing fits within the statute's list of lawful homicides. The speaker does carefully address whether his actions satisfy the governing lawful homicide statute, but it is not clear throughout the speech – as it is in cases before the Areopagus – that the speaker views the application of the governing statute as, de facto, a mandatory subject of discussion. One gets the impression that the speaker thinks the lawful homicide statute's provision permitting cuckolds to kill adulterers caught *in flagrante delicto* is only one (albeit the most important) piece of evidence for his contention that the killing was, in a general and non-technical sense, "justifiable." Euphiletus notes, for example, that adultery is considered an abomination not just in Athens, but in all of Greece.[99] The legal argumentation of *On the Death of Eratosthenes*, then, is not as clearly different from that of the popular courts as the homicide courts' extraordinary reputation and the superior legal definition of the lawful homicide statute might lead one to expect.

This brief examination of legal argumentation in the surviving homicide speeches suggests that, at least in intentional homicide or wounding suits before the Areopagus, speakers were markedly more focused on discussing the elements of the charge at issue than popular court speakers. Although the speakers in our other two homicide suits – Antiphon *On the Chorus Boy* and Lysias *On the Death of Eratosthenes* – take care to argue their case according to the governing statute, it is

---

[95] Lys. 1.30. The statute is not preserved in the manuscripts, but most scholars have assumed that it is the lawful homicide statute quoted in Demosthenes 23.53.

[96] Lys. 1.24, 37–46.

[97] In fact, he provides a deliberately misleading interpretation of this law by implying that the law required, not merely permitted, him to take Eratosthenes' life under the circumstances Lys. 1.34:

> Well then, gentlemen, not only have the laws acquitted me of having done wrong, but even directed me to exact this penalty.

Creative and zealous advocacy such as this should not be surprising in any Athenian court, homicide or popular.

[98] Lys. 1.30–32.

[99] Lys. 1.2.

difficult to say (particularly in the case of *On the Death of Eratosthenes*) whether the mode of legal argumentation in these speeches differs significantly from speeches delivered in the popular courts. It is, however, possible to make a few general observations about the surviving homicide court cases that suggest a greater degree of legal argumentation than that found in the popular courts. With the exception of *On the Death of Eratosthenes*, no laws are cited in any of the homicide speeches. It seems likely that speakers assumed that the experienced judges in the homicide courts were well aware of the basic laws governing their jurisdiction. In these five orations, the speakers repeatedly refer to the requirements of intentional and *bouleusis* of unintentional homicide without reciting the statute. The defendant in Lysias *Against Simon*, for example, summarizes the prosecutor's argument that the judges should infer *pronoia* from his assertion that the speaker was armed with potsherds, and begins his refutation with the statement "But it seems to me, O Council, that not only for you, who are experienced in looking into such cases, but also for all other men, it is easy to determine that he is lying."[100] It is understandable that the one case in which a law was cited involved a plea of lawful homicide: A defendant in such a case was obliged to show that his actions were not merely moral or just, but lawful under one of the several statutes listing specific types of killing that were not punishable.[101] One other factor suggests that the speeches in the homicide courts were more focused on legal argumentation than popular court speeches. It has been shown that whereas prosecutors in Athenian courts tend to focus more on the law, Athenian defendants use a variety of strategies to cast doubt on the prosecutor's case without necessarily providing a discussion of the relevant charge and its application to the case at hand.[102] Because all but one of our surviving homicide speeches are delivered by defendants, it may be revealing that all our speeches do include some discussion of the elements of the charged offense.

LEGALISM IN THE HOMICIDE COURTS: RELEVANCE

In the previous section, we examined the degree of legal argumentation found in the homicide courts – that is, the extent to which speeches in these courts focus on satisfying the specific criteria of the offense under which the charge was

---

[100] Lys. 3.28.

[101] cf. Carawan 1998:283. The speaker may have also quoted the law because it may have been an archaic and rarely-used statute. For discussion, see Phillips 2000:18–22.

[102] Johnstone 1999:54–60, 97–100. For discussion, see Chapter 3.

brought. In this section, we turn to a related issue, that of relevance – the types of arguments and information that were considered useful to a jury in making its decision. The Athenian notion of relevance in the popular courts was quite broad, and encompassed a variety of extra-legal information, such as discussion of the background of the dispute, appeals to pity based on the likely effects of a guilty verdict, and evidence related to the character of the parties.[103] By contrast, the homicide courts had a relevancy rule limiting the use of irrelevant statements. The Athenian definition of material "outside the issue" (ἔξω τοῦ πράγματος) for purposes of the homicide courts appears to have centered on character evidence. Although this rule was not adhered to in all respects, and although our sources exaggerate the effects the rule had on the nature of argumentation and decision making in the homicide courts, there are significant differences between our surviving homicide and popular court speeches.

The most striking divergence between the Areopagus and the popular courts is the Areopagus' relevancy rule.[104] A similar rule appears to have applied in the other homicide courts as well. The speaker in Antiphon's *On the Chorus Boy*, a case before the court at the Palladion, suggests that the rule applies to all homicide prosecutions: "But in this suit, when they are prosecuting for homicide and should, under the law, make accusations only regarding the charge itself. . . ."[105] The relevancy rule was incorporated into the *diômosia*, the special oath taken by litigants in homicide trials. One homicide court speaker states that the oath included a provision that the prosecutor limit his accusation to the facts of the homicide itself (*auton ton phonon*), so that neither the defendants' past crimes nor his good deeds would affect the verdict.[106]

None of our sources gives an exhaustive list of items which were considered "legally irrelevant" (ἔξω τοῦ πράγματος), but the context of Lysias *Against Simon*, Lycurgus *Against Leocrates*, and Antiphon *On the Murder of Herodes* makes it clear that lists of services and attacks on an opponent's character were, at least formally, forbidden.[107] Pollux, writing in the second century C.E., adds that litigants before the Areopagus were not permitted to include a *proem* or emotional appeals in their

---

[103] See Chapter 3.
[104] Lys. 3.46; Lyc. 1.11–13; Poll. 8.117.
[105] Ant. 6.9.
[106] Ant. 5.11.
[107] Lys. 3.46; Lyc. 1.11–13; Ant. 5.11.

speeches, and Lucian includes a similar formulation.[108] However, as we will see below, speakers in the homicide courts do not shy away from appealing to the Areopagites' pity. It is difficult to say whether these two non-classical sources are correct in including emotional appeals in the list of material considered outside the issue. One possible explanation is that this stricture was not as carefully observed as the limitation on character evidence. Another is that in the homicide courts, just as in the popular courts, information regarding the effects of an adverse verdict on a defendant was not considered irrelevant to the verdict. If this is the case, it may be that later writers were aware of the Areopagites' reputation for focusing on the merits of the case and not being misled by rhetoric, emotional appeals, or the speaking ability of litigants,[109] and mistakenly included appeals to pity as one type of argument considered outside the issue under the relevancy rule. In any case, the only thing we can be sure of is that arguments based on character, such as discussions of public services or past crimes, were considered irrelevant in the homicide courts.

We do not know for certain how, or how strictly, the relevancy rule was enforced, but an (admittedly very late) source suggests that the herald would squelch litigants who strayed from the subject:

> As long as they [the litigants] spoke to the issue, the Council tolerated them and listened quietly. If someone either delivered a *proem* prior to his argument in order to make them [the judges] more well-disposed, or dragged into the issue an extraneous appeal to pity or a rhetorical exaggeration – which are the sort of things that the students of rhetoricians devise against the judges – the herald came forward and immediately silenced him, forbidding him from talking nonsense to the Council and disguising the issue with his words, so that the Areopagites could look at the events unadorned.[110]

---

[108] Poll. 8.117: "It was not permitted to include a *proem* or to lament [i.e., make an appeal for pity]. Lucian, (*Anach.* 19), another late source, also suggests that emotional appeals were proscribed by the relevancy rule. If these statements were taken literally, this rule would require the judges or the herald to perform a quick feat of literary analysis during every speech.

[109] See, e.g. Arist. *Rhet.* 1354a; Aesch. 1.92. For discussion, see below.

[110] Lucian *Anach.* 19. In the *Laws* (948a8ff), Plato suggests a similar mechanism:

> And, on the whole, in a lawsuit the presiding officers are not to allow the litigants either to swear for the sake of persuasiveness, nor to call down curses on themselves and their family, nor to use shameful supplications nor womanly weeping, but to keep on explaining what is right and inquiring what is right, and if they do not, as he is speaking outside the point, the archons are to draw him back again to argument concerning the issue.

There is no indication that the herald in the Areopagus was any more experienced than other Athenian officials, who generally were chosen by lot to serve one-year terms.[111] It is unlikely that the herald would be entrusted with the responsibility for determining when a litigant's arguments strayed from the point. If the herald did enforce the relevancy rule, he presumably took his cue from the reaction of the more experienced homicide judges. In fact, it is likely that the relevancy rule was enforced entirely through informal means. Hard looks and grumbling from the Areopagites may have been enough to remind speakers of the expectation that they avoid irrelevant material.

Regardless of whether a formal mechanism for enforcing the relevancy rule existed or whether the experienced Areopagites would simply make their displeasure known to a litigant who strayed from the point, our sources reveal that it was widely believed that irrelevant material had no place in the court of the Areopagus. In the opening of the *Rhetoric*, Aristotle suggests that the Areopagus' relevancy law places the discussion in that court outside the realm of rhetoric and states that if all trials observed this rule there would be nothing left for a rhetorician to say.[112] Other passages indicate that the decisions made by the Areopagus were not affected by the character and social standing of the litigants, but do not specify whether this is because litigants refrained from addressing character issues, or because the judges successfully ignored character evidence and speaking ability in reaching their verdict. Aeschines, for example, states:

> Use as an example the Council of the Areopagus, the most exacting court in
> the city. For I have earlier seen many men in this court who, though they
> spoke very well and provided witnesses, were nevertheless convicted; and on
> the other hand I know that some men who spoke badly and had no
> witnesses were successful.[113]

A statement in Lucian, though not likely to be literally true,[114] suggests a strong and remarkably persistent belief that the identity and social standing of the litigants played no role in trials in the Areopagus: he states that the Areopagus judged at

---

[111] On heralds in Athens, see Kahrstedt 1969:303–306.

[112] Arist. *Rhet.* 1354a.

[113] Aesch. 1.92. Aeschines suggests the Areopagites reach the correct result without regard to the quality of the speakers or their witnesses in part because they base their decisions on their own knowledge and investigations as well as the proceedings in court. *Cf.* Lys. 7.25 for the Areopagus' monthly supervision of the sacred olives protected by law.

[114] A few scholars (e.g. Burkert 1987:240) have accepted Lucian's account.

night in the dark "in order that it would not pay attention to the man who is speaking, but only to what is said."[115]

One problematic text runs counter to the rest of our evidence. According to *The Constitution of the Athenians*, in private cases heard by the popular courts, litigants took an oath to speak to the point: "and the adversaries in a private suit swear to speak to the matter in dispute."[116] Even if this report is accurate, the required oath has left no trace in our surviving private speeches. Whereas speeches made before the homicide courts or referring to them make frequent mention of the relevancy rule,[117] speeches delivered in the popular courts never mention such a legal requirement. In the very few popular court allusions to speaking to the issue, most of which are found in a single speech, Demosthenes *Against Eubulides*, nothing in the phraseology suggests a duty imposed by law to avoid straying from the issue at hand.[118] One speaker begs the jury not to be irritated[119] if he seeks to demonstrate that his opponents are villains, as their villainy truly does pertain to the event that befell him: "For I think that in demonstrating the baseness of these men I am speaking to the very matter that befell me."[120] Another says that it is inappropriate for his opponents to discuss his character: "Are they [my opponents] unaware that it is fitting for them to speak on the issue?"[121] By contrast, the speaker before the Areopagus in *Against Simon* asserts that "it is not lawful to speak outside the issue in your court."[122] Thus, whereas the speaker in the popular court uses the word *prosêkei*, which connotes an informal duty, in the Areopagus the speaker refers to a legal prohibition, stating that speaking outside the issue is illegal (*ou nomimon*).[123] The speaker in Antiphon *On the Murder of Herodes* also suggests that

---

[115] Lucian *Hermot.* 64.13.

[116] For varying interpretations of this problematic text, see Rhodes 1993:718–719; Lipsius 1905–1915:918–919; Harrison 1998:163. The dikastic oath quoted in Demosthenes 24.149–151 includes a reference to jurors casting their vote concerning the charge, but most of the provisions of this lengthy oath have been rejected as inauthentic.

[117] E.g., Ant. 6.9; Lys. 3.46.

[118] Lys. 9.1–3; Dem. 57.7, 33, 59, 60, 63, 66. Because admonitions to the jurors to be faithful to the dikastic oath are common, the complete absence from our texts of this supposed litigants' oath is striking. For a discussion of references to the dikastic oath, see Johnstone 1999:33–42.

[119] Dem. 57.59: πρὸς Διὸς καὶ θεῶν μηδεὶς ὑπολάβῃ δυσκόλως, "by Zeus and the gods let no one take it ill."

[120] Dem. 57.59.

[121] Lys. 9.1: πότερον ἀγνοοῦντες ὅτι περὶ τοῦ πράγματος προσήκει λέγειν;

[122] Lys. 3.46: παρ' ὑμῖν οὐ νόμιμόν ἐστιν ἔξω τοῦ πράγματος λέγειν.

[123] See also Antiphon 6.9: "But in this suit, when they are prosecuting for homicide and should, under the law as it is, make accusations only regarding the charge itself. . . ."

a formal rule applied in the homicide courts. He speaks of an obligatory oath, applicable in homicide trials, to bring no charge other than the homicide itself.[124] And we have seen that a number of texts praise the Areopagus for its distinctive prohibition of irrelevant matter.[125] It is most likely, then, that the homicide courts had a unique procedural stricture forbidding the introduction of any matter not germane to the charge, some provision different from the putative oath for private litigants mentioned in *The Constitution of the Athenians*.

Examination of the four surviving speeches written for delivery in the Areopagus (Ant. 1, Lys. 3, 4, 7) and the two written for the other homicide courts (Ant. 6; Lys. 1) gives some indication of the extent to which the composition, rules, and procedures of these special courts affected litigants' use of material "outside the issue in dispute" (ἔξω τοῦ πράγματος). Speakers in the homicide courts are more skittish about citing their services to the state or slandering their opponents than popular court speakers, but irrelevancy was by no means absent from litigation in these courts. Although the relevancy rule was not adhered to in all respects, there are significant differences between the surviving homicide and popular court speeches, and litigants seem to be aware that the homicide courts enjoyed a reputation for having different expectations than the popular courts had.

Litigants before the homicide courts were reluctant to adduce evidence of their good deeds or to criticize their opponent's character. Although such references occur frequently in the popular courts,[126] litigants in our surviving six homicide speeches employ this strategy in only three passages.[127] In two of the three instances,[128] the speaker does not mention character without citing the relevancy rule and immediately checking himself, not unlike the modern trial lawyer who deliberately refers to inadmissible evidence in the hope that it will have an effect on the jurors despite the inevitable admonition from the bench that they disregard it. The speaker's unease is clear in Lysias *Against Simon*, where he squeezes in a quick attack on his opponent's conduct as a soldier but stops short with a *praeteritio*. He begins by stating, "I wish I were permitted to prove to you the baseness of this

---

[124] Ant. 5.11.

[125] Lyc. 1.11–13; Ant. 5–11; Arist. *Rhet.* 1354a.

[126] For discussion see Chapter 3; see also Carey 1994b; Ober 1990:226–233.

[127] Lys. 3.44–46; Lys. 7.31, 41.

[128] The exception is Lysias 7.31. This speech concerns the removal of a sacred olive stump, a religious offense within the Areopagus' jurisdiction unrelated to homicide and the other violent offenses associated with the homicide courts. The speaker indicates that the relevancy rule did apply in this type of case. Lys. 7.41–42.

man with evidence of other things [i.e., acts or events outside the charge]. . . . I will exclude all the other evidence, but I will mention one thing which I think it is fitting that you hear about, and that will be a proof of this man's rashness and boldness." After briefly recounting how his opponent beat up his military commander and was the only Athenian publicly censured for insubordination by the generals, he stops himself: "I could say many other things about this man, but because it is not lawful to speak outside the issue before your court. . . ."[129] Lysias *On the Olive Stump* includes a similar formulation.[130] In a survey of our entire corpus of court speeches, Johnstone has shown that defendants were much more likely than prosecutors to cite their liturgies and discuss issues of character.[131] The small number of references to character in the homicide courts becomes even more significant when we consider that all but one of our surviving homicide speeches were delivered by defendants.

In addition to the rare and reluctant use of character evidence in the speeches themselves, in one homicide case – Antiphon *On the Chorus Boy* – the speaker accuses his opponent of violating the relevancy rule by slandering him rather than restricting his prosecution to the homicide charge.[132] On closer inspection, however, the speaker's complaint appears to be unfounded. He indicates that the allegedly irrelevant material introduced by his opponent chiefly concerns his conduct in training the chorus.[133] As we have seen, the issue in this unusual case of *bouleusis* of involuntary homicide is whether the speaker is responsible for actions taken by his subordinates and therefore may be held liable for accidents that occur in connection with his training of the chorus, or whether "planning" requires a

---

[129] Lys. 3.44–46. Later in this same passage the speaker states that he performed many public services.

[130] The speaker boasts that he has fought in many battles and has been a model citizen before calling himself to order, as it were. ". . . I who have been involved in many sea and land battles on [Athens'] behalf, and have acted moderately in both the democracy and the oligarchy. But, O Council, I do not know what I should say here [i.e., the Areopagus]" (Lys. 7.41–42).

[131] Johnstone 1999:93–100. He shows that in private cases, defendants cite their liturgies 50% of the time, whereas prosecutors do so only 23% of the time.

[132] Ant. 6.7–10.

[133] Ant. 6.9:

Where it was possible for them, if I did any wrong to the city either in performing my duties as *choregus* or in any other way, to get revenge on their enemy and to assist the city by revealing and proving these crimes, not one of them was ever able to prove that I committed either a great or a minor crime upon your city. But in this trial, when they are prosecuting for homicide and should, under the law, make accusations only regarding the charge itself, they are scheming to put together false statements against me and to slander me before the city.

more direct connection to the giving of the poison. It was therefore natural for the prosecution to argue that the defendant was negligent in his handling of the liturgy, and indeed the speaker begins his own defense by stating that he discharged the office efficiently and scrupulously.[134] The purported irrelevant slanderous statements in the prosecution speech were thus more probably criticisms of the speaker's supervision over the choral training, a question directly relevant to the charge at issue.[135]

The unusual approach to relevance in the homicide courts can be seen clearly by comparing the use of extra-legal material in our surviving homicide court speeches with three popular court speeches involving similar charges: Antiphon *On the Murder of Herodes*, Lysias *Against Eratosthenes*, and Lysias *Against Agoratus*. *On the Murder of Herodes* and *Against Agoratus* are both homicide cases argued in a popular court via the *apagôgê* procedure.[136] The speaker in *On the Murder of Herodes*, a young Mytilenean defending himself on a charge of homicide, feels the need to give an explanation of his father's conduct when Mytilene revolted from Athens a decade earlier, and notes that his father has served Athens by sponsoring choruses and paying his taxes.[137] The prosecutor *in Against Agoratus* devotes six sections and witness testimony to an attack on the character of Agoratus and that of his family. He is, according to the speaker, a slave and the descendant of slaves, a convicted sycophant, and an adulterer who corrupts the wives of citizens.[138] The speaker also recounts the crimes of each of Agoratus' three brothers: one was executed for treason during the Sicilian expedition; one was imprisoned as a slave smuggler;

---

[134] Ant. 6.11.

[135] The speaker also devotes several sections of this speech to the argument that the prosecutor was bribed by his enemies to bring the case and thereby prevent the speaker from proceeding against them in court on unrelated charges (Ant. 6.33–40). Although some scholars have viewed this argument as irrelevant material, there is no reason to believe that the Athenians considered specific evidence that the prosecutor was bribed to bring a false charge *exô tou pragmatos*. Indeed, even in the restrictive evidence system of the modern United States, evidence that the plaintiff has filed prior false claims in similar cases and evidence suggesting that a witness had ulterior motives for his testimony generally are considered admissible. Because the prosecutor in an Athenian homicide case was required to swear that the accusation was true and that the accused had committed the homicide, such litigants were akin to witnesses in some ways.

[136] The details of the types of *apagôgê* have been vigorously debated in recent scholarship. For discussion, see Macdowell 1963:130–141; Hansen 1976, 1981a; Gagarin 1979; Evjen 1970; Volonaki 2000.

[137] Ant. 5.74–79.

[138] Lys. 13.18–19, 64–67.

and one was executed as a clothes stealer.[139] In *Against Eratosthenes*, Lysias accuses Eratosthenes, a member of the Thirty tyrants, with the killing of his brother Polemarchus during the Thirty's short-lived reign of terror. The legal context of this speech is not entirely clear from the text, but it appears to have been delivered before a popular court at Eratosthenes' *euthunê* in 403/2.[140] The *euthunê* was a procedure whereby magistrates examined each public official's conduct at the end of his term; private citizens could bring charges of misconduct against the official at any point in the procedure. Less than half of Lysias' prosecution speech concerns the murder of Polemarchus: Lysias details Eratosthenes' other evil deeds, beginning with his involvement with the oligarchic revolution of the Four Hundred in 411 B.C.E.,[141] and engages in an extended attack on the political figure and associate of the defendant, Theramenes.[142] We must be careful about drawing conclusions from the argumentation in this unique case.[143] Nevertheless, the unabashed use of references to character in *On the Murder of Herodes* and *Against Agoratus*, as well as *Against Eratosthenes*, supports the conclusion that speakers were more likely to stick to the issue in dispute in cases heard by the homicide courts than in similar popular court cases.

The one consistent exception to the relevancy rule we find in the homicide speeches is the appeal for sympathy from the Areopagites.[144] It is possible that under the stress of such a serious charge litigants could not maintain composure and refrain from appeals for pity, and that such appeals were allowed a degree of forbearance. But there is another possible explanation. We have seen that only non-classical sources include appeals to pity among the list of legally irrelevant

---

[139] Lys. 13.67.

[140] It may have been written for circulation rather than delivery in a court. Less likely is a prosecution via *dikê phonou*. For discussion, see Carawan 1998:376–377.

[141] Lys. 12.42–52.

[142] Lys. 12.62–78.

[143] It is possible that multiple offenses could be brought against a defendant in his *euthunê*, if indeed this speech was delivered as part of that procedure, in which case some of the material in the speech unrelated to the murder may have been regarded as germane to the charges. It is unclear what types of charges were suitable for prosecution through *euthunê*, but presumably they would be limited to wrongs allegedly committed by a magistrate in his official capacity against either individuals or the city (Arist., *Ath. Pol.* 48.4: εὔθυναν . . . τ᾽ ἰδίαν . . . τε δημοσίαν). The *Constitution of the Athenians* here states that the man bringing a charge must write out the specific offense (τὸ ἀδίκημα) of which he accuses the magistrate. Whereas we do not know what specific charges Lysias brought against Eratosthenes, it is improbable that they ranged as broadly as the accusations included in the speech.

[144] Lys.3.48; 4.20; 7.41; Ant. 1.3, 21, 25.

arguments. As discussed above, it may be that, just as in the popular courts, discussion of the effect of a conviction on the defendant was considered relevant to the Areopagites' decision.

Our examination of homicide court speeches suggests that although our sources overstate the differences between the rules and procedures of the Areopagus and the popular courts and exaggerate the effects of these differences, speakers would make significant alterations in their arguments when appearing before a homicide court.

THE MIRROR OF THE AREOPAGUS

By the classical period the homicide courts were considered – and, to a lesser extent, were – distinctive in their approach to relevance and legal argumentation. When, how, and why did this process of differentiation occur? Or, stated differently, what is it about homicide that explains its unusual treatment? Because we know very little about the history and development of either the homicide or the popular courts, any answer to these questions is necessarily speculative. In my view, it is the peculiar development of homicide law in the archaic period, *not* a sense that homicide was more serious or in some way different from other charges, that accounts for the unusual character of the homicide courts in the classical period. Although the early history of the homicide courts is murky, the more formal, legal approach of these courts appears to reflect the concerns of a state just beginning to assert control over private violence in the seventh and early sixth century B.C.E. The popular court system was introduced about a century or a century-and-a-half later as part of the creation and development of the democracy. In constructing the new popular court system, the Athenians consciously declined to adopt the strict approach of the existing homicide courts, but permitted these courts to continue to decide cases involving homicide in the traditional manner. The existence of a parallel court system for homicide can tell us a great deal about the aims and ideals of the popular courts and, more generally, about Athenian notions of law.

THE DIFFERENTIATION OF HOMICIDE AND POPULAR COURTS

The association between homicide and substantive legal argument is already evident in what is almost certainly Athens' first written homicide law, Draco's law of 621/0 B.C.E. This law, which survives in fragmentary form inscribed on a stone stele, appears to provide the first example of the formal distinction between offenders' mental states familiar in classical homicide law.[145] Draco's law sets out a legal procedure whereby cases of unintentional homicide appear to be judged by *ephetai*.[146] In a fragmentary portion of the inscription, the law also appears to provide for two types of justifiable homicide: self-defense in a fight started by another, and defending oneself from highway robbers.[147] The law as we have it mentions neither intentional homicide nor the Areopagus.[148] It is unclear precisely how homicide prosecutions worked in Draco's time: was jurisdiction divided among different courts as it was in the classical period?[149] Did the *ephetai* judge all cases of homicide, or did the Areopagus exist at this time as a homicide court as well?[150] How, if at all, was intentional homicide treated?[151] What were the consequences of an ephetic finding of unintentional or justifiable homicide?[152] The surviving evidence does not permit confident answers to these questions, but it does seem reasonably clear from the inscription that the *ephetai* were charged with determining a defendant's intent when he argued that he had killed unintentionally.[153] Just

---

[145] Carawan (1998:48) argues that the idea that intent was relevant in the treatment of homicide had been in circulation for some time before Draco, but was not formally recognized until Draco's law.

[146] IG I³ 104, lines 11–13. The inscription is lacunose. I follow Stroud's text and Gagarin's translation as given in Gagarin 1981a: xiv–xvii).

[147] IG I³ 104, lines 30–36.

[148] It is unclear whether the law originally included a provision addressing intentional homicide. For discussion, see, e.g., Gagarin 1981a:111–145; Carawan 1998:35; Sealey 1983:292; Wallace 1989:16–18.

[149] Most scholars now assume that the classical division of courts did not exist at the time of Draco. For three different reconstructions of the development of the various homicide courts, see Humphreys 1991:30ff; Carawan 1998:133–135; Sealey 1983.

[150] The traditional view, relying primarily on ancient legends of the Areopagus' history, held that the Areopagus was the first court for homicide and that Draco transferred some of the Areopagus' jurisdiction to the newly created *ephetai*. For a review of literature subscribing to this "Areopagite model," see Carawan 1998:7–8. For a recent variation on the Areopagite model, see Wallace 1989:3–47. Recently, several scholars have argued that the *ephetai* judged homicide cases in the time of Draco and that the Areopagus did not become a homicide court until the time of Solon or later. See, e.g., Humphreys, 1991:32; Gagarin 1981a:135ff; Carawan 1998:134; Sealey 1983:290–294.

[151] On this question, see, e.g., Humphreys 1991:36; Gagarin 1981a:111–145; Carawan 1998:35–6.

[152] See, e.g., Humphreys 1991:23; Gagarin 1981a:111–145; Carawan 1998:35–36; Sealey 1983:290–294.

[153] So Humphreys 1991:23. The *ephetai* may also have decided whether a killing qualified as justifiable homicide and was therefore not punishable, but this portion of the inscription is too fragmentary to draw any firm conclusions. Carawan (1998:35–36) argues that under Draco's law intentional and unintentional homicides resulted in the same penalty – exile with the possibility of pardon by the victim's relatives – and therefore that the *ephetai* would not ordinarily have made rulings based on intent. It is unclear from the inscription whether the victim's family could grant pardon in all homicide cases, or only in the case of unintentional killings. However, even if it is true that intentional killers were

as in the classical period, the distinction between intentional and unintentional homicide in Draco's law provided greater legal definition and presumably served to focus both litigants and *ephetai* on the narrow question of intent. From the very first written statute, then, homicide law exhibited greater legal definition and substantive content than the laws governing the popular courts in the classical period.[154]

We do not know how or why the distinction between types of homicide came to be recognized in Draco's law. Many early written statutes appear to have been ad hoc responses to quite specific pressing problems.[155] It is possible that the legal specificity of Draco's law reflects an attempt to address a specific controversy – whether to punish men who had killed fellow Athenians during a recent civil war. A little over a decade before the enactment of Draco's law, an Athenian aristocrat named Cylon attempted to establish a tyranny. The Athenian archons, led by the elite Alcmeonid clan, drove Cylon out of Athens and killed his supporters. Draco's law may have been enacted specifically to prevent the political enemies of the Alcmeonidae from charging them for the killing of the Cylonians and thereby driving them into permanent exile. It is possible that the law was designed to classify the actions of the Alcmeonidae as a form of unintentional or justifiable homicide.[156] It may be that the first step in differentiating homicide procedure was thus an historical accident of sorts, unrelated to the unique nature of the crime of homicide. However the differentiation between types of homicide first developed, once in place Draco's law provided substantive guidance to those judging cases of homicide, focused the attention of litigants and judges on the issue of intent, and, presumably, fostered an association between homicide proceedings and legal argument that took on a life of its own and would in time become self-reinforcing.

---

technically granted the possibility of pardon, an *ephetic* finding of unintentional homicide would have the effect of putting pressure on the victim's family to come to a settlement with the killer. There is no reason to believe that the *ephetai* were not charged with determining intent under Draco's law.

[154] Draco's law includes substantive content on other issues as well. It appears to instruct the *ephetai* to treat "the planner" of a homicide in the same manner as one who kills with his own hands (lines 11–13), and it declares that killing an exiled killer calls for the same sanction as one who kills an Athenian (lines 26–29).

[155] Hölkeskamp 1992b; 1999.

[156] This theory was suggested to me by Sara Forsdyke. Various provisions support this view of the law's purpose: prosecution is limited to the relatives of the victim; the law appears to be preoccupied with addressing unintentional and justifiable homicide; and a retroactivity clause makes it clear that the law would apply to those involved in the Cylonian conspiracy. For discussion, see Forsdyke (2005: xx).

The early history of the homicide courts' relevancy rule is even murkier. Classical sources state that that the unusual homicide procedures are ancient in origin and have remained unchanged since the time of Draco.[157] It is difficult to know whether to credit such statements, as these passages may simply reflect fourth-century ideology rather than seventh-century historical reality. A passage in Lucian describes the operation of the relevancy rule in the time of Solon,[158] but this source is too far removed from our period to offer secure evidence. My own, necessarily speculative, view is that the relevancy rule, which seems so "advanced" in comparison to the free-for-all approach to relevance in the popular courts, developed well before the creation of the popular courts.[159] The prohibition against irrelevant material likely grew out of an urgent need to foster obedience of and respect for verdicts in a fledgling legal system that was just beginning to assert control over the private use of violence. The traditional response to homicide in pre-Draconian Athens was retaliatory murder carried out by the victim's family unless they agreed to accept a blood price.[160] Draco's law sets limits on the family's power over a homicide: unintentional killers are to be permitted to flee the city unharmed; at least one type of justifiable homicide is proclaimed to be *nêpoinei* (without penalty); and, although the family retains the final decision on whether to accept compensation from unintentional homicides, a finding that a killing was unintentional likely put pressure on the family to do so. The process of convincing the relatives of a man who had been killed to relinquish the traditional right of immediate retaliation and abide by the findings of the *ephetai* must have been a slow and difficult one.

A relevancy rule may have been thought to assist in this process in two ways. First, by limiting the judges' discretion and discouraging evidence about the litigants' social background the relevancy rule may have fostered a belief in the impartiality of the judges,[161] and thereby encouraged families to appeal to and

[157] E.g., Ant. 5.14; 6.2.

[158] Lucian *Anach.* 19.

[159] Perhaps the relevancy rule was introduced sometime between Draco's law (621/0 B.C.E.) and the reforms of Solon (ca. 590 B.C.E.).

[160] Gagarin 1986:5–18.

[161] Hesiod's *Works and Days* (248–273) suggests that the possibility of unfair judgments meted out by corrupt or partial judges was a source of anxiety among litigants in the archaic period. It was particularly important that the Draconian *ephetai* establish a reputation for impartiality because by their nature their verdicts would disappoint one or other of the parties. By contrast, Gagarin (1986: 22, 43) has suggested that judges in early Greece tended to use compromise settlements acceptable to both sides to insure compliance.

abide by the results of the official homicide procedures. Second, the rule forced 2) families to cast their arguments in terms of the narrow question of the individual homicide. The relevancy rule would therefore promote the view that a homicide specific was an isolated event to be resolved rather than simply one part of an ongoing and escalating cycle of violence that reached beyond the individual killer and victim to encompass their families as well.

It was only after the homicide courts had been operating for about a century or so that a popular court system resembling the classical courts in structure and function was introduced. We can't put a precise date on the creation of the popular court system, but it seems most likely that this institution came about during the period of the creation and development of the democratic system. That is, sometime between Cleisthenes' political reorganization of 508/7 B.C.E. often thought of as the "invention" of the democracy, and the Periclean reforms that brought the radical democracy to full maturity in the mid-fifth century.[162] The formalism of the homicide courts was available as a potential model at the inception of the popular courts, but was rejected in favor of a more flexible approach.[163] The chronological priority of the homicide court procedures belies an evolutionary account of the development of law and legal thinking in Athens.

The legalism of the homicide courts grew out of the fledgling state's attempts to curb the violence and social disruption associated with this unique crime. Once the distinction between the two types of law court was established, however, it seems likely that it was inertia and the tradition of legalism in the homicide courts rather than a sense that homicide by its nature required different treatment that led to the decision to maintain the homicide courts as islands of formalism in a sea of highly informal popular court cases. Factors such as the seriousness of the offense and concern over pollution may also have played a role in the continued existence of the homicide courts' strict approach.[164] But our evidence suggests that these

[162] Though there may have been some form of popular judicial decision making prior to this period, a court system similar to the classical courts, with selection of jurors by lot and a clear differentiation between the Assembly and the court, was most likely a creation of the democracy. Whatever the nature of the archaic *hêliaia*, it is likely to have been radically transformed with the introduction of the democracy in the early fifth century. For a review of the evidence regarding the *hêliaia* and a new proposal, see Hansen 1981–1982; see also Sealey 1983:295–296.

[163] Later in this chapter I discuss why the Athenians rejected the homicide model for their popular court system.

[164] Parker 1996a:104–143; Arnaoutoglou 1993; Carawan 1998:17–19.

characteristics of homicide were less important in the classical period than one might expect. It is not clear, for example, that the Athenians shared the modern view of homicide as the most serious possible crime. Homicide was a private rather than a public matter; it was only one of many crimes that could result in the death penalty;[165] and, indeed, a man accused of intentional homicide could avoid death by voluntarily going into exile after the first of his two defense speeches. In addition, recent scholarship suggests that the relative importance of pollution in the treatment of homicide has been exaggerated, and that by the fourth century concern over pollution in relation to homicide was in steep decline.[166] The thesis that the differentiation of the homicide and popular courts was not primarily linked to the nature of the crime of homicide is supported by the introduction near the end of the fifth century of an alternative procedure, *apagôgê*, for dealing with at least some types of homicide through the popular court system. Further, we have seen that the praise of the homicide court procedures was not limited to their ability to resolve homicide cases alone; Athenian attitudes toward relevance cannot be explained simply by a clear preference for different modes of decision making when judging different types of offense.

The Homicide Courts and Athenian Notions of Law

The homicide courts' special procedures can tell us something about the Athenian notion of law and the aims of its popular courts. The existence of a rule forbidding irrelevant statements demonstrates that the Athenians were capable of imagining a legal process that entails the regular application of abstract principles to particular cases. There was a notion that in the homicide courts, at least, judicial decisions were to be based on the narrow legal and factual issues of the case detached from

---

[165] In addition to homicide, the death penalty could be used for treason, impiety, theft, robbery, assault, public corruption, extortion, debasing the coinage, violation of the grain laws, illegal exploitation of the silver mines, and forging a will. For discussion, see Barkan 1935:5–41.

[166] Some aspects of the homicide procedures appear to suggest concern about pollution: those accused of homicide were ordered to avoid holy places and the agora (Dem. 20.158), homicide trials took place in the open air (Ant. 5.11), and pardoned killers had to perform sacrifices and purify themselves before returning to Attica (Dem. 23.72). Litigants in homicide trials also took special oaths in an elaborate religious ritual (Dem. 23.67–68). But the importance of pollution in the development of homicide law and procedures has been questioned in recent scholarship and there may be other explanations for these provisions. For discussion, see, e.g., MacDowell 1963:144–146; Parker 1996a:104–143; Arnaoutoglou 1993; Gagarin 1981a:164–167; Carawan 1998:17–19.

their social context, and without regard for the character or social standing of the litigants and the impression that their rhetoric made on the judges.

The antiquity and conservatism of the homicide courts invested them with great prestige, even apart from any perception of the merits of their mode of decision making. The fact that the Athenians did not introduce similar constraining procedural and evidentiary rules in the popular courts despite these older examples seems to indicate a conscious reluctance to embrace that mode of notably stricter legal argumentation. Opportunities for an assimilation to the perceived methods of the homicide courts were not lacking: there were several episodes of major and minor legal procedural reform in the classical period, including the revision of the laws at the end of the fifth century, the transition from oral to written depositions, and the creation in the fourth century of a new set of legal procedures (the *emmênoi dikai*) for certain types of case. It is true that the enforcement of a relevancy rule might have presented more practical difficulties in the popular courts than in the homicide courts because the Areopagite judges were more experienced and presumably therefore more likely to express their displeasure when a speaker strayed from the issue at hand. But we should not underestimate the ordinary Athenian's familiarity with legal procedures. It is not improbable to suppose that knowledgeable jurors and spectators would be able to enforce a relevancy rule by shouting down speakers who introduced character evidence.[167] Even if a relevancy rule similar to that used in the homicide courts would be unenforceable in the popular courts, we would expect to see some mechanism similar to the jurors' oath that was in practical terms unenforceable, but which speakers nevertheless referred to often and milked for its rhetorical value.

The Athenian decision not to emulate the special procedures and apparent rigor of the homicide courts, most notably the relevancy rule, in the popular courts may be attributed to countervailing values in their political culture: the widespread participation of ordinary men, and the broad discretion extended to juries to temper strict legality with equity. The broad view of relevance evident in the popular courts reflected not only a normative judgment about the value of individualized justice but also a commitment to popular decision making in the new democracy. It is one thing to hold that a wide range of extra-legal information and argumentation, such as the prior relationship and interaction of the parties and the effect an adverse verdict would have on a particular defendant,

---

[167] On the possibility of knowledgeable bystanders heckling jurors, see Lanni 1997:187–188.

is potentially relevant to the resolution of a legal dispute.[168] But it is quite another to unleash a popular jury to determine, without being provided with any rule of decision, what types of legal and extra-legal information and argumentation should be credited in reaching a just decision in a particular case. Support for an open-ended system of relevance like that used in the popular courts cannot be separated from the critical question: who decides what is most relevant in a specific case? The discretionary approach of the popular courts was thus intimately linked to the creation of a participatory democracy in which, in Aristotle's words, the *dêmos* was *kurios* (supreme) in all things, including the popular courts.[169]

Why did the homicide courts not assimilate themselves to the more flexible procedures of the popular courts in the classical period? The sheer force of conservatism and reluctance to alter the traditional procedures of the Areopagus must have played some role. It is possible that the fact that the homicide courts did take into account the most important type of contextual information relating to a homicide – the intent of the offender – made it seem less necessary to reform the homicide procedures. The most important factor may have been the rarity of traditional homicide procedures. Homicide appears to have been unusual in Athens. Our sources mention only fifteen cases of homicide between 507 and 322 B.C.E.,[170] and only three homicide speeches for delivery in the special homicide courts survive.[171] The frequency of traditional homicide trials may have further declined in the fourth century because *apagôgê*, an alternate procedure for bringing at least some types of homicide cases in the popular courts, was introduced near the end of the fifth century.[172] *Apagôgê* avoided the formalities, oaths, relevancy

---

[168] For a discussion of categories of extra-legal evidence that Athenian jurors appear to have found relevant, see Chapter 3.

[169] Arist. *Ath.Pol.* 41.2.

[170] Herman 1994:101.

[171] Including non-homicide cases, six speeches for delivery before the homicide courts survive. It may be that the rarity of special homicide court trials is not the only explanation for the relatively small number of remaining homicide speeches. Bruce Frier has suggested to me that because homicide speeches were focused more on the legal and factual issues and less on rhetoric, speechwriters might be less inclined to publish these speeches and ancient scholars less likely to preserve them.

[172] The dating and types of *apagôgê* used in homicide cases have been the subject of scholarly dispute for some time. The defendant in Antiphon 5, delivered around 420 B.C.E., complains that the prosecutor's use of the *apagôgê kakourgon* procedure (the procedure normally used against street criminals) for an ordinary homicide is unprecedented. It is unclear whether this case marks the first instance of the expansion of *apagôgê kakourgon* to homicide cases, or whether this suit was merely an aberration. Another type of *apagôgê* applicable only in homicide cases (sometimes referred to by scholars as *apagôgê phonou*)

rule, and jurisdictional complexities of the traditional homicide courts and was heard in a popular court before ordinary jurors. Although the homicide courts continued to hear cases throughout the classical period,[173] the existence of this alternate homicide procedure, as well as the overall infrequency of homicide trials, may have weakened any inclination to change the traditional homicide procedures.

Even if the Areopagus and other homicide courts rarely heard cases in the classical period, the Areopagus remained prominent in the Athenian legal imagination, serving as a notional antithesis to the flexible approach of the popular courts. Indeed, if the homicide courts rarely sat in judgment, that probably only enhanced their reputation by promoting an idealized view of their operation undiminished by frequent or apparent departures from the ideal. The idealization of the Areopagus and other homicide tribunals in the classical period may reflect Athenian anxieties about the decision making process of its mass juries. Praise of the Areopagus and the homicide courts was particularly focused on the special ability of the judges and their tendency to ignore the social standing and character of the litigants. The use of character evidence in the popular courts was controversial,[174] and praise of the Areopagus may reflect a widespread unease about the potential for misuse of this type of information, especially at the hands of a popular court jury. In fact, litigants in the popular courts who use character evidence are careful to explain how this contextual information is relevant to reaching a just result.[175]

The Athenians were aware of, and uneasy about, the aspects of their legal system that discouraged strict legal argument divorced from the social context of the dispute. Theirs was a conscious choice to favor contextualized justice and broad jury discretion over the more formal, legal approach represented by the homicide courts. Nevertheless, there appears to have been a decided ambivalence about the decision not to follow the Areopagus' paradigm of expertise and legal

---

may have been introduced at the end of the fifth century. For an account of the dating and reasons behind the rise of the use of *apagōgē* in homicide cases, see Volonaki 2000. It is unclear whether *apagōgē* was available in all types of homicide (compare Gagarin 1979 with Hansen 1981a). What is important for our purposes is that in the late fifth- and fourth century some homicide suits were brought not through the special homicide court procedures, but in the ordinary popular courts via *apagōgē*. Carawan (1998:164–167) has suggested that *apagōgē* gradually eclipsed the *dikē phonou*.

[173] Carawan (1998:164 n.45) catalogues only six possible examples of traditional homicide prosecutions in the fourth century.

[174] See Chapter 3.

[175] See Chapter 3.

argumentation in the popular courts. The social construction of the Areopagus reveals anxieties about the dangers of broad-ranging jury discretion in the popular courts, particularly the potential misuse of character evidence. In the next chapter, we will explore a different source of ambivalence in the popular court system, namely the need to sacrifice some measure of consistency and predictability to produce contextualized and individualized judgments.

5 LEGAL INSECURITY IN ATHENS

▣⑤

THE PAST FEW CHAPTERS HAVE DESCRIBED SOME ASPECTS OF THE ATHENIAN JUDICIAL
system as a sign of tension between contradictory goals. The Athenians' idealization of the homicide courts reveals their ambivalence about the broad conception
of relevance employed in the popular courts, and in particular their unease over the
potential misuse of character evidence. In this chapter I explore another disadvantage of the popular courts, a defect inherent in any system favoring flexible justice:
the unlikelihood that there will be even a rough consistency and predictability in
judgments. Whereas much recent scholarship emphasizes the positive role played
by the popular courts in fostering social stability and cohesiveness in Athens,[1]
this chapter assesses the social and economic costs associated with the Athenians'
discretionary system of justice.

Legal consistency is the notion that like cases should be treated alike. Predictability is the ideal that the law is sufficiently certain to permit citizens to
confidently conform their conduct to the law in most situations. These are two
basic, closely related prerequisites of what lawyers today call the "rule of law."[2]
Of course, even modern legal systems do not provide near-perfect consistency
or predictability. Determining whether two cases are so alike that the decision in
the first case should control the second is far from a straightforward process.[3] In
today's common law legal cultures, this task of comparing past cases to insure
consistency is generally undertaken only with respect to legal, not factual, determinations.[4] Moreover, most contemporary trials are, by definition, unpredictable:
cases that reach the trial stage are generally considered winnable by the attorneys
on both sides. Nevertheless, in most cases one can determine one's legal rights
and liabilities in a particular situation by examining the relevant statutes and decisions interpreting those statutes. The rules elucidated through this process are

---

[1] E.g., Ober 1990:145; Johnstone 1999:106–108, 124–125.
[2] For a general discussion of the requirements of a "rule of law," see Rawls 1999:206–235. For a recent
discussion of the rule of law as an ideology, see Burns 1999:13–31.
[3] For discussion, see MacCormick 1994:60.
[4] Of course, the jury instructions come in the form of rules and interpretations of those rules that reflect
appellate decisions in past cases.

sufficiently clear that very few modern disputes result in the creation of a new rule of law.

Athens, by contrast, lacked clear, well-defined rules that permitted potential litigants to predict the likely result in even the most straightforward popular court case. We have seen that within the popular courts Athenian jurors were presented with a wide variety of legal and extra-legal information and argument and were left to their own devices to assign weight to different types of evidence as they saw fit, unguided by an authoritative rule of decision. As a result, popular court verdicts were largely ad hoc determinations. In the process of choosing a highly individualized form of justice in the popular courts, the Athenians were forced to sacrifice a good measure of consistency and predictability in their legal system.

"Sacrifice" may be too strong a term, for the Athenians do not seem to have been as troubled by the lack of consistency and predictability as a modern might expect. Nevertheless, legal insecurity – that is, pervasive uncertainty about legal rules and likely verdicts – did have significant negative consequences. The Athenian ideal of equality before the laws (*isonomia*)[5] implies treating like cases alike, and the lack of consistency across cases detracted from the lawcourts' perceived legitimacy and authority. On a more concrete level, legal uncertainty meant that the law did not provide reliable ex ante guides for behavior in many situations, which increased the risk and cost of private transactions. Nevertheless, the advantages of an individualized, ad hoc system of justice appear to have outweighed these disadvantages, at least in the popular courts. This chapter examines the extent and effect of legal uncertainty in Athens, and explores why the legal (and social) system managed to function surprisingly well despite this climate of legal insecurity.

LEGAL UNCERTAINTY AND POPULAR COURT DECISION MAKING

Modern legal systems generally attempt to achieve predictable and consistent verdicts by (1) applying reasonably precise statutes and codes whose meaning may be elucidated in legislative or academic commentary, and/or (2) following

---

[5] In the classical period, equality before the law was often appealed to as a particularly democratic virtue and was specifically associated with the Athenians' form of democracy, which put a premium on strict "arithmetic" equality of citizens. See, e.g. Aesch. 1.5; Dem. 21.188; 23.86; Eur. *Supp.* 429–434. For discussion, see Hansen 1999:84. The notion of equality before the law is found as early as Solon (fr. 36), but is only later associated with democracy.

precedents set forth in decisions in previous similar or analogous cases.[6] In the case of classical Athens, we must consider a third possibility: predictability and consistency in court verdicts may have been achieved through the application of commonly shared values and norms – through cultural rather than legal knowledge. The following sections examine each of these possibilities in turn. The wide array of factors considered by the jury in reaching its verdicts prevented the popular court system from developing a high level of consistency and predictability in most cases. But there is one important exception. It is likely that some level of predictability was achieved through shared norms in serious criminal matters that threatened public order.

STATUTES

The absence of carefully defined statutes, legislative history, or trained jurists made the consistent and predictable interpretation and application of laws impossible in Athens. This point is nearly self-evident and so need not detain us long. We have already seen that Athenian statutes generally did not define the essential elements of the offense in question. The vagueness of Athenian statutes and the lack of authoritative means of interpreting such statutes must have made it difficult to predict the likely outcome of a popular court case.

But one should be careful not to take this too far. The extent of legal uncertainty in Athens might not be as great as one might be led to assume by the absence of clear, authoritative legal rules: statutes might not have been nearly as vague to Athenians as they seem to us. Common values may have reduced the extent of legal indeterminacy in the Athenian system and provided the average citizen with a general sense of what sort of behavior might, for example, put him in danger of a suit for *hubris* even though this term is not defined by statute.

Nevertheless, shared norms could not compensate entirely for the absence of canons of statutory interpretation, legislative history, or academic commentary. In Lysias *Against Theomnestus*, for example, the defendant is charged with defamation (*kakêgoria*) for stating that the speaker killed his father. The defendant apparently argued that he was not guilty because he did not use the precise word prohibited in the defamation statute (*androphonos*, "manslayer"), but rather simply said that he had

---

[6] Many contemporary civil law systems (in theory, if not entirely in practice) do not include previous decisions among the sources of law and rely purely on statutes and codes as interpreted in academic commentary. For articles on precedent in various code systems, see MacCormick & Summers 1997.

"killed" his father.[7] The prosecutor rejects this defense as hairsplitting, arguing that it is not the text of the statute but the purpose of the law[8] that matters. One would expect that there would be a clear consensus among Athenians on whether defamation involved only the use of particularly offensive words enumerated by statute or should be interpreted broadly to include a variety of insults having the same effect. That both litigants apparently thought their respective interpretation of the statute could persuade the jury[9] suggests that shared norms did not eliminate uncertainty concerning the meaning of statutes in Athens. Indeed, Aristotle's call for precise definitions of offenses like theft (*klopē*) and adultery (*moicheia*) in the *Rhetoric*[10] suggests that Athenians lacked a clear idea of the criteria for even straightforward offences.

Perhaps more to the point, even if all Athenians shared a common understanding of the meaning of what appear to us to be hopelessly vague statutes, this consensus would not necessarily result in predictable or consistent outcomes. The relevant statute did not provide an authoritative rule of decision in the Athenian popular courts; the result suggested by the law would not necessarily trump the variety of extra-legal arguments raised by the litigants in a given case.

PRECEDENT

Another potential source of legal consistency and predictability is the application of custom and precedent. We should consider the possibility that Athenian verdicts were not simply ad hoc settlements for individual disputes, but rather perpetuated general principles embodied in previous court decisions. The Athenians had no notion of binding precedent, and in fact the absence of review of verdicts or accountability of jurors made it impossible to enforce any criteria of judgment on the jury. Nevertheless, speakers cite previous decisions in roughly one-fifth of our surviving speeches. Litigants also often state that the verdict in the instant case will deter or encourage particular types of criminals in the future, an argument that assumes that at least some value was placed on consistency across cases. It is tempting to interpret these references as evidence of a doctrine of "persuasive precedent" in the Athenian courts. This section examines the role

---

[7] Lys. 10.6–7.

[8] The speaker casts his argument in terms of the intent of the lawgiver, though this was of course a fiction. For discussion, see Johnstone 1999:25–33.

[9] As Johnstone (1999:25) points out, the defendant's arguments are not as absurd as the speaker portrays them, and in fact at the pretrial stage the arbitrator found for the defendant, not the speaker.

[10] Arist. *Rhet.* 1374a8.

of these examples of "legal" reasoning in Attic oratory in some detail in an effort to shed light on the extent of legal indeterminacy in classical Athens.

It may be helpful to summarize here my view of how litigants use previous cases before embarking on a detailed examination of the passages. A close examination of these passages indicates that Athenian litigants cited past verdicts in a manner vastly different from that of modern lawyers. Both in systems of binding and persuasive precedent, the touchstone of legal consistency is "treating like cases alike." Athenian speakers often make no attempt to demonstrate how the legal issues in the previous case relate to the current dispute and generally do not give enough information about the previous decision to provide meaningful guidance to the current jury. In most cases, speakers cite past cases not to elucidate the meaning of the law or proper application of the facts in the case at hand, but to provide general examples to the jury to establish that harsh penalties are acceptable and that even men with good reputations and exemplary records can be legitimately punished for crimes they commit.

Even in the relatively few instances in which speakers do compare aspects of the previous and the current case in some detail, the absence of an authoritative rule of decision diminished the effectiveness of arguments from precedent: cases that appear to be very similar with respect to one relevant factor, such as the seriousness of the offense, could in fact easily be distinguished by reference to one or more other legal or extra-legal considerations. Because Athenian popular court juries considered a wide range of factors relevant to their decision, very few (if any) cases would be similar enough on all relevant axes to serve as an authoritative precedent.

The references to past decisions in our surviving cases suggest that it was rhetorically useful for speakers to refer to past cases in a general way and to assume that verdicts were reasonably consistent for the purpose of making arguments based on deterrence, but that the type of detailed discussion of previous cases necessary to foster true consistency was considered impractical and ineffective. We will see a wide gap between the elevated rhetoric of consistency and precedent in the court speeches and the reality of the Athenian system, which made it virtually impossible for litigants or jurors to make individual verdicts consistent with previous cases.

Litigants refer to previous cases in 21 of our extant speeches, roughly one-fifth of the total.[11] However, the manner in which speakers discuss precedents differs

[11] Dem. 21.72–76, 175–184; 24.138; 19.273; 20.146–148; 34.50; 59.116–117; Lys. 12.35ff; 13.56–57; 6.17; 22.16; Aesch. 1.86–88, 173; 2.6; 3.252–253, 258; Din. 1.14, 23ff; 2.14, 25; 3.17; Lyc. 1.52ff, 111–116; Andoc. 1.29–30; Hyp. 4col. 1–3, 33–34; 5 col. 27; Ant. 5.67. This list was provided in Rubinstein 1993. For general accounts of the use of precedent in Athens, see Bonner 1994:181–183; Dorjahn 1928.

from modern legal reasoning in important respects. The key element in arguing for consistency between cases is isolating the *ratio decidendi* of a previous verdict and applying it by analogy to the case at hand.[12] Even in modern legal systems, in which arguments from precedents are based on decisions written by professional judges, the process of eliciting a clear, valid rule of law from a judge's verdict is far from an exact science.[13] Athenian juries did not announce reasons for their verdicts. In fact, juries did not formally deliberate and were not required to reach agreement on the basis for their decision; the verdict was based solely on a count of the votes. It is therefore likely that different jurors could be swayed by entirely different aspects of a litigant's case. Therefore any discussion of the *ratio decidendi* of a previous verdict by an Athenian litigant was by its nature entirely speculative.

As one of the basic criteria of legal consistency requires that no individual verdict conflict with existing rules or previous cases, explaining and distinguishing unfavorable precedents to show that one's position is not inconsistent with previous case-law is more important than adducing favorable precedents.[14] Athenian litigants, however, do not distinguish unfavorable precedents because they were not expected to ensure that their speeches were consistent with previous cases; precedents, like laws, did not offer an authoritative guide to a verdict, but were merely one type of argument a litigant might use if he thought it strengthened his case.[15] In three instances an Athenian litigant responds to his opponent's use of a previous case, but does not distinguish the facts of the current case from the precedent cited by his opponent.[16]

There is, to my knowledge, only one example of a speaker discussing an unfavorable precedent on his own initiative. And in that case the litigant merely rejects unfavorable recent verdicts as incorrectly decided, rather than attempting to explain why the facts in his case are different from them in some relevant way. In his defense of Euxenippus, a private citizen, Hyperides notes that the *eisangelia* procedure has traditionally been used only against orators and public men and lists several past instances.[17] He goes on to discuss three recent precedents for bringing a private citizen to trial for trivial offences by *eisangelia*, and, rather than arguing

---

[12] MacCormick 1994:60. Although MacCormick uses the term *ratio dicendi*, I use *ratio decidendi*, which is more commonly used by American lawyers.

[13] See generally Llewellyn 1990.

[14] MacCormick 1994:121.

[15] On the use of laws in our surviving lawcourt speeches, see Chapter 3.

[16] Andoc. 1.29; Aesch. 2.6; Dem. 21.36.

[17] Hyp. 4col.1.

that his position is not incompatible with these recent decisions, he simply states, "this recent development is ridiculous."[18] The fact that litigants could choose to ignore unfavorable precedents suggests that the discussions of previous cases did not greatly encourage consistency in the Athenian legal system.

How did speakers use favorable previous decisions in constructing their arguments? The references to past cases in our surviving speeches fall into three broad categories: citations of past penalties, comparisons of the social standing of past and current defendants, and passages that resemble modern notions of arguments from precedent. In more than half of the speeches that cite to previous decisions, Athenian litigants make no attempt to use the *ratio decidendi* of a past verdict as a guide for the proper interpretation and application of the laws in the current case. Eight passages record the penalties given in previous cases and urge the jury to treat the current defendant in the same spirit of severity.[19] These passages do not shed light on how the jury should interpret the facts or laws involved in the current case, and often involve examples of punishment for crimes completely unrelated to the case at hand. For example, when prosecuting Demosthenes for bribery, Dinarchus cites three unrelated precedents: Menon, who kept a free boy in his mill; Themistius of Aphidna, who committed hubris against a Rhodian lyre maker at the Eleusinian festival; and Euthymachus, who installed an Olynthian girl in a brothel.[20] Lysias mentions the severity with which the Athenian people have treated corrupt grain-inspectors (*sitophulakes*) in the past, though his case actually concerns grain-dealers (*sitopôlai*).[21] Most puzzling are the discussions of the punishments of the Arginusae generals[22] and

---

[18] Hyp. 4col.2.

[19] Dem. 24.138; 34.50; Lys. 12.36; 22.16; Din. 1.23; Hyp. 5col.27; Aesch. 1.173; 3.252. Prosecutors' inclusion of arguments related to punishment at the trial phase did not go entirely unchallenged. Andocides (1.29–30), for example, points out that his accuser's discussion of previous punishments for impiety presupposes that he is guilty. Andocides dismisses his accuser's recitation of the "frightening and horrific" stories of severe punishments suffered by previous offenders, asking, "What do these arguments and facts have to do with me? . . . I say that it was necessary to execute those men, because they committed impiety, but I should be spared, because I have committed no crime."

[20] Din. 1.23.

[21] Lys. 22.16.

[22] Lys. 12.36. In 406 B.C.E. the Athenians won a naval battle at Arginusae, but in the course of the battle several Athenian ships were sunk or disabled. A storm prevented the Athenians from rescuing survivors. In a special judicial procedure, the entire Assembly condemned the generals involved in the battle to death for the failed rescue mission. Xenophon tells us that the Athenians regretted this impulsive verdict almost immediately and scholars generally cite the loss of Athens' most experienced generals as one of the reasons for Sparta's victory just two years later. Xen. *Hell.* 1.7.7–35.; Kagan 1987:325–354.

Socrates[23] – hardly sterling exempla of Athenian justice – used by prosecutors to incite the current jury to convict.

Even when speakers refer to punishments in previous cases involving the same charge as the current suit, they do not attempt to compare factors relevant to punishment, such as the seriousness of the offenses or the past record of the defendant in the two cases. Nor do they explain how the "precedent" should be applied to the case at hand. In his action against Timocrates for an illegal legislative proposal (*graphê paranomôn*), to take one example, Demosthenes mentions two previous decisions involving illegal proposals, but does not discuss the circumstances of these cases or attempt to relate them to the facts of the current case in any way:

> Remembering how, not long ago, in the archonship of Evander, you
> executed Eudemus of Cydathenaeum for seeming to propose a law that was
> inappropriate, and you almost executed Philip, the son of Philip the
> shipowner, but when he proposed a stiff financial penalty, you fined him by a
> slim majority. You must now treat this defendant here with the same anger.[24]

The speaker does not explain why one of the offenders received death whereas the other was fined, nor does he tell the jury which of the two "precedents" it should follow in the current case and why. Demosthenes' discussion of examples of punishments given in the past for the same charge may provide the jurors with some general guidelines for choosing an appropriate penalty, but does not, as legal precedents are intended to do, point to a particular outcome. In all these passages, the speaker simply provides past examples of severe punishments and encourages the current jury to be strict in the current case. The recitation of past penalties may give the jury an idea of the upper range of punishments meted out by previous juries, and it may give the prosecutor's calls for severity the implicit authority of past juries, but it does not foster truly consistent verdicts in similar cases.

In seven other instances, the litigant citing a past case does not attempt to reason by analogy from the circumstances of the previous case, but simply compares the relative social positions of the past and current defendants.[25] Demosthenes *Against*

Presumably, the prosecutor is using this case to argue that if even good men like the generals can be punished the current defendant should be as well, but one wonders how this approach went over with the jury.

[23] Aesch. 1.173.

[24] Dem. 24.138; see also Hyp. 5 col. 27.

[25] Dem. 20.146–148; 34.50; 59.116–117; Din. 1.13; 2.14ff; 3.17; Hyp. 4.33–34. Social facts are also included in a more detailed discussion of precedents in Dem. 19.273.

Neaira involves the prosecution of Neaira for living as the wife of an Athenian citizen even though she was an alien. The speaker describes a case in which a priest was convicted for impiety, and argues that it would be outrageous that this man, who was from a priestly clan, had admirable and worthy ancestors, and was a citizen, was punished, if the jury did not also punish Neaira, a lowly prostitute.[26] In a similar vein, the prosecutor in *Against Phormio* notes that a previous jury felt no sympathy for a defendant who was the son of a general.[27] In prosecuting prominent politicians for corruption in the Harpalus affair, Dinarchus describes the past condemnation of Timotheus, a famous general, despite his distinguished services to the city.[28] One might object at this point that because a defendant's character, past record, and social standing were relevant to the jury's determination, comparing the social standing of the defendants in a past case to that of the current defendant would foster consistency across verdicts. We have seen, however, that this type of evidence was used in conjunction with information about the nature of the alleged crime and the context of the dispute; no litigant in our surviving speeches suggests that the jury should base its decision solely on the character of the defendant without reference to the event in dispute.[29]

Simply comparing the character and social position of the present defendant with that of the defendant in a previous case without comparing other aspects of the cases is insufficient to assist the jury in following the "precedent" cited by the litigant. In these seven speeches, the speakers do not extract a general rule or line of argument abstracted from the particular facts of the previous case that can be applied to future disputes. Just as in the citations of previous severe penalties, speakers note that men more prominent and honorable than the current defendant have been convicted in the past without detailing how the charges or other aspects of these past cases are similar to (or different from) the present suit. These passages reflect the general tendency of Athenian litigants to offer a highly contextualized

---

[26] Dem. 59.117. The speaker's very naming of Neaira in court showed his contempt for her status, for litigants carefully avoid shaming respectable citizen women by mentioning their name in court (Schaps 1977).

[27] Dem. 34.50.

[28] Din. 1.14; 3.17. To be sure, these passages are not entirely without relevance: they establish that even an exemplary past record was insufficient to save Timotheus from conviction of the charge of bribery, the same charge facing Demosthenes in the current suit. However, the speaker provides no details about the nature and seriousness of Timotheus' betrayal to permit the jury to determine whether Demosthenes' crime was equally serious and whether leniency therefore would be similarly inappropriate despite Demosthenes' public services.

[29] See Chapter 3.

and individualized account of a dispute. The discussion of previous decisions does not approach the level of abstraction necessary to encourage jurors to render verdicts which go beyond ad hoc settlements tailored to the particular facts and to the social positions of the current litigants.

Although more than half of the passages that discuss previous cases do not include enough information to significantly enhance consistency across verdicts, in eight of our 103 speeches litigants *do* attempt to apply the *ratio decidendi* of an earlier decision.[30] Demosthenes' speech *Against Meidias* includes the most extensive use of arguments from past precedents. Demosthenes tells the jury that when he was sitting in his official seat in the theater as *chorêgos* at the dramatic festival of the Great Dionysia, his longtime enemy Meidias strode up to him and punched him in the face in front of the entire theater audience. In his prosecution,[31] Demosthenes discusses several past cases involving the law regulating festivals to support his contention that Meidias violated the laws by assaulting Demosthenes while he was serving in an official capacity as *chorêgos*.[32] One such is the case of Euandrus, who was severely punished for arresting a private debtor during the festival. He lists the features, abstracted from the particular facts and social context of the case, which make Euandrus' actions less serious than those of Meidias: "This was one man, in a private matter, where *hubris* was not at issue, who was given such a [severe] penalty for breaking the law."[33] He explains to the jury that he is providing these precedents "in order that you might compare the crimes those men have committed to the actions of this man [Meidias]."[34] Elsewhere in the same speech,

---

[30] Dem. 21.72–76; 175–184; 19.273ff; Lys. 6.17; 13.56; Din. 2.25; Aesch. 1.86–88; Isoc. 18.22; Lyc. 1.52. The *Rhetoric to Alexander* (1422b20), generally attributed to Anaximenes in the mid-fourth century, notes that earlier verdicts can be used to substantiate a speaker's interpretation of a vague law and provides a sample argument:

> And it is not only I who say that the lawgivers enacted this law because of these considerations, but also in an earlier case, when Lysitheides was advancing arguments similar to those now put forward by me, the jurors cast this vote concerning the law.

However, only a small part of the treatise relates to arguments concerning legal issues (*to nomimon*).

[31] It is unclear whether this speech was ever delivered in court. Aeschines 3.52 suggests that Meidias bought a settlement after losing unanimously at a preliminary hearing in the case before the entire assembly. Such a hearing was a feature of the unusual judicial procedure, known as *probolê*, used by Demosthenes For discussion, see MacDowell 1989b:13–16, 23–24.

[32] Dem. 21.175–184.

[33] Dem. 21.177.

[34] Dem. 21.175.

Demosthenes speculates about the *ratio decidendi* of an earlier decision. He tells the jury how a certain Euaeon was condemned by only one vote for killing a man at a public banquet in revenge for one blow,[35] and then suggests how the jurors at the earlier trial might have interpreted the defendant's action:

> Let us posit that the men judging him guilty voted against him not because he was protecting himself, but because he acted in this way with the result that he killed him, while those voting to acquit conceded even this extreme form of revenge to the man who had suffered *hubris* to his person.[36]

Leocrates, the defendant in Lycurgus 1, does not seem to have violated any specific law. Compensating for this embarrassing deficiency in his case, Lycurgus turns to precedent to justify his prosecution of Leocrates for fleeing Athens when it appeared that Philip of Macedon was poised to strike the city. Lycurgus cites the case in which Autolycus was condemned for secretly sending his wife and children away when the city was in danger, carefully comparing his actions to those of Leocrates: "And yet if you punished a man who was blameworthy of sending away to safety those who were of no use in the war effort, what ought this one suffer who, being a man, did not pay back his country for nurturing him?"[37] The sophisticated use of previous cases in these passages is exceptional.

What is to be made of these rare instances of arguments from precedent? Athenian litigants (and their speechwriters) were certainly capable of reasoning by analogy, but rarely chose to do so. This is probably due in large part to the difficulty of obtaining information about prior verdicts for use as precedents. Athens did not keep detailed records of past cases that would provide litigants with sufficient information to compare the circumstances of the past and current suit.[38] Indeed, even verdicts were not regularly recorded for preservation and future

---

[35] Dem. 21.71–76.

[36] Dem. 21.75. Demosthenes discusses this past case to emphasize his own restraint in not immediately retaliating against Meidias. Demosthenes asks the jury "consider how much more anger is appropriate for me, having suffered in such a way because of Meidias, than was the case for that man Euaeon when he killed Boeotus," pointing out that while Euaeon was struck by a drunken acquaintance, at a dinner he attended voluntarily, and in the presence of his own friends who could support him, Demosthenes suffered deliberate *hubris* at the hands of a personal enemy in the presence of foreigners and citizens while he was acting in his official capacity (Dem. 21.73–74).

[37] Lyc. 1.53.

[38] Lanni 2004. Litigants and speechwriters would know about high-profile cases through gossip, but it is unclear how detailed and accurate such information would be. There is some evidence that orators in

consultation.[39] It is also possible that involved discussions of previous cases were not considered effective with a popular court jury. Arguments from precedent, like statutory arguments, were no more authoritative than many other types of legal and extra-legal argumentation. It seems likely that general references to past verdicts could instill the jury with the proper spirit for performing its task and remind the jury of its duty to enforce the law by imposing severe penalties, even on high status defendants. But a detailed discussion of a previous case could make the speaker's arguments appear overly legalistic and technical.[40] In any case, as mentioned above, arguments from precedent were inherently weak in Athens because the wide variety of potentially relevant factors in a jury's decision made even a very similar case easily distinguishable. A previous case with an almost identical legal issue might appear different to an Athenian jury because, for example, the prior relationship between the two disputants was different in the two cases, or because one defendant enjoyed a better prior record and reputation than the other.

Despite the absence of a meaningful system of precedent, the extant forensic speeches imply that court decisions did have an effect beyond the litigants in the particular case. Consequentialist arguments warning jurors that the effects of their verdict will extend beyond the current case is a topos often met in forensic oratory.[41] Prosecutors commonly argue that a conviction will have a deterrent effect.[42] For example, the speaker in *Against Neaira* urges the jury to punish the

training and speechwriters watched trials, but it seems that such spectators focused on the rhetoric of the speeches and the delivery of the speaker rather than facts and outcome of the case (Aesch. 1.77; 173; Plu. *Dem.* 5.2). Indeed, the precedents that are cited in the surviving speeches tend to involve famous individuals or high-profile public offenses, such as treason, bribery, and impiety.

[39] Lanni 2004. However, the notion and even the practice of recording court decisions were not unheard of in the Greek world. Aristotle (*Pol.* 1321b35) thought that all states should have a magistracy that held private contracts and the verdicts of the lawcourts. In the fifth-century lawcode at Gortyn, one of the duties of the *mnamon*, or "rememberer," is to inform the judge of previous decisions. For *mnamones* generally, see Thomas 1996:19–22.

[40] Although an Athenian jury would likely be receptive to the general notion of consistency across cases, any suggestion that the jury should take a mechanical approach to reaching a decision or be bound by the verdict in a previous case, especially if the just result appeared to dictate otherwise, was likely to be ineffective. On Athenian jurors' reluctance to accept arguments based on legal technicalities, see Chapter 3.

[41] For a discussion of such consequentialist arguments as examples of persuasive precedent, see Rubinstein 1993.

[42] E.g., Lys. 1.36, 47; 12.35; 14.12; 22.20; 27.7; 30.23; Dem. 50.64; 54.43; 56.48; 59.112; Rubinstein 1993.

defendants "in order that they might pay the penalty for their misdeeds, and also so that others might take thought in advance and be afraid to commit a crime against the gods and the city."[43] In another case, Aeschines counsels the jury, "come down hard on one man, and you will not have to do so with a crowd [of offenders]."[44] In a similar vein, speakers claim that an acquittal will encourage criminals and promote lawlessness in the city.[45] The speaker in Lysias *Against Nicomachus* paints a lurid picture of malefactors poised to strike:

> Those who want to steal from the state are paying attention to how
> Nicomachus fares in the trial. If you do not punish him, you will give these
> men carte blanche, but if you, voting against him, give him the harshest
> penalty, with the same vote you will make the others better and you will be
> doing justice with respect to the defendant.[46]

These consequentialist arguments presuppose some consistency and predictability in Athenian courts: for a verdict to deter criminals effectively, citizens must, at a minimum, have some reason to fear that future cases will be treated in a similar manner. For this reason, it is tempting to interpret these statements as "prospective precedents" which indicate an awareness that the current verdict may affect future juries.[47]

It is important to note, however, that whereas litigants often claim that the verdict will influence the behavior of the community at large, there are, to my knowledge, only two passages in which the speaker contemplates the putative effect of a decision on a future *jury*.[48] Because there is no law which directly applies to Leocrates, Lycurgus argues that in this case "you must be act not only

---

[43] Dem. 59.77.

[44] Aesch. 1.193.

[45] E.g., Lys. 1.36, 27.7; Dem. 59.112. This sort of argument is first made by the Furies in Aeschylus *Eumenides* (503–515). Litigants also tell jurors to be mindful that an individual verdict may have wide-ranging effects on Athens' trade (Dem. 35.51; 56.48; Lys. 22.21).

[46] Lys. 30.23.

[47] Rubinstein (1993) discusses these passages as prospective precedents "on the level of rhetoric," while E. Harris (1994a:136) suggests that individual cases, though not "formally binding, could be appealed to by future litigants and thus have an influence on later cases."

[48] Whereas the speaker in Dem. 56.48 does use the verb *nomotheteô* ("to make laws") when referring to the jury's decision, the passage discusses the effect of the verdict on the behavior of lenders rather than on future juries.

as judges of the current offense but also as lawmakers (*nomothetai*)."[49] Using similar language, the speaker in Lysias 14 argues that because this is the first such case since the peace of 404, the jurors must be "not only jurors but lawmakers" and warns the jury, "however you decide these cases now, so will the city treat these issues for all time."[50] In both cases, the speaker calls attention to the fact that the case at hand is unusual, so unusual, indeed, that it requires the jurors to take on a role beyond their normal constitutional function. It seems, then, that the Athenians did not have a strong sense that individual verdicts serve as persuasive precedents for future juries.

We have seen that the haphazard recording of verdicts, taken with the way in which litigants discuss previous cases, makes it difficult to believe lawcourt speakers when they claim that Athenians would carefully note court verdicts and alter their behavior accordingly, confident that one verdict was an accurate indication of future decisions. Nevertheless, the assumption met in the speeches that the effects of court decisions extend beyond the particular case, along with the frequency of citations of past cases, indicate that the general norm that verdicts should be consistent and predictable had some force in Athens. It seems likely that speakers exploited this norm for rhetorical purposes on occasion, using the consequentialist topos to encourage jurors to dole out severe punishments in the name of deterrence,[51] to induce the jurors, who were not accountable in any way for their verdicts, to decide responsibly by emphasizing the wide-ranging effects of their verdict, and perhaps to give an aura of consistency to a system that was all too unpredictable.

SHARED NORMS AND CULTURAL KNOWLEDGE

The final possible source of consistency and predictability in the Athenian legal system is shared cultural norms and values. We must consider the possibility that most Athenians would react similarly to any particular case and arrive at roughly

---

[49] Lyc. 1.9.

[50] Lys. 14.4.

[51] Indeed, Rubinstein (1993) points out that this topos occurs twice as often in prosecution speeches as in defense speeches. She also notes that this topos is more common in public cases, and suggests that while in private suits the function of the court is primarily to settle an individual dispute, in public cases the jury took on the additional function of upholding general principles embodied in previous decisions. I suspect, however, that even in public cases notions of precedent were very weak. The uneven distribution of our topos may indicate that whereas consequentialist arguments could be effective, if somewhat dubious, in public cases, in private suits they became absurd.

the same conclusion as to the fair result. Under this view, the legal system would exhibit consistency across cases, and judicial outcomes could be predicted from Athenians' shared norms.

At first glance, this interpretation appears to have much to recommend it. Modern societies often have two separate sets of rules: legal rules known primarily by legal experts, and informal social norms that govern everyday interactions.[52] In Athens, by contrast, popular norms of fairness and cooperation were precisely those at play in the courts, allowing potential litigants to draw on their cultural knowledge to predict the likely outcome of a lawsuit. Moreover, there is reason to believe that most Athenians would have a similar moral and emotional response to various types of offenses. In contrast to the diversity in economic class, ethnicity, and religion characteristic of most contemporary Western nations, Athenian society – and in particular the subset of adult male citizens who judged, and for the most part, were judged, in court – was fairly homogenous,[53] with a considerable stock of shared common values and beliefs.[54] Individual conscience was to be subordinated to *homonoia* ("same-mindedness" or "unanimity"),[55] and the core values of democratic civic ideology were regularly reinforced through shared community service and public speech, most notably in funeral orations for the war dead.[56]

Nevertheless, shared norms and values are insufficient to create true consistency and predictability in a legal system that considers a vast array of factors relevant to any legal decision. Whereas there may have been consensus on whether each type of legal or extra-legal argument favored the prosecutor or the defendant and which pieces of evidence were particularly damning for either side, it often must have been difficult to predict the interaction of all the evidence in a particular case. To take an example, most Athenians may have endorsed general values such as the importance of public service, family obligations, and honest fair dealing.

[52] For a case study of the relationship between legal rules and informal norms in a close-knit cattle-ranching community, see Ellickson 1991:40–120.

[53] In theory, at least, all Athenians shared a common ancestry, though in practice citizenship may have been more porous. On the role of the myth of autochthony in Athenian identity, see Loraux 1993:35–70; on the likelihood that citizenship was much more fluid than the strict laws seem to allow, see Scafuro 1994:156–198; E. Cohen 2000:79–103.

[54] For a basic introduction to Athenian values, see Chapter 2.

[55] Ober 1990:296–298.

[56] Loraux 1986; Ober 1990:336–339.

Most Athenians also recognized many specific norms promoted by the sanction of law:[57] the duty to care for and properly bury elderly relatives, the importance of respecting a man's wishes to will his money to whomever he wishes, the immorality of forcefully seizing a disputed inheritance rather than pursuing legal avenues, and the wrongfulness of attempting to bribe witnesses to lie at the suit's arbitration. Potential litigants in an inheritance case in which each side was supported by some of the values and norms listed above would find it difficult to predict a given jury's decision.

It is important to distinguish here between predictability of outcomes as opposed to arguments. The types of arguments likely to be raised on either side of a particular case could easily be anticipated.[58] Cultural knowledge can help predict the issues and arguments a jury will find relevant and how it is likely to react to each of those arguments, but cannot predict how the jury will weigh competing norms in any particular case. There was no consensus on a hierarchy of norms in Athenian society. This is most evident in Attic tragedy. Tragic dramas often dramatize a conflict of norms – to name the most famous example, duty to family versus duty to the state in *Antigone* – with no clear moral resolution. In the law courts, too, the jury was often presented with conflicting norms and left to decide on a case-by-case basis which arguments to credit.[59]

THE EXCEPTION: PROTECTING PUBLIC ORDER

There is one class of case that may well have achieved some level of predictability despite these difficulties. The community's outrage at what we would consider serious criminal matters, such as crimes of violence resulting in grave injury, may have been so great that one could anticipate that the seriousness of the offense could not easily be outweighed by other relevant factors in the case. For example, although the precise charge and penalty for jumping someone in the street might be unclear, basic, widely shared notions of acceptable behavior made it fairly certain

---

[57] For the distinction between values and norms, see Luhmann 1982:107.

[58] Hence the frequency of topoi in the surviving speeches. Litigants would in any case have a good idea of their opponent's arguments prior to trial from the *anakrisis*. We do not know how often parties decided to settle their case after getting a look at their opponent's hand at the *anakrisis*, but the frequency of court trials in Athens suggests that uncertainty as to the likely jury verdict often remained after these preliminary proceedings.

[59] See Chapter 3. For an argument that modern trials also often involve a competition between competing values drawn from the legal, political, moral, and economic sphere, see Burns 1999:201.

that some punishment would be forthcoming in the absence of extremely strong mitigating factors. The need to maintain public order in the absence of a police force undoubtedly reinforced the belief in the seriousness of such transgressions.[60] Even if the precise outcome in such a case was uncertain, the likelihood that the behavior would result in some sanction may have been sufficient to deter some potential offenders.

With the exception of cases involving serious criminal matters, however, the Athenians' shared norms and values did not result in legal consistency and predictability. The failure of statutes, citation to past cases, and shared norms to produce legal consistency stems from a single characteristic of the Athenian legal system: a broad notion of relevance that called for considering such a variety of factors that it was impossible to construct explicit or implicit abstract rules and principles that could be consistently applied across cases.

THE COSTS OF LEGAL INSECURITY

The ad hoc, discretionary nature of popular court decision making vested ordinary Athenian jurors with enormous power. Scholars of Athenian democracy have argued that broad jury discretion played a vital role in maintaining social order and stability in Athens.[61] One scholar, for example, has pointed out that the interactions in the courts may have eased the tensions and conflicts that naturally arise in a society like Athens where citizens were politically equal but socially very unequal. Under this view, the courts provided a forum for ongoing communication and negotiation between elite litigants and mass jurors "in a context which made explicit the power of the masses to judge the action and behavior of elite individuals."[62]

But broad jury discretion also brought serious disadvantages. The lack of consistency and predictability in the Athenian courts resulted in widespread uncertainty regarding one's legal rights and duties. This relatively high level of legal insecurity had a pervasive effect on Athenian social interactions. The capability of the written

---

[60] Indeed, we will see below that many offenses that threatened public order – certain types of theft, burglary, highway robbery – were disposed of through summary arrest and execution. Offenders caught red-handed engaging in these types of crimes were denied the opportunity to present a contextualized account to a popular court jury.

[61] E.g., Ober 1990:145; Johnstone 1999:106–108, 124–125.

[62] Ober 1990:145.

law to guide conduct and order social relations was extremely limited, and legal uncertainty imposed significant costs on many private transactions. Oliver Wendell Holmes' well-known "bad man" theory of the law may help highlight the importance of legal security in the ordinary functioning of law.[63] Holmes described the function of law by imagining a "bad man" who viewed the law purely instrumentally and planned his behavior based on what he predicted he could (and could not) get away with under the existing rules. Legal indeterminacy such as that found in Athens makes this task difficult or impossible, reducing the effectiveness of law as a means of social control.

In the absence of clear rules, it was not possible for Athenians to conform their conduct to the law with any confidence, at least in cases that did not involve what we would consider serious criminal matters. Even in situations apparently governed by a precise rule, as was the case in many inheritance disputes, public awareness that a jury might rely on extra-legal arguments to reach a verdict contrary to the outcome suggested by the statute or will reduced the law's ability to influence conduct. In private law transactions, this state of affairs must have increased the risk and cost of every transaction and created inefficiencies. Sellers and buyers could never be reasonably sure that they would be able, if necessary, to have the terms of a contract or the protections afforded them by law[64] enforced by a court. Citizens with what would appear to be a clear legal claim to an estate or other form of property could find themselves mired in lawsuits.

Of course, Athenians would have tried to reduce the effects of legal uncertainty by conducting their affairs with men with whom they had close ties whenever possible.[65] This would make it easier to settle their disputes through informal means without reference to the laws or recourse to the courts.[66] Members of the local community would be susceptible to informal pressures to honor agreements and to conduct business honorably. Men who regularly did business together

---

[63] Holmes 1997 (originally published 1897).

[64] There was very little state regulation of private transactions, but there were some laws designed to protect buyers, such as a law prohibiting the making of false statements in the agora, a law regulating the process by which an Athenian official would declare silver coinage valid (Rhodes & Osborne 2003: No. 25) and various rules regarding the sale of slaves (Hyp. 3.14–15).

[65] For examples of Athenians transacting with relatives, neighbors, or close friends, see, e.g., Dem. 33.6–7; 53.9; cf. Dem. 35.6–7.

[66] Ellickson (1991) has shown that contemporary Americans in close-knit communities, who have imperfect access to predictable legal enforcements because of the high cost of litigation, are able to order their affairs effectively "without law," by reliance on trust and informal control over anti-social behavior.

could be assured that each party had incentives to act fairly to preserve the ongoing relationship.[67] Even when concluding single transactions with men outside the local community, one could expect that the fear of a tarnished reputation and negative gossip might prevent merchants and other businessmen from engaging in extremely unscrupulous behavior.[68]

But informal means of social control can not compensate completely for the absence of precise legal rules and predictable judicial outcomes. Informal norms are least effective in regulating conduct when the actors lack close social ties or an ongoing business relationship, or when the stakes of a dispute are high.[69] Most Athenians would find it difficult to deal exclusively with members of one's local community. Although residents of any particular deme would likely constitute a close-knit community,[70] the city of Athens and the area around the port of the Piraeus were teeming commercial centers filled with citizens, resident aliens, and foreigners. Athens was not a face-to-face society. Whereas a man might well sell his crops to and obtain his staples from men with whom he had an ongoing relationship, he would likely purchase some items in the market of Athens or the Piraeus from merchants whom he did not know (or know of).[71] City dwellers were likely to encounter strangers on a regular basis.[72] As already noted, fear of negative gossip may have induced merchants and businessmen based in Athens to refrain from the worst sort of unfair dealing. However, gossip about merchants reaching those outside or in other parts of the city would most likely be limited to extremely negative or positive stories and would therefore be insufficient to fully enforce informal norms of fair dealing. Finally, men performing liturgies, such as outfitting a trireme or funding a dramatic production, would be obliged

---

[67] There is an extensive law and economics literature on "relational contracting" – the tendency of market players to abandon short-term self-interest in individual exchanges for the sake of developing and maintaining an ongoing trading relationship (Bernstein 1992; 1996).

[68] On the importance of gossip as a means of informal social control, see Hunter 1994:96–119.

[69] Ellickson 1991:94, 250–251.

[70] Of course, many deme members lived outside the boundaries of their deme. Those resident in the deme, however, would approximate what we think of as a close-knit community.

[71] Swords and shields for military service, perfume, pottery, and other such items were unlikely to be produced in local areas and may have been obtained while visiting the city to attend festivals, the assembly, or to serve in the courts. Theophrastus' citizen *agroikos* (*Char.* 4) attends the Assembly while he is in the city shopping and running errands.

[72] To cite just one example, the speaker in Hyperides 3 appears to have had no prior relationship or knowledge of Athenogenes when he purchased his perfume shop, and Athenogenes apparently did not suffer from informal reprisals after tricking the speaker with a misleading contract.

to deal with particular specialized vendors and skilled employees. In cases such as these – where the parties share a shallow relationship and are unlikely to engage in repeated transactions – informal norms are ineffective and the failure of the formal law to influence conduct and to order transactions becomes most costly and burdensome.[73]

A private suit for damages involving a one-off transaction between two strangers, Demosthenes *Against Polycles*, may present an example of the inability of the law to curb clearly illegal behavior. The case involved a dispute over the performance of the trierarchy, a liturgy which required a rich individual to pay the costs of manning and maintaining a ship in the Athenian navy for one year. The defendant, Polycles, was slated to replace the speaker as trierarch and assume the costs of the ship. Unless the story told by the speaker is a complete fabrication and his witnesses are shameless perjurers, Polycles boldly and repeatedly flouted the law and refused to pay for the ship, forcing the speaker to sue to try to recoup his losses. If Athenian judicial outcomes predictably and consistently followed the written law, we would expect that Polycles would not submit to a trial he would almost certainly lose, but rather would have agreed eventually to take over the ship or at least attempted to settle the claim prior to trial for less than the full amount owed.[74] The difficulty of predicting Athenian judicial outcomes encouraged Polycles to take his chances at trial and forced the speaker to waste time and effort on litigation in an attempt to vindicate a clear legal claim.

Even when disputants had close social ties, such as a familial or neighborly relationship, informal means of social control would often prove inadequate to order private transactions if the stakes in the dispute were high.[75] Where a significant inheritance was in dispute, for example, family members often turned to the formal legal rules and processes. The costs associated with legal insecurity are particularly evident in our surviving inheritance cases, where the lack of finality exacerbated the problems caused by legal uncertainty and unpredictability. We have already seen that jurors in inheritance disputes appear to have been particularly receptive

---

[73] For a discussion of why informal social control works best in close-knit communities, see Ellickson 1991:250–251.

[74] Of course, blatant violations also occur in legal systems with a relatively high degree of legal certainty, though one would expect that in such cases once the victim evinced the willingness and resources to litigate, the case would likely be settled prior to trial.

[75] Ellickson (1991:94) notes that in a modern context parties are more likely to turn to formal legal rules and processes if they estimate that the intrinsic or extrinsic stakes of a dispute are high.

to equitable arguments that contradicted the written rules of testate or intestate succession. Under Athenian inheritance law, a claimant could make a claim on an estate at any time until five years after the death of the man who held it as heir, and we know of one example of an heir's right to an estate being challenged in court over 20 years after he inherited it.[76] Unsuccessful claimants could even sue more than once for the same estate as long as they used a legal theory not addressed in the previous case. In addition to the costs related to protracted litigation, an heir had little incentive to maintain or enhance the inherited property if he could not be reasonably certain that he would be able to ward off a legal challenge.

The most striking evidence of the failure of both the laws and informal norms to order private transactions is the high level of litigation in Athens. In the absence of reliable ex ante guides to behavior, a remarkably high number of Athenians resorted to litigation to resolve their disputes. We have seen that the Athenians had a reputation for being *philodikoi*, "lovers of litigation."[77] Frequent litigation imposed a cost not only on individuals conducting transactions, but also on the legal system as a whole. Case-by-case decision making carried out by paid juries numbering in the hundreds is far more costly and less efficient than ex ante rulemaking.

The negative effects of legal insecurity were social as well as financial. Because litigation was always a distinct possibility, Athenians carefully planned events that might have legal significance in preparation for a possible trial. It was customary to gather a group of kin, friends, or neighbors to serve as potential witnesses before undertaking any action that might result in litigation, such as agreeing to a contract, paying a debt, making a will, or introducing one's son to deme membership.[78] It has been pointed out that the presence of witnesses gave these events a "staged" quality.[79] The process of self-consciously choreographing every-day dealings in anticipation of litigation may have caused these common social

---

[76] Is. 3.58; 5.7, 35. For discussion, see Harrison 1998:220 & n.3.

[77] See Chapter 2.

[78] Is. 3.19–20; cf. Dem. 57.14; Lys. *fr.* VI.i (Albini). For a detailed discussion of the use of such *Solemnitätszeuge*, see Scafuro 1997:42–50. The habit of gathering witnesses for a potential court case was not limited to pre-planned events. From Lysias 3 we learn that a boy who was attacked in the street had the presence of mind to call for passersby not only to protect him, but also to act as witnesses: as they were dragging him away, the boy was "screaming and yelling and calling for witnesses." According to the speaker many people rushed to help (Lys. 3.15–16).

[79] Scafuro 1997:46.

interactions to become more impersonal. This tendency toward the formalization of social interactions in preparation for a possible trial may have contributed further to the litigiousness of Athenians by creating a negative feedback loop of sorts. The common practice of bringing witnesses along when concluding a transaction brought the specter of litigation into the interaction, formalizing the entire process and reducing the emphasis on interpersonal trust and informal norms of fair dealing.[80] This practice undermined informal means of social control and helped to push disputants into the formal legal procedures.[81] A high level of litigation in turn encouraged more Athenians to prepare by gathering witnesses and carefully staging any social interaction that might lead to a court case. The Athenians thus had all the disadvantages, but few of the advantages, of a formal legal system. The ever-present possibility of litigation undermined settlement efforts and informal means of social control, but in the absence of precise, predictable rules the capability of Athenian substantive law to guide conduct was limited.

MITIGATING THE EFFECTS OF LEGAL INSECURITY

Why were the Athenians willing to tolerate a system that so often failed to reliably guide behavior? The short answer is that they didn't tolerate it completely. Street crime such as burglary, theft, and common violence was effectively dealt with outside the popular court system through summary procedures and informal methods. At the end of the fifth century a short-lived set of legal reforms sought to enhance legal certainty in some respects. Further, we will see in Chapter 6 that the need for greater legal certainty in large-scale commercial transactions led to the development of a special legal procedure that employed a more formal, predictable means of reaching a verdict. But the fact remains that in the vast majority of cases nothing was done to boost legal certainty or predictability in the long term. In most cases, the Athenians valued the discretionary approach used in the popular courts more highly than legal certainty and predictability. In this section I examine a variety of factors that helped Athenian society to function smoothly despite the decision to sacrifice predictability for flexibility in legal decision making.

---

[80] Ellickson (1991:53–56, 76–79) notes, for example, that neighbors in a close-knit ranching community consciously shy away from formalizing relationships through making written agreements, maintaining precise records of credits and debits in their interactions, or exchanging money, so as not to undermine the informal, trusting atmosphere of the relationship.

[81] Private arbitration, which represented something between formal legal procedures and informal settlement, was also a possibility. For discussion of private arbitration, see Todd 1993:123–125.

Maintaining Public Order

We have seen that the absence of legal consistency and predictability limited law's ability to order private law transactions. Legal insecurity does not, however, seem to have hindered the maintenance of public order in Athens. In stark contrast to classical Rome, Athenians did not routinely carry weapons and there appears to have been relatively little violent crime.[82] Why was this the case?

For one thing, there was simply less legal uncertainty with respect to public order offenses than other types of suit. We have seen that the lack of precise legal rules probably had less of an effect on the predictability of verdicts in what we would consider serious criminal matters because it was unlikely that mitigating defense arguments would completely outweigh the community's outrage at the offense and lead to an acquittal. But the most important reason is that many crimes that threatened the public order – certain types of thefts, house burglary, and robbery – were commonly dealt with in a summary (and severe) manner. When *kakourgoi* ("wrongdoers") were caught red-handed engaging in such crimes, they could be brought before a board of magistrates and executed without trial if they admitted the charge.[83] One wonders why anyone would confess in such circumstances. It has been suggested that an accused thief may have been required to explain how he came by the stolen property, a more difficult task than merely remaining silent and refusing to confess guilt.[84] In this way, legal uncertainty was virtually eliminated for many types of street crime, because a man caught red-handed would be killed without the opportunity to argue to a jury for acquittal or a lesser penalty based on mitigating factors.

In addition to greater certainty and predictability of formal legal sanctions, informal means prevented and punished men who threatened the public order, including those criminals who were not members of the immediate community and thus were impervious to reputational sanctions. In the absence of a public police force, bystanders commonly assisted victims of theft or violence.[85] The classic example of bystander intervention in Athens is described in Lysias *Against Simon*. When a man and his boy lover are attacked in the street by a group of

---

[82] Herman 1994:101.

[83] For a brief discussion of this procedure, with secondary references, see Chapter 2.

[84] Todd 1993:80–81. Hansen (1990b:234 n.93) suggests, based on evidence concerning the behavior of criminals in other societies, that the guilty tend to confess in the face of undeniable evidence, regardless of the adverse consequences of doing so.

[85] For discussion of bystanders and other forms of social control in Athens, see Hunter 1994:96–117, 120–150, 185–189.

men, the speaker tells us, several passersby jumped into the fray on the side of the victims, and a large crowd formed condemning the aggressors.[86] A man contemplating an act of theft or violence may well have been deterred by the likelihood of detection and intervention by a crowd of bystanders as well as by the knowledge of potential legal sanctions. The use of summary procedures and informal methods to maintain public order effectively limited the burdens of legal insecurity to private law transactions. Whereas legal uncertainty made business dealings more difficult, it did not disrupt the basic functioning of social order in Athens.

The Lack of Economic Innovation

Another factor that mitigated the effects of legal insecurity was the lack of dynamism and innovation in Athenian social and economic interactions. It is easy to forget that the polis responsible for radical innovation in government, philosophy, and the arts was socially and economically a conservative place. In his seminal work on the ancient economy, Finley argued that notions of economic rationality and productive investment have no place in descriptions of ancient economic behavior.[87] Whether one fully accepts this controversial thesis, it is clear that there was very little drive for change or innovation in business dealings in Athens. There were no complex financial instruments, no development of new business organizations such as corporations. Business arrangements and the uses of property kept to traditional, simple forms.

Where, as in Athens, individuals generally enter into familiar and well-worn types of transactions – simple loans, contracts for sale, and mortgages on property – there is less need for precise legal rules to provide guidance on how to arrange the deal and on what the parties should expect from each other in the arrangement. Of course, familiarity with the type of transaction does not eliminate the problem of legal insecurity. Uncertainty as to whether the particular contract will be enforced by a court or rejected for any of a variety of reasons unrelated to the specific terms of the contract remains, but custom surrounding the making of contracts makes it easier for parties to make deals. A society in which social and economic arrangements were a small, known quantity might never develop a strong sense that law should act as a guide to future behavior. In these circumstances it would be only natural to assume that the best justice is ex post justice, that is, a different rule for every case as the circumstances require.

[86] Lys. 3.15–16.
[87] Finley 1999:116–122.

Maintaining Authority and Legitimacy

Unpredictable verdicts not only limited the reach of Athenian substantive law, but also taxed the authority and legitimacy of the formal legal system. In traditional societies, ad hoc dispute resolution procedures often achieve legitimacy largely through the reputation for wisdom and fairness associated with the individual judge(s) or the official position that he holds.[88] For example, in the archaic Greece depicted in Homer and Hesiod, kings and elders serving as judges wield the scepter, a gift of Zeus and thus a symbol of the divine authority for their rulings, and the Muses assist kings as they deliver "straight" judgments by endowing them with honeyed speech.[89] In classical Athens, by contrast, ordinary men without any legal expertise delivered ad hoc judgments that could not be reliably predicted from statutes or previous verdicts. Where did such a system draw its authority and how did it maintain legitimacy?

The belief in the collective wisdom of the masses is a centerpiece of Athenian democratic ideology and must have played an important role in fostering respect for jury verdicts. The most famous expression of the virtue of collective wisdom appears in Aristotle's *Politics*:

> For it may be that the many, though each of them may not be an excellent
> man, nevertheless when gathered together they are better, not man-by-man,
> but all together.... for when there are many people, each one has some
> aspect of virtue and practical wisdom and coming together they become like
> a single human being with many feet, hands, and perceptions. The effect is

[88] In many societies, the tendency of judges to select a compromise solution acceptable to both parties fostered adherence to and public acceptance of individual decisions, which in turn enhanced the public's respect for the legal procedures. This appears to have been the case, for example, in early Greece and in African tribal societies such as the Tiv and the Barotse (Gagarin 1986:22, 30–31, 43). Classical Athenian jurors did not arrive at a compromise decision acceptable to both litigants but rather chose between them, which excluded this source of legitimacy.

[89] Hes. *Th.* 79–83. On the importance of the scepter and the association of kingship with judging, see MacDowell 1978:14; Gagarin 1986:27 n.28. Zeus reportedly provided not only the scepter, but also the *themistes*, rules of proper behavior, to kings to assist in judging cases. Hom. *Il.* 2.205–206 On the intervention of the Muses, see Hes. *Th.* 79–93; Gagarin 1986:24–25. On the reputation for exceptional wisdom enjoyed by popular judges, see Gagarin 1986:23. For a negative representation of the early judges as liable to bribery and flattery, see Hes. *Op.* 33–39. In the trial scene depicted on the shield of Achilles, the crowd played a vital role in the decision making process: various elders take turns wielding the scepter and suggesting a ruling, but it is the crowd who decides by acclamation which ruling is accepted. Hom. *Il.* 18.497–508. For a recent discussion of this controversial passage, see Gagarin 1986:26–33. Although the public makes the final determination in this case, the involvement of wise elders in suggesting just solutions gives the procedure more legitimacy than a simple vote of the people.

the same when it comes to character and thought. For this reason the many
are superior in judging works of music and of the poets; various men
[perceive] a portion, all [perceive] everything.[90]

The elaborate system of selecting and assigning jurors to court cases in the
fourth century – far more elaborate than was required to insure random selection
and prevent corruption – may have served as a public ceremony designed to
communicate to juror, litigant, and spectator alike that the body about to give
judgment was greater than the sum of its parts.[91]

The Athenians also maintained a number of legal fictions that downplayed the
potential for inconsistent and unpredictable verdicts by emphasizing the stability
and continuity of the laws and legal decisions over time. When discussing previous
cases speakers maintain the fiction that the former and current juries are identical.
For example, Aeschines could ask a jury in 345 B.C.E., 54 years after the event,
"so then, men of Athens, did *you* execute Socrates the sophist . . . ?"[92] Athenians
referred to Athens' laws as "the laws of Solon" and regularly attributed many of
the city's laws, including quite recent enactments, to the ancient lawgiver.[93] The
fiction of a stable, unchanging body of laws of ancient and venerable lineage may
have diverted attention from and eased anxieties about the often unpredictable
and inconsistent results produced by jurors applying those laws.

What sociologists term the "procedural justice effect" may have been another
mechanism that contributed to the legal system's legitimacy. The procedural justice
effect is simply that "participants and observers evaluate procedures as more or less
just or fair independent of their outcome, and that this estimation is quite relevant
to whether the distribution resulting from a procedure is accepted as just."[94]

---

[90] Arist. *Pol.* 1281 b1–11. In the Sicilian debate in Thucydides, Athenagoras defends democracy by stating
that the rich are the best people for looking after money, the intelligent are the best counselors, but
it is the many who are best at listening to the different arguments and judging between them (Thuc.
6.39.1). For a discussion of collective wisdom in the orators, see Ober 1990:163–165.

[91] See Bers 2000.

[92] Aesch. 1.173; Wolpert 2003. The United States Supreme Court maintains a similar fiction: nearly two
hundred years after the original case, the Court could refer to "*Marbury v. Madison*, where we held. . . ."
Webster v. Reproductive Health Services, 492 U.S. 490, 533 (1989) (citations omitted). Early in the Court's
history, John Marshall replaced seriatim opinions with majority opinions in an effort to boost the
Court's legitimacy by clarifying the reasons behind the opinion of the Court and fostering a sense of
intergenerational continuity. On the various fictions used to bolster the legitimacy of the American
legal system, see Kahn 1997.

[93] For discussion, with examples, see Thomas 1994:119ff.

[94] Röhl 1997:1.

Where the criteria for reaching a just outcome are complex, hard to determine, or controversial, the judgment of the fairness of the procedures will serve as a "social heuristic" for the perception of the fairness of the outcomes themselves.[95] Aspects of the Athenian legal process, particularly its strong adversary procedure, may have fostered a belief that the procedure as a whole was fair, thus bolstering respect for individual verdicts and the legitimacy of the legal system.[96]

Sociologists suggest that disputants across a variety of modern cultures prefer strong adversary procedures to other forms of dispute resolution.[97] Litigants tend to find a strong adversary procedure like that found in classical Athens satisfying because it permits them to tell their story in their own way and to be involved in the process of arriving at a rule of decision for their particular case.[98] Disputants prefer procedures in which the parties have control over the presentation of evidence and argument, but then relinquish control over the resolution of the dispute to a third party who is perceived to be neutral and fair.[99] It is interesting to note that observers and disputants evaluating the fairness of a procedure often value the ability of the decision maker to adjust the rules to reach just outcomes in particular cases ("the correctability rule").[100] According to these criteria, Athenian legal procedures are precisely the type that would attract litigants and impress observers as being fair. The widespread acceptance by litigants and observers of the fairness of judicial procedures may have fostered respect for and compliance with individual verdicts,[101] and helped the Athenian legal system maintain legitimacy in the eyes of the public.

---

[95] Wasserman 1997:37–8.

[96] Frier (1985:237–241, 246–251) has argued that in the Roman Republic the legitimacy of the legal system was bolstered in part by just this sort of effect. Frier (1985:229–231) also points to the value of unreasoned and inappellable verdicts in bolstering legitimacy by producing a quick and dispositive result and by insulating the reasons for the verdict in the "black box" of the *iudex*, thereby allowing participants to intuit their own reasons for the decision. These effects also apply to the unreasoned verdicts of Athenian juries.

[97] For a summary and discussion of the studies, see Röhl 1997:7–18. It is interesting to note that disputants living in societies that employ an inquisitorial system of justice also prefer adversary procedures (Röhl 1997:11).

[98] For discussion of this topic in the context of republican Rome, see Frier 1985:246–51.

[99] Vidmar 1997:125.

[100] For discussion, with references to specific studies, see Röhl 1997:10.

[101] Though, of course, unsuccessful individual litigants could, and likely often did, remain unsatisfied with the specific outcome of their case. One might wonder why, in the absence of formal means of enforcing judgments, unsuccessful litigants would ever comply with an adverse court judgment. First, the widespread acceptance of the fairness of the legal procedures created informal norms of abiding by verdicts. In addition, by the conclusion of a trial, a litigant had already signaled to society by

In sum, although there were significant costs associated with the high level of legal uncertainty in Athens, a variety of informal mechanisms permitted Athenian society to function reasonably well, particularly with respect to the maintenance of public order. A combination of democratic ideology, legal fictions, and psychological effects fostered respect for and compliance with jury verdicts despite the absence of consistency and predictability. In the next section we will see that for a brief period the Athenians considered large-scale reforms to reduce legal uncertainty. They ultimately abandoned these efforts, however, perhaps because the public process of legal revision undermined the ideology and legal fictions that fostered public respect for the laws and the legal system, without greatly improving social order.

THE LEGAL REFORMS AT THE END OF THE FIFTH CENTURY

At the end of the fifth century, two political crises pushed the Athenians from an uneasy acceptance of legal uncertainty to large-scale legal reform. In 411 the Athenian Assembly was persuaded to vote the democracy out of existence. Two short-lived oligarchic regimes ruled Athens before the democracy was restored the following year. In 404, not long after Athens surrendered to Sparta to conclude the Peloponnesian War, an oligarchic coup ushered in the spectacularly violent reign of the Thirty Tyrants. In both cases, legal reforms were instituted shortly after the restoration of the democracy. The revolutions revealed the fragility of the democratic constitution and the need for safeguards in the process of lawmaking to protect the most important Athenian laws from hasty repeal or amendment. The political crises also raised questions about the character of the *patrios politeia* ("ancestral constitution"): both democrats and oligarchs claimed the *patrios politeia* laid down by Solon and Draco as their own, and the focus on collecting and reorganizing the laws of Solon and Draco after the restoration of the democracy may have been an attempt to establish the bona fides of the democracy.[102]

his participation that he recognized the legitimacy of the procedure and would accept the outcome, making it socially untenable to reject the verdict. Luhmann (1975) discusses the process by which legal procedure insures compliance with decisions quite apart from the perception of procedural or outcome fairness through a learning process that changes the structure of the expectations of the participants and socially isolates the unsuccessful litigant.

[102] Hansen 1999:162.

Although the oligarchic revolutions provided the impetus for reform, the nature of the reforms suggests an attempt to address the longstanding problem of inconsistency and uncertainty in the laws as well. The paucity of our evidence and the difficulties involved in interpreting our literary sources[103] make it impossible to determine the precise extent and aims of the legal reforms with any certainty. But the conclusion that the Athenians were striving for coherence, or at least the absence of contradictions, in their legal rules seems beyond doubt. We depart here from a largely synchronic study of the legal system to examine the legal developments of a single decade not because the reforms had an important impact on the functioning of the courts – in fact, we will see that the various reform measures were either short lived or ineffective. Rather, this episode is of interest because in the attempts at reform we can see both a widespread ambivalence about the uncertainty inherent in the legal system, and the limits of Athenian willingness to alter their legal system to reduce legal insecurity.

THE REVISION OF THE LAWS, 410–404 AND 403–399

Soon after the restoration of the democracy in 410, a board of magistrates known as *anagrapheis* was set up to research and write up the laws. According to Lysias *Against Nicomachus*, this board, which included Nicomachus, was instructed "to write up the laws of Solon."[104] A separate decree of 409/8 also ordered the *anagrapheis* to republish Draco's law of homicide.[105] Modern accounts of the legal revisions tend to interpret the evidence in one of two ways.[106] For some, the board was charged with collecting and publishing only the laws of Solon and Draco that were

---

[103] Our two main literary sources for the reforms are Lysias *Against Nicomachus*, and Andocides *On the Mysteries*. *Against Nicomachus* concerns the prosecution of Nicomachus, who served in 410–404 and again in 403–399 as one of the officials involved in collecting and publishing the laws as part of the reforms. Because this speech accuses Nicomachus of overstepping his powers, it may exaggerate the actions taken by the board on which Nicomachus served, and/or understate the mandate given to this board. *On the Mysteries* discusses at some length the second phase of the reforms that began in 403. Andocides was involved in a religious scandal in 415, and as a result was barred from attending the Eleusinian Mysteries. In this suit, Andocides is charged with breaking the ban in 400 or 399, and Andocides argues in part that the original provision banning him from participation, along with all other laws passed prior to the reforms of 403, was made invalid by the revision of the laws. It is therefore in his interest to portray the reforms as a sweeping revision of the entire law code.

[104] Lys. 30.2.

[105] IG i³ 104.5–6.

[106] Robertson (1990) has proposed a third interpretation, namely that the *anagrapheis* were appointed to transcribe all the laws for Athens' new central archive, and did not permanently "publish" the body of laws, but merely, during the second phase of reforms, temporarily posted individual statutes for

currently in force; that is, the *anagrapheis* replaced those Solonian or Draconian laws that had been clearly superseded by later legislation,[107] but otherwise did not concern themselves with valid laws unrelated to subjects addressed by these ancient lawgivers.[108] On this view, the revisions were aimed at collecting the valid laws of Solon and Draco in one place[109] and eliminating inconsistencies that had developed in one part of their statute law, but did not include an attempt to publish a single, comprehensive, and coherent body of law.

However, because the phrase "the laws of Solon" is commonly used to refer to the Athenian laws in general, it seems likely that the Lysias passage should be interpreted somewhat more broadly to mean that the *anagrapheis* were charged with collecting all the laws currently in force and publishing them in a single place.[110] This broader account of the mission of the board gains strength from epigraphical evidence suggesting that the *anagrapheis* did in fact write up recent laws in addition to the laws of Solon and Draco.[111] If this interpretation is correct, the legal reforms of 410 were aimed in part at producing a single, consistent code of laws that would foster legal certainty by eliminating obvious inconsistencies among statutes. However, this reform did not address the indeterminacy and inconsistency created by the application of the laws by juries in court cases. The process of revising the laws was terminated six years later when the Thirty Tyrants came to power.

When the democracy was restored in 403, the *anagrapheis* were reappointed for a second term to continue their work. It seems likely that the revision of the

---

inspection. This provocative thesis has thus far not won many adherents. See, e.g., Rhodes 1991:91; Todd 1996:128.

[107] The prosecutor in Lysias 30 states that Nicomachus not only collected and published the laws but also deleted regulations he found in his research (Lys. 30.2). The speaker implies that deleting laws went beyond the mandate of the *anagrapheis*, but it is more likely that one of the functions of the board was to discard outdated, inconsistent, or redundant laws. For discussion, see Todd 1996:109.

[108] E.g., K. Clinton 1982.

[109] Laws were inscribed on stone stelai and generally displayed near the offices of the relevant magistrates (Todd 1993:56 & n.7). As a result, the texts of laws were scattered throughout Athens. Sometime around the end of the fifth century, a public archive was constructed to house copies of the laws (Boegehold 1972).

[110] Sickinger 1999:98. Other, slightly different, accounts that also posit the revision of all the laws then in force include Rhodes 1991 and Hansen 1999:162–163. Presumably the *anagrapheis* ignored nonce enactments, like honorary decrees, in the process of revision (Rhodes 1991:91–92).

[111] Inscriptions on stelai that scholars have associated with the *anagrapheis'* first term from 410–404 include laws recent enough to mention the trierarchs and the *dikastêrion* (Rhodes 1991:90).

laws was completed fairly soon after reappointment, as the *anagrapheis* appear to have devoted much of their second term to producing a sacrificial calendar which survives in fragmentary form.[112] Our most important source for the second phase of legal reform is Andocides' speech *On the Mysteries*. In the course of his defense, Andocides quotes a decree moved by Teisamenos in 403 that outlined which laws were valid in the restored democracy. The decree provided in part that the Athenians should be governed in accordance with tradition, using the "laws of Solon" and "the decrees of Draco which we used in the past."[113] The "laws of Solon" and "decrees of Draco" in this statute probably refer to the revised code of laws collected and published by the *anagrapheis*.[114] The decree also describes a process for vetting new laws: two boards of *nomothetai* were set up, one, elected by the Council, proposed laws and temporarily displayed them in public, while the second, selected from the demes, voted on whether to ratify each law and add it to the code.[115] Andocides claims that all the laws were examined through this process before being included in the new law code, and some scholars have taken him at his word.[116] But a straightforward reading of the decree itself (rather than Andocides' interpretation of the decree) suggests that the laws published by the *anagrapheis* were automatically included in the new code and only new laws that were deemed necessary additions to the code underwent this examination and ratification procedure.[117]

Andocides also quotes a series of related laws, two of which are of interest here. "The magistrates shall not use an unwritten law concerning any matter;" and "No decree, whether originating from the Council or the Assembly, can supersede a law."[118] The first law is generally interpreted to mean that magistrates were to enforce only the laws that were written up by the *anagrapheis* and amendments ratified by the *nomothetai*; other laws that were not included in the revisions were now void.[119] The second law created a distinction between laws (*nomoi*) of general application included in the new law code, and decrees

[112] Sickinger 1999:99.
[113] Andoc. 1.83.
[114] Rhodes 1991:97.
[115] Andoc. 1.83–84.
[116] E.g., Hansen 1999:163.
[117] MacDowell 1962:194–199.
[118] Andoc. 1.87.
[119] E.g., Rhodes 1991:97; Sickinger 1999:100.

(*psêphismata*), which were generally temporary or more specific enactments passed by the assembly and could not contravene a valid law. Taken together these laws indicate that the laws collected and published in the process of legal revision were intended to be an exclusive, authoritative law code that could not be contravened by the assembly alone (the elaborate process for amending a law or creating a new law after the completion of the codification is discussed below). The revision of the laws from 410–399 thus attempted to eliminate inconsistent, outdated, or redundant laws, and to create a single, at least superficially coherent law code.

The codification should have alleviated the legal uncertainty in Athens to some degree by providing a single, authoritative collection of laws in a central location that could be consulted by litigants.[120] But the law code is not mentioned again after Andocides' speech in 400. When litigants do state their source for a law, they mention either the individual stele or the archive where copies of laws were kept.[121] I find the interpretations of the revisions put forward by Hansen and Todd most plausible: the Athenians did indeed strive for legal codification in 403 in an attempt to increase consistency and coherence among their body of legal rules, but seem to have abandoned the idea almost immediately.

We cannot know for certain why the Athenians became so quickly disenchanted with codification. It seems likely that the completed code did not remain unchanged for long and required numerous amendments and additions.[122] Perhaps the process of constant revision and republication of the laws seemed impractical.[123] More attractive is Todd's speculation that the public process of constant revision of the law code would highlight the reality that the Athenian laws were not, in fact, the unchanging ancestral laws of Solon and Draco, but were in constant flux. Todd suggests that "the Athenians collectively preferred chaos and a sense of continuity to coherence at the price of admitting change."[124] Stated another way, the Athenians may have felt that the authority of the law was diminished rather than enhanced by codification, and that the gains in legal certainty (which

---

[120] Some scholars who characterize the legal reforms as a "codification" of the laws nevertheless doubt that all the laws were published on stone in a single location. See, e.g., Rhodes 1991:98–99; cf. Hansen 1999:163–164.

[121] E.g. Dem. 59.75–76 (stele); Dem. 25.99 (archive); Lyc. 1.66 (archive).

[122] Hansen 1999:164.

[123] See Hansen 1999:164. He suggests that once codification was abandoned new laws were kept in the archive on papyrus and that some were also inscribed on individual stone stelai.

[124] Todd 1996:130.

were in any case modest because the reforms did not change the ad hoc nature of jury decision making) were outweighed by the reduction in the respect for and authority of the laws.[125]

NOMOTHESIA

The process of lawmaking in the fourth century, known as *nomothesia*, was also designed in part to foster coherence and consistency in the Athenian corpus of laws. It is not clear when the *nomothesia* procedure was introduced, but it may have been conceived as part of the legal reforms and enacted sometime not long after the revision of the laws of 403–399.[126] The three laws concerning *nomothesia* that are most interesting for our purposes are the "review," "repeal," and "inspection" laws.[127] The "review law," quoted in Demosthenes *Against Timocrates*, provided that each year the Assembly was to reconsider the entire body of laws and vote on whether to retain or reject each law.[128] If any law was voted down, anyone who wished could make a proposal to replace the old law. A board of *nomothetai* (chosen by lot from the jury pool, unlike the one-time board of *nomothetai* involved in revision of the laws from 403–399) heard arguments and decided whether to accept the new proposal or retain the original law. Under the "repeal law," any citizen could at any time, on his own initiative, make a proposal to replace an old law with a new one to be considered by the *nomothetai*.[129] The "inspection law" described in Aeschines *Against Ctesiphon* provided a procedure for eliminating inconsistent laws. Under this measure, the *thesmothetai* were charged with examining the laws and informing the Assembly "if any written law is contrary to any other law, or if an invalid law is included among the valid ones, or if more than one law has been written on the same subject."[130] In such a case, the Assembly arranged for a board of *nomothetai* to sort it out.

---

[125] The Athenian approach to legal consistency may not be as foreign as might at first appear. In modern legal theory judicial consistency is generally justified either as a requirement of fairness, and thus an end in itself, or merely as a policy that serves to enhance the authority of the law and the predictability of decisions.

[126] Hansen 1999:165–166. Some scholars have argued that the various surviving laws relating to *nomothesia* were introduced gradually throughout the fourth century. For discussion, see D. M. MacDowell 1975; Rhodes 1985; cf. Hansen 1985.

[127] There is some dispute as to whether or not there were additional laws related to *nomothesia*. See Hansen 1985; MacDowell 1975; Rhodes 1985.

[128] Dem. 24.20–23.

[129] Dem. 24.33.

[130] Aesch. 3.38.

Unlike the revision of the laws, *nomothesia* remained in force throughout the period of Athenian independence and, in some scholars' view, had a profound impact on the nature of the Athenian democracy. By taking the power to make laws out of the hands of the popular Assembly, so the argument goes, *nomothesia* contributed to the transition in the early fourth century from a radical to a more moderate democracy.[131] However, the effect of *nomothesia* on the workings of the legal system was much more limited: although *nomothesia* fostered some coherence and consistency among the laws,[132] this process did nothing to alleviate the uncertainty and inconsistency caused by the highly particularized, ad hoc nature of popular court jury decision making.

It seems that the problems created by legal insecurity, serious though they were, were not troublesome enough to trigger changes in the basic workings of the popular courts. Apparently there was no political will to limit the popular court jury's discretion in order to create greater legal certainty and to improve the capability of the law to guide conduct. In the next chapter, we will see that in one area of law – maritime suits – the costs associated with contextualized justice outweighed the benefits, and steps were taken to narrow the range of evidence considered relevant to the jury in an effort to enhance the predictability of verdicts.

---

[131] For the argument that the distinction between the nature of fifth- and fourth-century Athenian democracy is overdrawn, see Ober 1990:95ff.

[132] The Athenians were not entirely successful at avoiding inconsistencies: Demosthenes and Aeschines introduce conflicting laws regarding the awarding of honorary crowns. Compare Dem. 18.120–122 with Aesch. 3.32–48. For discussion, see Rhodes 1980:306.

6 MARITIME CASES

፬ſſ

IN THE MIDDLE OF THE FOURTH CENTURY B.C.E., THE ATHENIANS CREATED A SPECIAL procedure for maritime suits, the *dikê emporikê*.[1] *Dikai emporikai* were most likely heard in the ordinary popular courts,[2] but were exceptional in the frequency of non-citizen participation as litigants and witnesses, and in the rule that only disputes over written contracts could be heard through this procedure. Maritime suits, like Athenian homicide cases, exhibit a distinctive notion of relevance and mode of legal argumentation. Speeches in *dikai emporikai* appear to be more focused on the terms of the written contract and less likely to appeal to arguments from fairness or to evidence regarding the character and social standing of the litigants than ordinary popular court speeches. The unusual mode of argumentation in maritime cases can be traced to two interrelated causal factors: the common participation of foreigners in *dikai emporikai*, and the need to facilitate trade and attract non-Athenian merchants[3] by offering a predictable procedure that focused on the enforcement of contracts as written.

A few words regarding the nature of our sources for the *dikai emporikai* are in order. In discussing characteristics of the homicide courts that set them apart from ordinary popular courts, it was possible to draw on numerous texts explicitly remarking on the differences between them. There are no comparable discursive comments regarding the procedures of the *dikai emporikai*.[4] Consequently, the analysis offered here must be based on the evidence from the five surviving maritime speeches themselves, which are virtually silent on the significance of the

---

[1] *Dikê emporikê* (pl. *dikai emporikai*) refers both to the special maritime procedure and to a maritime case brought under this procedure.

[2] For the possibility that *dikai emporikai* were heard in special courts before specialist judges, see below.

[3] On the domination of Athenian maritime trade by non-Athenians, see Reed 2003:27–33.

[4] Demosthenes 7.12 may be suggestive in this regard:

And yet, at that time we had more dealings with each other than we have now, Macedonia was in our control and paid us tribute, and at that time more than now we used their markets and they used ours, and maritime suits (*dikai emporikai*) were not *akribeis* ("by the book" or "carried out according to rule") as they are now, carried out monthly, making it unnecessary for those who are so far away from each other [i.e., Macedonia and Athens] to make an interstate legal agreement [*symbolôn*].

distinctive procedures at issue, and on inferences drawn from comparisons of the argumentation found in maritime and non-maritime cases. Judgments about the extent to which maritime speeches are distinctive in their approach to legal and contractual as opposed to extra-legal argumentation is inevitably somewhat subjective. However, the written contract requirement for *dikai emporikai* sets these procedures clearly apart from ordinary popular court cases.

THE CREATION AND CHARACTERISTICS OF THE *DIKÊ EMPORIKÊ* PROCEDURE

ECONOMIC DECLINE AND THE CREATION OF THE *DIKÊ EMPORIKÊ*

Among the many advantages of empire was the ability to force delivery to Athens of vital items that it could not provide for itself, such as timber, iron, and, most important, grain. When Athens lost the Peloponnesian War in 404 B.C.E., it lost not only its fleet and imperial tribute, but also its position as the dominant commercial center in Greece.[5] The market and the new Spartan hegemony now dictated the activity of merchants and the flow of goods. The grain supply became a perennial source of concern.[6] In the decades following the defeat, Athens gradually fought its way back to military and economic prominence and formed the Second Athenian League in 378 B.C.E. In 357, Athens' fortunes again took a turn for the worse. Athens was hit by a severe grain crisis and the revolt of four of its most powerful allies. After two years of fighting, Athens relented and made peace. In 355 the city was near bankruptcy and could no longer rely on its imperial power to insure an adequate supply of grain and favorable trading conditions. During this period the statesman Eubulus initiated a number of wide-ranging reforms that greatly improved the finances of the city and the prosperity of its citizens. It was in this context that the law creating the special maritime procedures was introduced.

It is not entirely clear what Demosthenes means when he refers to the *dikai emporikai* as *akribeis*. He may simply be referring to the requirement that these suits be initiated at a specified time each month or to the strict procedural requirements of the new procedure, such as the need for a written contract. On the other hand, he may be suggesting that maritime cases under the *dikê emporikê* procedure are conducted in a more formal manner, adhering more strictly to the terms of the contract than commercial cases heard before the introduction of the special *dikê emporikê* procedure.

[5] On Athenian foreign trade and economy in the fourth century, see, e.g., Mossé 1973:12–17, 32–49; Isager & Hansen 1975:11–84; Strauss 1986:42–69; Eder 1995.

[6] See Garnsey 1998.

From the fifth century, cases involving merchants had been tried by a board of magistrates known as *nautodikai*.[7] We know very little about the procedures used in these cases during the fifth and early fourth century.[8] In his 355 tract *On Revenues*, Xenophon suggested that Athens could attract traders and thereby boost its economy by taking steps to provide quicker and more just legal procedures for merchants.[9] It appears that the Athenians did just that by introducing a special procedure, the *dikê emporikê*, for cases involving a written contract for shipment to or from Athens. The *dikê emporikê*, most likely created sometime between 355 and 347 B.C.E.,[10] had a variety of distinctive features, including equal standing for foreigners and metics, expedited procedures, and special measures for enforcing judgments.[11]

No source explicitly discusses the motivation behind the creation of the *dikê emporikê*. But it seems likely that these maritime procedures were designed to encourage foreign merchants to come to Athens by offering them legal protection equal to that enjoyed by Athenian citizens in ordinary cases, and, in addition, expedited procedures with special provisions to insure compliance with judgments. The requirement of a written contract would presumably foster precision in business dealings and predictability in court verdicts, and lessen merchants' fear of being haled into court on baseless charges. Gernet notes that one litigant's use of the dative in describing the maritime procedures – "private suits for merchants and shipowners" – suggests that the law was conceived as a benefit for wronged merchants, though of course merchants were defendants as well as plaintiffs in such suits.[12] It may have been hoped that by attracting foreign merchants and making it easier for citizens and non-citizens resident in Athens to do business, the *dikai emporikai* would stimulate the city's flagging economy.

When it came to the protection of its endangered grain supply, Athens used the stick as well as the carrot. In the fourth century the city passed a series of protective measures designed to safeguard the supply of food: any resident of

---

[7] The *nautodikai* first appear in an inscription dating from about 444 B.C.E. (IG i² 41).

[8] We know even less about the board of magistrates called the *xenodikai*. For discussion, see Harrison 1998:23–24. There was another route for resolving disputes available to some foreigners from the fifth century: some states had bilateral agreements with Athens that granted the citizens of each state full access to the courts of the other. On such *symbola*, see, Gauthier 1972.

[9] Xen. *Poroi* 3.3. Xenophon did not make specific proposals to reform the existing procedures.

[10] The special procedures must have been introduced sometime after Xenophon's *Poroi*, but before Demosthenes' prosecution of Meidias in 347, which contains a reference to a *dikê emporikê* (Dem. 21.176).

[11] Each of these features is described in more detail later in the chapter.

[12] Dem. 33.1; Gernet 1938: 184.

Athens who shipped grain anywhere except its harbor could be punished with death;[13] residents were not permitted to lend money for maritime voyages that did not transport grain to Athens;[14] and it seems that any grain ship that docked in its harbor was permitted to re-export only one-third of its cargo.[15] Although the *dikai emporikai* were not limited to cases involving the shipment of grain, the importance of securing food for Athens lurks behind both the motivation for and practice of these special maritime suits.

Special Features of the *Dikê Emporikê*

The unusual rules and procedures used in *dikai emporikai* have led some scholars to credit the Athenians with developing the seeds of international commercial law.[16] Five cases survive in which speakers indicate that the case is being tried using the *dikê emporikê* procedure (Demosthenes 32–35 and 56). It is largely from these cases that we must discern the basic features of this special procedure. All arose out of a *nautikos tokos*, a high interest loan[17] on the security of shipping cargo. In such an arrangement, the debtor was obliged to repay only if the ship arrived safely; otherwise, the lender was responsible for the loss. These transactions therefore seem to have served as a form of insurance, because creditors who invested in a large number of ships bore the considerable risk of shipwreck and theft.[18]

It has been argued that *dikai emporikai* were heard in separate courts before specialist judges drawn from men familiar with commercial matters.[19] This hypothesis rests on two passages in which the speaker in Demosthenes *Against Lacritus* suggests that "those judging the *dikai emporikai*" will not be fooled by his opponent's specious arguments.[20] Neither passage clearly suggests a panel of experts; both remarks, part of the same speech, may just as plausibly be explained as attempts

---

[13] Dem. 34.37; 35.50; Lyc. 1.27.

[14] Dem. 35.51; Dem. 56.6, 11.

[15] Arist. *Ath. Pol.* 51.4.

[16] E.g., E. Cohen 1973: 69; Gernet 1938; Paoli 1974a:111–115; cf. Todd 1993: 323, 336.

[17] Interest rates in our sources range from 12.5% (Dem. 50.17) to 30% (Dem. 34.23).

[18] de Ste. Croix 1956. Millett (1983) disputes the characterization of these loans as a form of insurance. For a balanced discussion of this dispute, see Todd 1993:337–340. For a detailed treatment of the institution of maritime loans, see Isager & Hansen 1975:74–84.

[19] E. Cohen 1973:93–95.

[20] Dem. 35.43: "Let him persuade you of whichever of these arguments he wishes. For if he is able to persuade you who judge cases concerning merchants' contracts, then I agree that this man is most expert;" Dem. 35.46: "But this man is so abominable and so far exceeds all men in wickedness, that he

to flatter the jury.[21] Although we cannot rule out the possibility that there were special commercial judges, it seems most likely that cases brought under the *dikê emporikê* procedure's special rules were heard by ordinary jurors in the popular courts.

The most revolutionary feature of the *dikai emporikai* was that foreigners, metics, and possibly even slaves were given standing equal to Athenian citizens in these suits. In ordinary non-maritime cases, a foreigner could not bring suit in Athenian courts except by special arrangement, for example if his polis had a bilateral agreement with Athens giving the citizens of each state access to the others' courts. The admission of metics, or resident aliens, as litigants and witnesses in *dikai emporikai* was not quite as unusual: metics could sue or be sued in other types of private case (*dikê*) as well.[22] Precisely because the court did not distinguish between citizens and others in *dikai emporikai*, it is difficult to identify many individual litigants in our five surviving maritime suits, but the presence of metics and foreigners as well as citizens is certain.[23] It is important to note that citizens participated regularly in the maritime suits; by one count, roughly the same number of Athenians and non-Athenians appear in our surviving speeches.[24] *Dikai emporikai* were not special procedures for foreigners but events in which citizens and non-citizens were, at least in a formal sense, on an equal footing. Indeed, it is an Athenian in a suit against a foreigner who asks, "Aren't the same laws written for all of us, and do not the same rights apply for all in *dikai emporikai*?"[25]

---

is trying to persuade you to vote that this mercantile case is inadmissible, with you now judging the *dikai emporikai*."

[21] MacDowell 1978:84; Todd 1993:336.

[22] Arist. *Ath. Pol.* 58.2–3; Lys. 23.2. The capacity of metics with respect to *graphai* (public cases) is unclear. Our surviving statutes indicate that at least some, and perhaps most, types of *graphê* were by their terms limited to Athenians (e.g., Dem. 21.47; 59.16), but we know of at least one public case that was prosecuted by a metic (Dem. 59.64). Some scholars have suggested that a metic could bring a public case only when he himself was the victim, and was forbidden from serving the more public-spirited role of *ho boulomenos*. For discussion, see, e.g., Whitehead 1977:92–5; Patterson 2000.

[23] Foreigners: e.g., Hegestratus and Zenothemis of Massalia (Dem. 32. 4–5); Metics: e.g., Chrysippus (Dem.34.38–39); Citizens: e.g., Androcles (Dem. 35.10). For a full list of *nauklêroi and emporoi* mentioned in the surviving maritime speeches with tentative status identifications, see Isager & Hansen 1975: 72 & nn. 77–79.

[24] Isager & Hansen 1975: 72.

[25] Dem. 35.45. For discussion, see MacDowell 1978: 234. The speaker attempts to capitalize on his citizen status elsewhere in the speech.

It is probable, though not entirely certain, that slaves were also permitted to serve as litigants and witnesses in *dikai emporikai*. This hypothesis rests largely on a single example: Lampis, a shipowner mentioned in Demosthenes *Against Phormio*. Lampis is described as an *oiketês* ("house servant")[26] and one of the *paides* ("boys")[27] of Dio, language that in itself strongly suggests slave status. Yet the speaker tells us that Lampis was a witness at the arbitration and implies that he could have prosecuted the case himself.[28] Although the case of Lampis suggests that slaves enjoyed standing in *dikai emporikai*, it has been pointed out that there is reason for caution: speakers sometimes refer to former slaves simply as slaves in our surviving speeches, and it is possible that Lampis was a free man at the time of the trial.[29] If, as seems likely, slaves were permitted to litigate on an equal basis in the *dikai emporikai*, these suits represent a radical departure from ordinary popular court cases, in which slaves were not given the right to litigate and were not even permitted to participate as witnesses without being subjected to torture.[30]

The maritime suits had a number of distinctive features designed to facilitate merchants' use of the city's legal institutions. The speaker in Demosthenes *Against Apaturius* states:

> For merchants there are monthly opportunities for the lodging of written complaints from Boedromion to Munichion [approximately September to April] in order that, having obtained justice straightaway, they might put to sea.[31]

[26] Dem. 34.5.

[27] Dem. 34.10.

[28] Dem. 34.18; Todd 1993: 193.

[29] Todd (1993:193) notes that Apollodorus referred to Phormio as a slave long after he had been freed, and that in two cases Lysias calls his opponents, whom we know to have been citizens, slaves. Dem. 45.76, 84, 86; Lys. 13.18, 64; 30.5. Cohen (2000: 136) proposes another candidate, arguing that Zenothemis, one of the litigants in Demosthenes *Against Zenothemis*, is a slave based on reference to him as "underling of Hegestratus (ὑπηρέτης Ἡγεστράτου) (Dem. 32.4). However, this moniker need not denote slave status, and we can draw no conclusions from this passage.

[30] There are some notable exceptions to this general statement: a slave who acted without instructions from his owner might be sued directly (Dem. 55), and in a few special circumstances a slave could inform against his master without torture through a process known as *mênusis* (Osborne 2000). Uncertainty surrounds the case of Pittalakos, a public slave (*dêmosios*) who, according to Aeschines (1.54–62), brought suit against his rival in Timarchus' affections. For discussion, see, e.g., E. Cohen 2000: 136, 168–169; Todd 1993:192–194; Fisher 1993:57. E. Cohen (1992) has argued that slaves could litigate in banking suits as well (cf. Todd 1994).

[31] Dem. 33.23.

Some scholars have argued that the two months are falsely transposed in the manuscript, and therefore that maritime suits would be heard only during the summer months to insure quick resolution of disputes during the sailing season.[32] Cohen has challenged this view, maintaining that most merchants would spend the winter in Athens and would prefer to delay their cases until the off season.[33] Regardless of which interpretation is correct, it is clear that the special scheduling of cases tried under the *dikê emporikê* procedure was designed to provide merchants with convenient access to the courts.

Maritime cases are also unusual in that they are among the "monthly suits," (*dikai emmênoi*),[34] meaning that cases of this sort could be initiated at a specified time during each month.[35] The details of these suits are obscure, but it seems likely that the monthly suits followed an expedited procedure.[36] Finally, presumably because the risk of flight was greater in the case of foreign merchants, there were special provisions to insure compliance with judgments in maritime suits. The *dikai emporikai* required that unsuccessful litigants be incarcerated until they paid the judgment.[37]

For our purposes, the most important feature of the *dikê emporikê* was that only disputes over written contracts could be heard through this procedure. Four of our five surviving maritime speeches are *paragraphai*, counter-suits in which the defendant argues that the plaintiff is bringing an illegal prosecution.[38] Because the central issue in these cases is the admissibility of the claim under the *dikai emporikai*,

---

[32] Paoli 1974b:177–186; see also Hansen 1983.

[33] E. Cohen 1973:42–59; Carey & Reid 1985:234–235.

[34] Arist. *Ath. Pol.* 52.2. The *Constitution of the Athenians* lists several other examples of monthly suit, many but not all of which involve commercial matters. The reason for this particular grouping of types of case remains obscure. For discussion, see, e.g., Gernet 1938:173–179; E. Cohen 1973:12–22; Harrison 1998:22–23.

[35] For a detailed defense of this interpretation of *emmênoi*, see E. Cohen 1973:23–36; see also Carey & Reid 1985: 234. For the alternative view that monthly suits were those that had to be completed within one month, see, e.g., Gauthier 1974; Isager & Hansen 1975: 85; Hansen 1983:165–177.

[36] Monthly suits likely dispensed with public arbitration, and D. Cohen (1983:36–40) suggests that there may have been no *anakrisis* in these suits. See also Carey & Reid 1985:119–120.

[37] Dem. 33.1: the law "commands prison as punishment for wrongdoers until they pay whatever amount is required by the judgment, in order that no one may heedlessly wrong any merchant"; see also Dem. 35.46–47; 56.4; E. Cohen 1973:75–79.

[38] Demosthenes 32 (*Against Zenothemis*); 33 (*Against Apaturius*); 34 (*Against Phormio*); 35 (*Against Lacritus*). For discussion of the *paragraphê* procedure, see Wolff 1966; Harrison 1998:105–130; Isager & Hansen 1975:123–137.

these speeches provide valuable evidence about the requirements for bringing suit under the special maritime procedures. The speaker in *Against Zenothemis* offers the clearest definition of the *dikai emporikai*:

> The laws, gentlemen of the jury, order that there will be private suits for shipowners and merchants for contracts regarding shipments to and from Athens, and concerning which there are written agreements.[39]

This passage can be interpreted to mean either that disputes properly brought under the *dikai emporikai* procedure must concern written contracts for a shipment to or from Athens, or that oral agreements concerning shipments to or from Athens *and* written contracts of any sort come under the jurisdiction of this procedure.[40] The former, the conjunctive translation, seems the more natural, and the disputes in our surviving speeches seem to satisfy both these requirements. All of the speeches except one explicitly discuss a written contract for shipment to or from Athens.[41] Moreover, the speaker in Demosthenes *Against Zenothemis* suggests that shipment to or from Athens is a *sine qua non* for his opponent's

---

[39] Dem. 32.1. The speaker in Demosthenes 34.42 offers a similar formulation:

> The law itself serves as a witness to the admissibility of this private suit, ordering that *dikai emporikai* are those that concern contracts entered into in Athens and for the Athenian market, and not only those made in Athens but also as many as are made for a sailing trip to Athens.

In Demosthenes 33.1, the speaker reports:

> The law, gentlemen of the jury, orders that suits for merchants and shipowners shall be under the jurisdiction of the *thesmothetai*, if they are wronged in any way in the market sailing either here or outbound to some other destination....

The speaker's suggestion that the maritime procedure is available for merchants "wronged in any way" is clarified in the next sentence, where he notes that a contract is required for a *dikē emporikē*, and that where there is no contract the case is subject to dismissal through the *paragraphē* procedure (Dem. 33.2).

[40] For the conjunctive view, see Lipsius 1905–1915:632; E. Cohen 1973: 100ff. The main proponent of the disjunctive view is Gernet (1938: 186). Scholars also disagree on whether the *dikē emporikē* also required that one of the litigants be an *emporos* or a *naukléros*. Compare Carey & Reid (1985: 233) and Isager & Hansen (1975: 86), both of whom argue for such a requirement, with Gernet (1938: 185) and E. Cohen (1973:114–129).

[41] Dem. 32.16; 34.6; 56.6. Demosthenes 35.10–13 contains what appears to be an authentic maritime contract in full. It is not clear whether the contract at issue in *Against Apaturius* was written, but all the other agreements mentioned in the speech were. See Dem. 33.12 (loan for Apaturius' creditors); 33.15 (written arbitration agreements). The details of the deals involved in this suit are far from clear and have generated a great deal of scholarly debate, but more than one plausible interpretation of the speech is consistent with a written contract requirement in *dikai emporikai* (see, e.g., Isager & Hansen 1975:151–52; E. Cohen 1973:108–110).

dikê emporikê; such a statement would not help the speaker's cause if any written contract were sufficient to bring the case within the maritime procedure.[42] The most straightforward argument is perhaps the most persuasive: it is difficult to understand why the Athenians would provide access to these special procedures to litigants in cases that had no connection with Athens merely because a written contract was involved. Indeed, it seems to be now generally agreed among scholars that a written contract was required to bring a *dikê emporikê.*[43]

THE PERSISTENCE OF ORAL PROOF IN THE POPULAR COURTS

A written contract requirement such as that used in the *dikê emporikê* procedure was unprecedented in Athens. The first reference to a written contract in our surviving popular court speeches occurs in Isocrates *Trapeziticus*, tentatively dated to 393 B.C.E.[44] Although references to written agreements become more frequent in the later court speeches, it has been pointed out that purely oral agreements continue to be used and enforced in non-maritime cases throughout the classical period.[45] The speech from the Demosthenic corpus *Against Spudias*, for example, concerns a complex dowry arrangement that appears to have been entirely oral. There is no definitive statement as to what constitutes an enforceable contract in Athens,[46] but those remarks in the orators' speeches that approach such a statement are strikingly devoid of references to writing.[47] The term for enforceable agreement we meet most frequently, *homologeô*, means literally "speaking the same way." In *Against Athenogenes*, a case that involves a written contract for the sale of a perfume shop, Hyperides notes that "the law says that whatever agreements one man makes with another are binding."[48] That the Athenians generally considered oral and written agreements interchangeable is clear from a passage in Isaeus describing a

---

[42] Dem. 32.22–3; E. Cohen 1973:101–102.

[43] E.g., Isager & Hansen 1975: 87; Carey & Reid 1985: 233; MacDowell 1978:233; Todd 1993: 336.

[44] Isoc. 17.20.

[45] Thomas 1989:40ff.

[46] The nature of Athenian notions of contract has been the subject of some debate. Compare Beauchet (1969:10) with Pringsheim (1950:86ff). More recently, Todd (1993:264–8) has suggested that the Athenians had no real doctrine of contract at all. For our purposes, it matters only that in non-maritime cases the Athenians do not seem to have distinguished between written and oral agreements.

[47] E.g., Dem. 56.2; 48.11,54; 42.12; 44.7; Hyp. 3.13; Dem. 18.24–25; *Cri.* 52e; *Leg.* 11.920d.

[48] Hyp. 3.13.

complicated contract in which some of the terms were written down and others verbally agreed to before witnesses.[49]

Thomas has pointed out that where written contracts are used in our surviving non-maritime speeches, they seem primarily to have supplemented the speaker's evidence rather than to have served as decisive proof.[50] We have only two examples of contracts offered as evidence without accompanying witness testimony.[51] When discussing a written contract, speakers generally furnish witnesses who testify to the nature of the agreement between the parties as well as to the authenticity of the document.[52] Even bankers' records (*grammata*), which were routinely recorded in writing and used in litigation, were not necessarily considered the best evidence of a banking transaction.[53] In *Against Timotheus*,[54] for example, Apollodorus, the son of the banker Pasion, is suing to recover debts owed to his father after his death. Although Apollodorus mentions the bank records as one source of information as to the amount of the various debts,[55] he never enters the records into evidence but instead calls as witnesses the clerks in the bank who had paid out the money.[56] Noting that when his father became ill he told Apollodorus and his brother the details of each particular debt owed to him, Apollodorus also calls his brother as a witness to the debts and has his own oath regarding them read out.[57]

---

[49] Is. 5.25.

[50] Thomas 1989:40–45.

[51] Hyp. 3.8; Lyc. 1.23. The speaker in Hyperides 3 feels compelled to explain the absence of witnesses by claiming that the transaction required unusual secrecy.

[52] E.g., Is. 3.19; 9.12; Dem. 27.21; 29.7; 30.32; 38.5. In the *Laws* (953e), Plato prescribes that written contracts be witnessed. For discussion, see Thomas 1989: 42; Pringsheim 1950:12ff, 1955.

[53] Cf. E. Cohen 1992: 125.

[54] Dem. 49.

[55] Dem. 49.5, 42.

[56] Dem. 49.33, 42. He states that at the arbitration he presented as evidence both the books and the testimony of the bank clerks (Dem. 49.44). It is notable that the speaker has both the records and witness testimony at his disposal, but chose to use only the latter, presumably because he believed the jury would find this approach more compelling. Because the water-clock was stopped for the reading of evidence, time was not a factor in this decision.

[57] Dem. 49.42–43. A word should perhaps be said regarding a famous passage in Isocrates *Trapeziticus* (17.2):

> For contracts with bankers are made without witnesses, and it is necessary for those who are wronged to take on risk in pursuing a claim against men of this kind, who have many friends and manage a lot of money, and are thought to be trustworthy because of their job.
> Nevertheless, under these circumstances I think that I will make it clear to everyone that Pasion [the banker] has defrauded me of money.

Thomas draws on recent work on the relationship between literacy and orality to explain the mixture of oral and written proof in the Athenian popular courts. Until recently it was widely thought that the introduction of literacy to a society brought immediate and comprehensive change marked by rapid growth in rational modes of discourse.[58] Scholars working in a number of periods and geographical areas have challenged this view, pointing out that the transition from orality to widespread literacy is often gradual, with considerable overlap of the spoken and the written.[59] Adopting this approach, Thomas interprets the persistent use of oral proof in non-maritime popular court cases despite the presence of written contracts as evidence of the gradual emergence of a "document-minded" attitude in classical Athens.[60]

The *dikê emporikê* procedure, however, constitutes an important exception to the persistence of oral proof in the Athenian lawcourts. By the mid-fourth century written contracts were a privileged form of proof, and indeed were required, in maritime suits. In this small class of cases, the Athenians appear to have become "document-minded" quite quickly. Scholars generally explain the *dikê emporikê* procedure's unique written contract requirement by arguing that maritime loans were too complex or involved sums that were too significant for oral agreements,[61] and that professional traders were able to become accustomed to using contracts more quickly than ordinary citizens.[62] Although these factors certainly contributed to the development of the written contract requirement, they cannot entirely

At first glance, this passage appears to suggest that banking transactions were generally concluded without witnesses and therefore that banking records were considered definitive evidence in court. In fact, the speaker is explaining his own lack of witnesses to the transaction at issue. This passage suggests that men dealing with bankers generally did not bring their own witnesses, which reveals little about the value accorded *grammata* because it is the banker, rather than his clients, who have access to the records and can bring them into court. (The absence of written receipts is one of the peculiarities of Athenian business practice (Dem. 33.12; 34.30; 48.46; Pringsheim 1950:287–297; E. Cohen 1992: 119.). We have seen that *Against Timotheus* suggests that when bankers press a claim based on the records, they rely on witnesses as much as on the written records.

[58] E.g. Havelock 1982; Goody 1986.

[59] Clanchy (1993) for example, traces the gradual adoption of a written record in medieval English law and records examples of the combination of oral and written proof. He argues that despite a familiarity with religious writing, the transition to a written administrative system took over a century.

[60] Thomas 1989:34–60.

[61] E.g., Jones 1977: 219.

[62] E.g., Finley 1985: 22. Indeed, writing appears to have been associated with trade from a very early period. It is not surprising that interaction with those outside one's trusted community would lead to more precise and formal business relationships, with commitments spelled out in written form.

explain the distinctiveness of the maritime procedures.[63] We meet complex oral agreements in our surviving non-maritime speeches,[64] and many mortgages on land did not merit a written contract despite the high value of the transaction.[65] It is particularly curious that there was no similar preference for writing in two types of suit that also involved complex commercial transactions between experienced businessmen: suits for capital loaned for the establishment of a business in the agora,[66] and mining suits (*dikai metallikai*). Both these procedures were among the "monthly suits" (*dikai emmênoi*) and thus experienced procedural changes at around the same time the written contract requirement was introduced in *dikai emporikai*.[67] One example of each type of procedure survives, and there is no hint of a preference for or requirement of written proof in either speech.[68]

[63] The suggestion that writing was part of a professional's repertory raises the difficult question of the extent of literacy among Athenians in this period. There is some indication that functional literacy extended well beyond a small class of professional merchants. For example, written wills were common, and in the early fourth century litigants were required to present written pleadings and witness depositions in written form (Calhoun 1919a). For an argument that "most of those who might be engaged in legal affairs could probably read well enough to serve their needs," see Gagarin (forthcoming); cf. W. Harris 1989:65–115. For a general discussion of literacy in classical Athens, see Thomas 1992. Although it is hardly surprising that there was no general requirement for written contracts, we might have expected a preference for written over oral contracts and other forms of proof.

[64] E.g., Dem. 45.

[65] Our primary source for secured transactions are the fourth-century *horoi*, large "mortgage-stones" placed on property indicating that the land was legally encumbered. The *horoi* served to warn potential buyers or creditors, but were not themselves contracts, because they generally do not even name the debtor. Of the 157 surviving stones, only fifteen refer to written contracts recording the transaction (Finley 1985; Millett 1982; Todd 1993:252–255).

[66] Arist. *Ath. Pol.* 52.2.

[67] Banking cases (*dikai trapezitikai*), were also included among the *dikai emmênoi* (Arist. *Ath. Pol.* 52.2) Our surviving *dikai trapezitikai* (e.g., Isoc. 17) predate the reform of the banking suits into a monthly procedure, making it impossible to know whether these suits included a written contract requirement. I am inclined to think that they did not, based on the differences in argumentation between cases involving banks and other commercial suits, on the one hand, and *dikai emporikai* on the other.

[68] In both cases – Demosthenes 36 and 37 – the speaker argues that his opponent's suit against him is illegal in part because he has been released from all claims. If these suits required a written agreement, we would expect that the speakers would take the argument one step further by maintaining that the suit was improperly brought because no agreement exists between the parties. Indeed, this is precisely the argument made by the speaker in Demosthenes 33, a *dikê emporikê* in which the speaker similarly brings a *paragraphê* on the ground that he has been released from all claims (Dem. 33.2–3). Demosthenes 36 offers little insight into the nature of the procedure used, but the speaker in Demosthenes 37.35–36 does briefly discuss the law defining the scope of *dikai metallikai*. The speaker argues that *dikai metallikai* were limited to physical encroachment or interference with another's workings in the mine and did not apply to loans concerning mining contracts. If this is an accurate depiction of the jurisdiction of

The following sections present the argument that the difference in the approach to written proof in maritime and non-maritime cases is due in part to the value placed on jury discretion and flexible justice in non-maritime popular court cases. The written contract requirement in *dikai emporikai* tended to focus the dispute on the terms of the written agreement and to discourage extra-legal argumentation. This effect was valuable in the context of maritime suits designed to attract foreigners and facilitate trade. A similar preference for written proof in the ordinary popular courts would, however, hinder the jury's ability to take into account the particular circumstances of each case in reaching their decision.

THE WRITTEN CONTRACT REQUIREMENT AND ARGUMENTATION IN MARITIME CASES

One would expect that the requirement of (or even a strong preference for) written proof would tend to focus the dispute on the terms of the written agreement. This narrow focus on the written contract would facilitate business deals by increasing the predictability of verdicts, but would also hamper the jury's ability to take into account a wide range of factors in reaching its decision.[69] Our five surviving *dikai emporikai* bear out this prediction: one of the most distinctive features of these speeches is the importance of the terms of the agreement to the speakers' arguments.[70] In the three maritime cases in which the speaker is not challenging the existence of a contract, the written contract is recited in full within the first ten sections of the speech.[71] It has been pointed out that of the 113 references to written contracts in the entire Demosthenic corpus, 100 occur in these three

mining suits, it is not at all surprising that there is no suggestion of a written contract requirement in this speech. However, the speaker acknowledges that the law also applies "if someone does wrong in other ways related to the mines" (Dem. 37.36). Carey and Reid (1985:144) point out that this statement suggests that the law had a clause including all wrongs concerning the mines within the purview of the *dikai metallikai*.

[69] For a different, but related, argument that the limited use of writing in litigation was intricately connected with the amateurism of Greek legal systems, see Gagarin (forthcoming). Gagarin argues that the extensive use of writing in the Roman legal process was critical to the development of the legal profession and a more "technical" body of law. Whereas Gagarin contends that the unusual approach to writing in the legal process extends beyond Athens to other Greek *poleis*, this chapter presents an explanation for the predominantly oral nature of litigation that is rooted in the specific concerns of the Athenian democracy.

[70] Carey & Reid 1985: 200n.50; Christ 1998b:220–221; D. Cohen 2003:94–96.

[71] Dem. 34.7; 35.10; 56.6.

speeches alone.[72] Demosthenes *Against Lacritus* is most striking in this regard. The speaker discusses the contract in painstaking detail, "addressing in turn each of the provisions written in the contract,"[73] and then has the entire agreement read out a second time.[74]

The contract in Demothenes *Against Dionysodorus* did not address the precise issue in dispute. The contract provided that the lender bear the loss if the ship was lost at sea, and that the borrowers pay a penalty if they did not return with their cargo to Athens. The contract made no provision for another contingency – rather than total loss of the ship, damage severe enough to preclude the return of the ship and require that her cargo therefore be sold outside Athens. This is what the defendant claimed to have happened, if we can trust the prosecution's account.[75] Although the contract is silent on the crucial question of the rights of the parties in this contingency, the speaker quotes from the written contract four times and repeatedly refers the jurors to the terms of the agreement as the proper guide to their decision.[76]

It is not only speakers who are pressing their contractual claims who emphasize that the terms of the written contract are decisive in maritime suits. The speaker in Demosthenes *Against Apaturius*, the defendant in the original contract action, refers to a written contract as "the exact agreement," (*akribês*)[77] and notes that contract disputes are to be resolved by reference to the written document:

> All men, whenever they make written contracts with one another, after
> sealing the agreement they deposit it with those whom they trust, for this
> reason, that if they disagree about something, it would be possible for them
> to go to the written contract and from this obtain the means of resolving
> their disagreement.[78]

In contrast to the importance of the contractual terms in *dikê emporikê* suits, speakers in other popular court suits involving written contracts rarely dwell on the specifics of the legal instrument or suggest that jurors should look, as modern lawyers put it, only within the "four corners of the contract."

---

[72] Carey & Reid 1985: 200 n.50. Christ (1998b:220–221) and D. Cohen (2003:94–96) also note the speakers' emphasis on the written contract in these cases.

[73] Dem. 35.17.

[74] Dem. 35.37.

[75] Dem. 56.35.

[76] Dem. 56.6, 36, 38.

[77] Dem. 33.36.

[78] Dem. 33.36.

The most famous contract case from classical Athens is Hyperides *Against Athenogenes*. The speaker fell in love with a slave boy who belonged to Athenogenes and offered to buy the boy's freedom. Athenogenes agreed to sell the boy, his brother, and his father to the speaker, and included in the deal the perfume business that the boy's father Midas had managed for Athenogenes. By purchasing the slaves and their shop rather than simply buying their freedom, the speaker agreed to take responsibility for their debts. Athenogenes assured the speaker that the assets of the perfume shop would easily cover any liabilities. He read aloud a contract he had prepared in advance, but the speaker, intent on securing access to the boy, did not pay close attention and did not inspect the document before concluding the transaction. It did not take long for creditors to appear and demand a total of about five talents. The speaker then examined the agreement for the first time and noticed that in addition to a short list of insignificant debts the contract included a catch-all clause: "and anything Midas owes to some other man."[79] It appears that the Athenians had no written law explicitly voiding a contract that was unconscionable, fraudulent, or even illegal; indeed, it appears that a contract provision that nothing, including laws, will have greater effect than the agreement was, at least formally, enforceable.[80] Nevertheless, the speaker in this non-maritime suit focuses solely on the circumstances surrounding the deal and argues that the jurors should ignore the contract because it is unjust (*mê dikaia*).[81] Although some scholars view this case as strong evidence of the

---

[79] Hyp. 3.10.

[80] The contract in Dem. 35.10–13 (a *dikê emporikê*) includes the provision, "concerning these issues nothing can override the contract." The speaker elaborates on this clause later in the speech, but does not suggest that such a clause was controversial or unusual:

> The contract does not allow anything to override its written terms, nor does it allow anyone to propose a law or decree or any other thing that is contrary to the contract's terms . . . Dem. 35.39.

Indeed, the speaker in Demosthenes 48 (discussed later in the chapter) attempts to enforce an agreement to commit a crime. Of course, popular court juries concerned with reaching a fair result in light of the particular circumstances of the case were unlikely to find such legalistic arguments persuasive, and it is not surprising that the speaker in Demosthenes 48 does not anchor his case on the contract terms alone.

[81] Hyp. 3.13. Adducing four laws relating to misrepresentation, mistake, and legal capacity in other contexts, the speaker constructs an ingenious argument that unjust contracts should not be binding (Hyp. 3.13–17). Modern scholars dispute whether this speech should be seen as an example of arguments based on equity or creative legal reasoning. Compare Scafuro (1997:61) and Christ (1998b:221–223) with Johnstone (1999:28ff) and E. Harris (2000:48–54). For our purposes, it is important only that the speaker does not focus on the terms of agreement and makes no effort to make a contractual argument.

willingness of Athenian popular jurors to overlook the terms of a written contract in the interests of fairness,[82] we must be careful not to make too much of this case: with the terms of the contract arrayed clearly against him, the speaker may have had little choice but to attack the contract itself.

Our other surviving non-maritime contract case,[83] Demosthenes 48 *Against Olympiodorus*, is biased in the other direction: the speaker is suing his partner in crime for breach of contract[84] for tricking him out of his share, and one would expect that the plaintiff would focus on the terms of the agreement in the absence of equitable sources of support for his claim. The speaker, Callistratus, and his brother-in-law, Olympiodorus, made a written contract to divide the estate belonging to Comon, a mutual relative, evenly between them and to exclude all other claimants. After the two managed to have the estate awarded to Olympiodorus by colluding in various misrepresentations to the court, Olympiodorus refused to give Callistratus half of the estate in accordance with their agreement. Predictably, Callistratus emphasizes that his opponent has breached their agreement, and he states that he would have had the contract itself read out in court, but that Olympiodorus prevented him from getting his hands on the document.[85] Callistratus does not rest his claim solely on the terms of the contract, however, but also includes a number of arguments rooted in fairness and cooperative values. He stresses that he offered Olympiodorus a fair settlement to avoid litigation but was rebuffed,[86] and he requests in the first instance not the enforcement of the contract as written but a compromise ruling:

> I beg you, gentlemen of the jury, once you have listened to both of us and examined for yourselves what happened, that you send us away, best of all reconciled to one another, and thus that you serve as benefactors to both of

---

[82] E.g., Christ 1998b:221–223. Christ compares this speech to the strongly contractual arguments in *dikai emporikai*.

[83] Many cases in the corpus include a contractual claim along with other legal charges. Only Hyperides 3 and Demosthenes 48 involve simply a contract action, making it possible to compare the extent to which the speakers in these cases focus on the contract with speeches delivered in *dikai emporikai*.

[84] The suit was technically a *dikē blabēs*, "an action for damage." There appears to have been no distinctive procedure for a breach of contract action (Todd 1993: 266).

[85] Dem. 48.9, 48. Callistratus challenged Olympiodorus to go with him to retrieve the contract from the man with whom they had deposited it and make copies to put into the sealed jar containing evidence for the trial, but he refused. Callistratus challenges his opponent to have the contract read out in court and urges the jurors to permit this (Dem. 48.51).

[86] Dem. 48.4.

us. But if you do not accomplish this, from the remaining options I beg that you place your vote for the man who makes just arguments.[87]

In addition to emphasizing his moderation and willingness to compromise to end the conflict, Callistratus points out that he has respected the obligations of *philia*. He notes that he arranged for Comon's burial, a fact often cited by contestants in inheritance cases to show their personal connection to the deceased and right to a share of the estate.[88] Finally, Callistratus reports that Olympiodorus is unmarried and has been wasting all his money on his mistress, a former slave, whereas Callistratus has a wife and daughter to support:

> Are not they [my wife and daughter] being wronged and suffering terribly
> when they see the courtesan of this man beyond decent limits, wearing many
> pieces of gold jewelry, and beautiful clothing, making showy excursions, and
> using what belongs to us to lord it over everyone, while they themselves [my
> wife and daughter] are in all these things in an impoverished state? Surely
> these women are being wronged even more than I am?[89]

Thus, although the plaintiff in Demosthenes 48 does mention the contract with his opponent several times, he does not confine his arguments to the terms of the agreement or suggest, as speakers in *dikai emporikai* do, that the contract should be the sole guide to the jurors' decision.

This comparison of two non-maritime speeches with the *dikai emporikai* suggests, but does not prove, that litigants in maritime suits were more likely to focus on arguments based on the written agreement than speakers in ordinary non-maritime cases. Wills are legal instruments similar to contracts in many ways, and an examination of Athenian litigants' approach to written wills may offer additional comparative material. Because wills were thought to be highly susceptible to forgery and fraud,[90] one might expect arguments in inheritance cases to center on the veracity and contents of the will. Unlike the speaker in the

---

[87] Dem. 48.3.

[88] Dem. 48.6.

[89] Dem. 48.55. Callistratus also argues that Olympiodorus has gone mad and is not responsible for his actions because he is under the influence of this mistress (Dem. 48.56). He cites a law of Solon providing that all acts done under the influence of a woman were void, though it is unclear how this law helped his case (Dem. 48.56–57).

[90] E.g., Is. 7.2; Arist. [*Pr.*] 29.3.

contract case *Against Athenogenes,* a litigant faced with a will containing unfavorable terms could always attempt to overturn it by alleging forgery rather than being forced to resort to more general arguments of fairness and justice unrelated to the legal instrument in question. It has been demonstrated, however, that litigants in inheritance cases also regularly appeal to a variety of arguments that are not focused on the will being disputed: they argue that they have a better claim to the estate than their opponent because they were closer in affection to the deceased, performed his burial rites, and are more likely to use any wealth awarded by the court to perform public services.[91] Even speakers defending a will or adoption from challenge utilize such extra-legal positions, arguing, for example, that by challenging the will their opponent will deprive the dead man of an heir and cause his house to become extinct.[92] Indeed, scholars have often noted that our surviving inheritance speeches seem to indicate that jurors were as concerned with distributing the property fairly as with interpreting the will in question.[93]

The foregoing survey of argumentation in maritime and ordinary popular court suits indicates that litigants in *dikai emporikai* appear to have focused their arguments on the terms of the contract, whereas speakers in non-maritime cases involving written contracts or wills include a more contextualized account, basing their claims on what they perceive to be the fair result as well as the proper contractual interpretation. It is impossible to say whether the written contract requirement in *dikai emporikai* is the cause or effect of this difference in approach in these two types of case, but it seems clear that a similar preference for written proof and narrow focus on the terms of an agreement in non-maritime cases would have detracted from the popular court jurors' ability to consider broader issues of fairness as well as arguments based on the contract or will at issue in reaching their verdicts. The value placed on a flexible and contextualized approach to justice may have made Athenian jurors reluctant to embrace written forms of proof in ordinary non-maritime cases.

[91] E.g., Is. 1.4,17,19,20,30,33,37,42; 4.19; 5.36–38; 41–43; 6.60–61; 9.4, 27–32. All of these cases involve a written will. For discussion, see Hardcastle 1980.

[92] Is. 2.1,10–14,22–27; Dem. 43.68; 44.2,11,43; Hardcastle 1980:14–15.

[93] E.g., Hardcastle 1980; D. Cohen 1995:171–173; Christ 1998b:222–223. For an argument that equity argumentation in Isaeus is a response to obscurities and gaps in the inheritance laws rather than an attempt to appeal to fairness, see Lawless 1991:110–135.

RELEVANCE AND ARGUMENTATION IN MARITIME SUITS

The unusual emphasis on the written contract in *dikai emporikai* is but one of the distinctive features of argumentation in this class of cases. It is impossible to draw firm conclusions on the basis of only five surviving maritime cases, but a comparison of these cases with similar commercial but non-maritime suits suggests that there may have been important differences between the mode of argument in these two types of case. To be sure, litigants in maritime cases, just as other law court speakers, use narrative and rhetoric to create a persuasive case.[94] However, these speeches include significantly fewer appeals to extra-legal argumentation, such as references to the character and social standing of the litigants than non-maritime speeches. Law court speakers appear to have had a notion of a distinct standard of relevance in *dikai emporikai*, though of course this "standard" was entirely informal, customary, and fluid, unlike the relevancy rule of the homicide courts.

We have seen that our surviving maritime speeches tend to focus narrowly on the contractual dispute at issue and to avoid more contextualized accounts of the transaction and arguments based on fairness and equity. One might expect that the presence of foreigners, metics, and perhaps even slaves, in addition to citizens in *dikai emporikai* would lead to a plethora of arguments in which the litigant of more favored status would exploit his superior social standing. With few exceptions, however, the social standing, character, services, and reputation of the litigants in business dealings play no role in the arguments in the maritime suits. Indeed, in several cases we are unsure of the legal status of the individuals involved in the transaction.

The one notable exception is Demosthenes *Against Lacritus*. The speaker, an Athenian citizen named Androcles, slanders his opponents because they are from Phaselis, a town well known, the speaker tells us, for producing the most wicked and dishonest men.[95] Androcles contends that Phaselites are prone to dirty tricks and sophisms (*sophismata*) both in the market and in the courtroom,[96] and calls

---

[94] For example, factual issues are often important in *dikai emporikai* (e.g., did the boat sink from natural causes, or was it the victim of foul play?), and speakers in maritime suits tend to do a particularly good job of presenting a coherent, plausible, and detailed account of their version of the facts.

[95] Dem. 35.1–2; 25–26.

[96] Dem. 35.2.

Lacritus a sophist, noting on two different occasions in the speech that he is a student of the rhetorician Isocrates.[97] Despite these vicious attacks on the character of his opponents, Androcles does not directly argue that this evidence should determine the jurors' votes; indeed, we have seen that the bulk of this speech is devoted to a close reading of the contract, which is twice read out in full in the course of the oration. Nevertheless, this speech is a striking exception to the general absence of information and argument based on reputation and character in the four other surviving *dikai emporikai*. A narrowed sense of relevance in *dikai emporikai* is also suggested by the complete absence of appeals to the jurors' pity, a well-known *topos* in our non-maritime cases.

Speakers in *dikai emporikai* do appeal to broader policy considerations with respect to one topic: the importance of insuring Athens' grain supply. In three of our five maritime cases, speakers argue that their opponents are complicit in a violation of Athens' protective legislation regarding the transport of grain.[98] In two of these cases, the speaker notes that his opponent denied grain to Athens in a time of shortage, in one case going so far as to accuse his opponent of being involved in a grain price-fixing scheme masterminded by the former ruler of Egypt.[99] It is important to note that when speakers refer to their opponents' failure to supply grain to Athens, they do not argue that the jurors should vote in their favor for this reason. In these cases, following the terms of the agreement is consistent with enforcement of the protective legislation, and it is the former rather than the latter argument that predominates in the speeches. Each of the speakers in these three *dikai emporikai* appears to adopt a long-term view, arguing that Athens' economic health and particularly her grain supply depend on the ability of the courts to enforce maritime contracts as written to encourage lending and facilitate trade. For example, the speaker in Demosthenes *Against Dionysodorus* emphasizes that predictable verdicts according to the terms of the contract are good for business.[100] In a similar vein, the speaker in Demosthenes *Against Lacritus*

[97] Dem. 35.15, 40. The speaker in Demosthenes 32.31–32 anticipates a similar attack by his opponent based on his relation to the orator Demosthenes.

[98] Dem. 34.36; 35.50–53; 56.3–4, 11–12. Non-residents, who were not subject to the laws' restrictions, could nevertheless be involved in a violation by taking a loan from a resident for a voyage and then failing to ship grain to Athens as agreed. For such a case, see Dem. 56.11–12.

[99] Dem. 34.36; 56.7–9. The speaker in Demosthenes 34.38–39 notes that he provided grain to Athens at fair prices, even in times of shortage.

[100] Dem. 56.48.

notes that when his opponent "renders shipping contracts invalid and dissolves them,"[101] he wrongs the people as well as the speaker. This sentiment is echoed by the speaker in Demosthenes *Against Phormio*, who argues that it is in the city's interest to protect lenders by holding borrowers to their contracts. He points out that lenders, not borrowers, put up the capital necessary for trade and states that "neither ship nor shipowner nor passenger is able to put out to sea, if the part played by those who lend is taken away."[102]

This distinctive mode of argumentation in maritime cases, in which the character of the litigants and issues of fairness in light of the specific context of the transaction are downplayed in favor of the terms of the written agreement and the general principle that contracts should be binding, can be usefully compared to other commercial, but non-maritime cases. Demosthenes *For Phormio* and Demosthenes *Against Pantaenetus* are promising candidates for comparison: these cases are also speeches in the Demosthenic corpus dating from sometime in the middle of the fourth century; they involve commercial transactions between litigants who are seasoned and successful businessmen, but not political figures; and, like four of our five *dikai emporikai*, they are part of *paragraphê* actions.

Although the subject matter in *For Phormio* and *Against Pantaenetus* – the leasing arrangement of a banking business and a series of transactions involving mining property – is similar to that of maritime suits, the speeches are not as narrowly focused on the business transactions at issue. The speaker in *For Phormio*, for example, disparages Apollodorus' performance of liturgies and ridicules his extravagant habits,[103] defends Phormio's career,[104] makes a standard appeal to win the juror's pity,[105] and argues that it is to the jurors' advantage to award the money to Phormio.[106] In *Against Pantaenetus* Nicobulus slanders his opponent's witnesses as foul, impure, most seductive, and most abominable.[107] He includes an extended discussion of his fear that his case will be prejudiced by the jury's dislike of money-lenders like himself, and the jury's disgust at what the speaker confesses are his unpleasant qualities: he apparently walks fast, talks loudly, and goes around with

[101] Dem. 35.54.
[102] Dem. 34.51.
[103] Dem. 36.42, 45, 52, 55–57.
[104] Dem. 36.56.
[105] Dem. 36.59.
[106] Dem. 36.58–59.
[107] Dem. 37.48.

a walking stick.[108] Most striking is the use in these two speeches of witnesses to testify solely to the good character of the speaker or the villainy of his opponent. The speaker in *For Phormio* offers testimony both of Phormio's good character, uprightness, and generosity,[109] and of the baseness of Apollodorus.[110] Nicobulus also presents character witnesses in *Against Pantaenetus*: he states, "Please read out the witness testimony regarding what sort of person I am toward men who lend money on bond and toward those who are in need."[111] Although speakers in our surviving popular court cases often boast of their character and slander their opponents, the use of character witnesses *stricto sensu* as in these two cases is quite rare. The emphasis of the litigants in both these cases on their reputation for fair business practices contrasts starkly with the narrow focus on the terms of the written contract typical in *dikai emporikai*.

Christ has pointed out a similar difference between cases involving banking transactions and the *dikai emporikai*: whereas litigants in banking suits present their cases in terms of breaches of intimate relationships of *philia* between the parties, speakers in maritime cases emphasize a breach of contract.[112] Thus in non-maritime commercial cases, enforcing the cooperative values of fair dealing and respect for *philia* appears to have been paramount, in contrast to the more formal approach used in *dikai emporikai*.

The narrower notion of relevance in *dikai emporikai* did not extend to what we might term procedural technicalities. In Demosthenes *Against Apaturius*, for example, the statute of limitations has run, but the speaker uses this information

---

[108] Dem. 37.52.

[109] Dem 36.55.

[110] Dem. 36.55–56:

> Moreover after having heard the evidence of these witnesses you will know the character of each of these men [Apollodorus and Phormio].

WITNESS TESTIMONY

Now come take those concerning the baseness of Apollodorus.

WITNESS TESTIMONY

Is this man here [Phormio] of the same sort? Consider. Read aloud.

WITNESS TESTIMONY

Read also in how many ways this man has been of service to the city.

[111] Dem. 37.54.

[112] Christ (1998b:180–91) discusses how litigants convert banker-client disputes into questions of *philia* in Isocrates 17, Demosthenes 49, and Demosthenes 37.

only as circumstantial evidence to support his factual claim that he was not a surety, and emphasizes that he is not arguing that the suit is barred by the statute of limitations.[113] Four of the five surviving maritime suits are part of *paragraphê* actions, counter-suits in which the defendant argues that the plaintiff is bringing an illegal procedure. We have seen that speeches in *paragraphai* actions do not concentrate exclusively on the legal issues of the counter-suit but include detailed discussions of the original dispute, and the maritime *paragraphai* are no exception. To cite two examples, all but three sections of Demosthenes *Against Lacritus* relate to the underlying contract action rather than to the narrower question at issue in the *paragraphê*,[114] and the speaker in Demosthenes *Against Zenothemis* notes his resolve to discuss more than the counter-suit: "now from the same speech you will learn that this suit is not admissible, and you will also see the whole treachery and evil of this man here."[115] It seems that even the desire for predictability in judicial decisions regarding commercial matters could not trump the Athenian aversion to excessive legalism and procedural technicalities.

WHY A DIFFERENT NOTION OF RELEVANCE IN MARITIME SUITS?

We have seen that speeches in *dikai emporikai* seem to be more focused on the contractual issue in dispute and less likely to appeal to evidence regarding the character and social standing of the litigants than similar non-maritime commercial cases, where a man's reputation for fair business practices and other issues beyond the specific terms of any written agreement, such as fairness and equity, become relevant to the jurors' decision. It seems likely that the specific aim of the *dikê emporikê* – to facilitate trade by providing a predictable procedure and attracting foreign merchants – accounts for the distinctive mode of argumentation evinced

---

[113] Dem. 33.27:

> Please take the law, which directs that sureties will be valid for one year. I do not rely heavily on the law [i.e., the statute of limitations] by arguing that I do not have to pay the penalty if I did act as a surety, but rather I am saying that the law serves as a witness that I did not act as a surety, as does this man himself, for in that case he would have initiated a suit against me as a surety within the time limit set forth in the law.

[114] The crucial question for purposes of the *paragraphê* – whether Lacritus is Artemon's heir – is addressed only in sections 3, 4, and 44. For discussion, see Isager & Hansen 1975:172–173.

[115] Dem. 32.2.

in these suits. The formalism of the maritime procedures was probably an accommodation to the specific needs of commercial suits, not an improvement on the popular court procedures. Though the *dikai emporikai* have more in common with modern courts, the Athenians may well have viewed the more "legal" approach in maritime cases as affording a judicial process inferior to the contextualized format of the popular courts, or at least inappropriate to the issues raised in the popular courts.

The policy to encourage lending and to facilitate trade, especially in grain, by offering a predictable procedure that focused on the enforcement of contracts as written made the wide-ranging discretion wielded by juries in non-maritime suits counter-productive in the context of maritime cases.[116] A focus on the terms of the written contract reduced the uncertainty associated with the ad hoc approach taken in the Athenian popular courts and gave lenders and traders confidence that they would be able to enforce their contracts in court if necessary. The speaker in Demosthenes *Against Dionysodorus* makes precisely this argument when urging the jurors to strictly enforce the maritime contract in his suit:

> For if you think that contracts and agreements made between men should
> be enforced, and you will show no forbearance toward those who break
> them, then those men who lend their own money will do so more readily
> and as a result your market will flourish ... For who will want to risk his
> money, when he sees written contracts having no effect, and arguments of
> this sort [i.e. contrary to the terms of the agreement] winning the day, and
> the accusations of criminals being placed before justice?[117]

This reassurance may have been particularly important in the maritime trade because it often involved doing business with men outside one's close-knit community, including foreigners whose reputation might not be well-known, who might not be repeat players, and who might not be easily influenced by the informal means of the marketplace.[118] Merchants dealing with strangers would be less trusting, and therefore more likely to want well-defined commitments spelled out in written contracts and enforced in a more formal procedure. Strict enforcement

---

[116] For speakers' statements regarding the importance of encouraging lending and facilitating trade by strictly enforcing written agreements, see Dem. 34.51; 35.54; 56.48–50.

[117] Dem. 56.48–50.

[118] For a discussion of how close-knit communities can order their affairs effectively "without law" by reliance on trust and informal control over anti-social behavior, see Ellickson 1991:40–123.

of contracts is an easy way to reduce legal uncertainty in a society without precise legal rules or legal experts because it does not involve the creation of a complex substantive law but permits the contracting parties to create their own law for each deal.

The narrower notion of relevance employed in *dikai emporikai* was also vital to attracting the foreign merchants who dominated maritime trade to Athens.[119] Foreigners would be at a distinct disadvantage in the ordinary Athenian popular courts, where they would be subject to judgment based on unwritten Athenian norms and values that they might not fully understand, let alone share. Few transient foreign merchants would have ready access to the witnesses necessary to present a contextualized account of their character, reputation, and manner of doing business. Even those who could present such a case might not be sanguine about their chances of prevailing in an Athenian court against an Athenian citizen who could point to military service and other hallmarks of good character familiar to popular court juries. The *dikē emporikē* procedure, by focusing on the terms of the written contract and discouraging extra-legal information and argumentation, offered foreign merchants the chance to resolve their disputes on a truly equal footing with citizens based on a transparent, straightforward, and non-culturally specific standard: the terms of the written contract agreed to by the parties.

If a more formal, predictable legal procedure facilitated business deals, one might ask why the Athenians employed this approach only in maritime cases and did not adopt it in other business contexts such as banking and ordinary contract cases. We have seen that Athenian jurors valued their ability to enforce informal social norms of fair dealing and good conduct in reaching their verdicts in the popular courts.[120] The adoption of a narrow relevance regime in non-maritime cases would have detracted from the democratic juries' ability to wield their influence on Athenian life. In *dikai emporikai*, on the other hand, the common participation of foreigners may have isolated maritime business activity from the everyday social interactions in which the Athenian juror took great interest.[121] Although citizens played an active role in maritime trade, the port of the Peiraeus was thought of as "a world apart" from city life, and commercial activity was always

---

[119] Reed 2003:27–33.

[120] For discussion, see Chapter 3.

[121] The locus classicus for the (idealized) quality of these interactions is the *epitaphios* in Thucydides (2.37.2–3).

considered different and separate from more respected economic pursuits.[122] In this sphere, Athenian jurors probably saw less value in enforcing fair play and insuring a just resolution that took account of the particular circumstances of the case. On the other side of the ledger were the considerable economic advantages associated with a more narrow, legal approach in maritime cases. In this one area of law, the costs associated with discretionary justice outweighed the benefits, and steps were taken to narrow the range of evidence considered relevant to the jury in an effort to enhance the predictability of verdicts and thereby facilitate trade.

[122] von Reden 1995; Garland 2001:58–100.

7 CONCLUSIONS

WE SEE IN CLASSICAL ATHENS THE FIRST SUSTAINED, WELL-DOCUMENTED APPROACH
to a perennial problem faced by all organized societies in constructing a legal
system: the tension between adherence to general rules and doing justice in specific cases. Under the democracy, the Athenians experimented with a variety of
responses to this problem. Rather than employ a uniform procedure for all cases,
the Athenians adopted a mixed system, with pockets of legal formalism surrounded by popular courts that granted juries a wide degree of discretion. For the
majority of cases, the Athenians chose what, by modern standards, is a remarkably
flexible approach to legal decision making. Greater formalism in homicide and
maritime cases is likely to have promoted the stability of the predominant, and
far less rigid, mode of the popular courts.

In this study, I have argued that the Athenian approach to law was more varied
and complex than has previously been recognized. A more fine-grained description
of the Athenian legal system must take account of not only popular court practice,
but also the more formal, legal approach used in homicide and maritime cases.
The special homicide and maritime procedures suggest that the Athenians could
conceptualize, and to some degree implement, a legal system in which abstract
principles were impartially applied. In popular court cases, by contrast, a much
broader notion of relevance prevailed, as juries made ad hoc determinations based
on the particular circumstances and context of the dispute, including the character
and reputations of the litigants.

These differences cannot be explained as part of an evolution or consistent
development over time toward a rule of law. When the popular court system
was introduced in the early years of the democracy, the legalism of the homicide
courts was available as a potential model. The Athenians opted instead for a
more discretionary system, declining, for example, to adopt a relevancy rule in the
new courts. This conscious choice reflects not only a belief in the importance of
contextual information in reaching a just decision, but also a political commitment
to jury discretion in the new democracy.

At the same time, the Athenians were keenly aware of the drawbacks of the
popular court system. They seem to have worried about verdicts based solely on

175

the character of the parties without any reference to the issue in dispute. The survival, indeed the idealization, of the homicide tribunals and their use of the relevancy rule in the classical period may reflect this anxiety. In addition, discretionary decision making by popular juries made the legal system less consistent and predictable. Athens managed to maintain public order and respect for the legal system despite the climate of legal insecurity, but the lack of predictability imposed significant risks and costs on private transactions. The creation of a special maritime jurisdiction can be seen as an attempt to alleviate the problem of legal uncertainty in one specific area. In these courts, arguments focused on the terms of the contract rather than on the parties, producing more consistent results that fostered commerce and attracted foreign merchants.

The constant negotiation between flexibility and consistency indicates that for the Athenians the primary aim of the courts was to resolve disputes justly, taking into account the circumstances of each case. In this sense, the courts of Athens served "legal" rather than social or political ends. But to say that Athenian courts served legal ends is not to endow them with all the legal powers that modern courts have: Athenian courts resolved the disputes before them, but they could not and did not attempt to speak (as many modern courts do) to whether future disputes should be resolved in the same way. On the contrary, Athenian decisions were entirely ad hoc, and probably did little to assure Athenians that a particular course of conduct was proper. Of course, Athens had norms and mores, and these must have been reflected in, reinforced by, and even influenced by court verdicts. But there was nothing authoritative about a particular decision the way there is in most modern common law jurisdictions. Overall, Athenian courts were backward-looking, a focus that is consonant with Aristotle's definition of judicial rhetoric as judging an action in the past.[1]

The Athenian popular courts also lacked a related power traditionally wielded by modern courts: the power to crystallize society's approval or disapproval of particular conduct. Some legal scholars argue that a key function of the law and of court decisions in particular is to express society's approval or disapproval of behavior.[2] Law probably served such an "expressive" function in Athenian society, but this function must have been attenuated in popular court cases. On the one hand, a popular court jury had the opportunity through its verdict to make a public

---

[1] Arist. *Rhet.* 1.3.
[2] E.g., Sunstein 1996; McAdams 2000; Kahan 1997.

statement about whether the litigants had abided by the community's values of fair dealing or decent conduct in the particular case, regardless of the result suggested by a strict reading of the statute, will, or contract at issue. But because a jury's verdict could turn on any of a number of specific legal or extra-legal factors raised in the case, the jury's ability to express a clear and precise moral statement, and thus to influence the moral and social values of Athenian society, was limited. The trial of Socrates is a good example: although the jury's overall condemnation of Socrates was well known, his precise crime and exactly what the jury thought of him is unclear (and seems to have been unclear even at the time); the guilty verdict may have represented little more than a rejection of Socrates' unorthodox manner of defending himself.

The emphasis on finding a just outcome to a particular case effectively precluded a court system capable of announcing stable rules or clear moral judgments. Why was informal, contextualized dispute resolution so highly valued, despite its costs? Part of the answer must be that although the disadvantages associated with discretionary justice – the risk of prejudice, the absence of predictability – were the same as they are today, the potential effect of these shortcomings was much less severe in classical Athens than they would be today. Because the Athenian citizen body was ethnically, socially, religiously, and ideologically (if not economically) far more homogenous than contemporary societies, broad jury discretion must have been more predictable than it would be today. In addition, we have seen that a variety of informal mechanisms rooted in the cohesiveness of Athenian society ensured that public order was maintained despite the law's inability to provide reliable guidance for future behavior.

Then there is the question of administrative costs: case-by-case decision making carried out by juries numbering in the hundreds is an extremely inefficient way to resolve disputes.[3] However, Athens' political culture helps to explain why high cost was not much of an issue. For the Athenians, popular court cases gave average citizens an opportunity to participate in the governance of their city. In fact, Athenians were sometimes buried with their juror's ticket (*pinakion*), indicating their pride at performing jury service.[4] In the Athenian view, jury trials were

---

[3] Many modern evaluations of the choice between predictable rules and flexible standards in constructing legal directives analyze the relative costs of rulemaking and ex post discretionary decisions (Kaplow 1992; Posner 1997).

[4] Kroll 1972.

important mechanisms of democratic participation, not costly procedures to be limited as much as possible.

In addition, ex post jury decision making may have been more efficient than detailed rule making. Passing a law or, in the fourth century, a decree, involved a meeting of the popular Assembly, where any male citizen was permitted to propose a rule or give a speech regarding the proposal under discussion. This was cumbersome. Where enhanced certainty and predictability were needed to attract foreign traders in maritime suits, the Athenians avoided the costs of rulemaking entirely by strictly enforcing the terms agreed to by the parties rather than creating substantive contractual rules. The unusual balance between formality and certainty on the one hand and flexibility and fairness on the other was thus well suited to the political and social context of classical Athens.

But there must be more to it than that. The discretionary approach benefited the poor citizen males who formed the dominant political constituency of the democracy. The judicial system placed all litigants, the rich included, squarely in the power of the predominantly poor jurors who enjoyed the right to reach verdicts by whatever reasoning they wished to apply. In the popular courts, the poor had the opportunity to express their notions of good and bad behavior, and thereby in a general way influence the ethical atmosphere of the city. The informality of legal procedures and broad notions of relevance gave the poor access to legal remedies, and the forensic rhetoric appropriate to contexualization allowed room for uneducated men to "tell their story" in a more-or-less natural way. Indeed, although no direct expression of the poor man's point of view survives, one treatise written by a man with oligarchic sympathies suggests that the aspects of the democracy that he detests, including the judicial system, were rationally seen by the poor and the masses (*hoi penêtes kai ho dêmos*[5]) as serving their interests.[6]

This system is nothing the rich would have created had they been given complete freedom of choice. In the last decade of the sixth century, Cleisthenes, in the words of the *Constitution of the Athenians*, formed a political connection with (literally "brought over") the *dêmos* and effectively ended the monopoly of leading families

---

[5] The term *dêmos* can mean either the population as a whole (*populus*) or the poor (*plebs*). On the ambiguity of the term, see Rhodes 1993:88.

[6] [Xen.] *Ath. Pol.* 1.1, 13. The *Constitution of the Athenians* is a prose piece perhaps written sometime around 425 B.C. that seeks to explain the success of the Athenian democracy. Originally incorrectly ascribed to the fourth-century historian Xenophon, scholars generally refer to the author as the "Old Oligarch," a name doubtless linked to the author's clear antidemocratic sentiment.

in Athenian politics.[7] The rich could no longer compete successfully against each other without making at least some gesture to the ordinary Athenians assembled in the city's legislative and judicial bodies. Regrettably, we have only a sparse record of trials conducted between the reforms of Cleisthenes and the earliest years of recorded logographic activity, starting in about 430, but it must have been within this period that the popular court procedures as we know them took shape to accommodate the newly acquired power of lower class citizens.[8]

The most important factor in the adoption of a discretionary judicial system was Athens' political structure. As a direct, participatory democracy, Athens rarely placed men with expertise in official positions, preferring to rely on ordinary citizens selected by lot. Whenever possible, important decisions – including such specific tactical matters as the number of ships to send on a military expedition – were made by the citizen body rather than entrusted to individuals. In the legal sphere, the preference for amateurism and popular decision making meant that legal decisions were left entirely to the popular court juries. Magistrates exercised little power in dismissing cases on legal grounds at preliminary stages, and there was no equivalent of the modern judge to influence the arguments of the parties and to instruct the jurors about the laws and how to reach their verdict. We have seen that laypersons naturally tend to think about social interaction in the form of a story that includes the broad social context, and find the restriction of evidence demanded by formal legal reasoning counterintuitive. It is not surprising that amateur Athenian jurors embraced contextual information and argumentation as relevant and even vital to their task. Moreover, the commitment to popular decision making dictated that juries be given maximum discretion in reaching their decisions. After all, it was not only through the Assembly but also through the popular courts that the people ruled Athens. The justice they dispensed there was popular, democratic, and uniquely Athenian.

[7] Arist. *Ath. Pol.* 20.1.
[8] Boegehold (1995:21–22) assigns a date of not long after 460 B.C.E.

BIBLIOGRAPHY

Adeleye, G. (1983) "The Purpose of the Dokimasia" *Greek, Roman and Byzantine Studies* 24: 295–306

Adkins, A. W. H. (1975) *Merit and Responsibility: A Study in Greek Values*, Chicago

Adkins, A. W. H. (1972) *Moral Values and Political Behaviour in Ancient Greece: from Homer to the End of the Fifth Century*, New York

Alfieri, A. V. (1991) "Reconstructive Poverty Law Practice: Learning Lessons of Client Narratives," *Yale Law Journal* 100: 2107–2147

Allen, D. S. (2000) *The World of Prometheus: The Politics of Punishing in Democratic Athens*, Princeton

Anderson, G. (2003) *The Athenian Experiment: Building an Imagined Political Community in Ancient Attica, 508–490 B.C.*, Ann Arbor

Andrewes, A. (1963) *The Greek Tyrants*, New York

Armour, J. (1996) "Just Deserts: Narrative, Perspective, Choice, and Blame" *University of Pittsburgh Law Review* 57: 525–548

Arnaoutoglou, I. (1993) "Pollution in the Athenian Homicide Law" *Revue Internationale des Droits de l'Antiquité* 40: 109–137

Arnaoutoglou, I. (1998) *Ancient Greek Laws: A Sourcebook*, London

Avramović, S. (1990) "Plaidoyer for Isaeus, or. IX" in G. Nenci & G. Thür, eds. *Symposion 1988: Vorträge zur griechischen und hellenistischen Rechtsgeschichte*, 41–55, Cologne and Vienna

Avramović, S. (1997) *Iseo e il diritto attico*, Naples

Barber, B. R. (1996) "Misreading Democracy: Peter Euben and the *Gorgias*" in J. Ober & C. Hedrick, eds. *Dēmokratia: A Conversation on Democracies, Ancient and Modern*, 361–375, Princeton

Barkan, I. (1935) *Capital Punishment in Ancient Athens* (PhD. Dissertation, University of Chicago)

Bateman, J. J. (1958) "Lysias and the Law" *Transactions and Proceedings of the American Philological Association* 89: 276–285

Bateman, J. J. (1962) "Some Aspects of Lysias' Argumentation" *Phoenix:* 16: 157–177

Beauchet, L. (1969) *l'Histoire du droit privé de la République athénienne*, Amsterdam

Benedict, R. (1989) *The Chrysanthemum and the Sword: Patterns of Japanese Culture*, Boston

Bennett, W. L. & M. S. Feldman (1981) *Reconstructing Reality in the Courtroom*, New Brunswick

Benseler, G. E., ed. (1927) *Isocrates Orationes*, Leipzig

Bernstein, L. (1992) "Opting Out of the Legal System: Extralegal Contractual Relations in the Diamond Industry" *Journal of Legal Studies* 21: 115–157

Bernstein, L. (1996) "Merchant Law in a Merchant Court: Rethinking the Code's Search for Immanent Business Norms" *University of Pennsylvania Law Review* 144: 1765–1821

Bers, V. (1985) "Dikastic Thorubos" in P. A. Cartledge & F. D. Harvey, eds. *Crux: Essays Presented to G.E.M. de Ste. Croix on his 75th Birthday*, 1–15, London

Bers, V. (1998) "Professional and Amateur Speech in the Athenian Courts," Address delivered at the American Society for Legal History, Toronto

Bers, V. (2000) "Just Rituals. Why the Rigmarole of Fourth-Century Athenian Lawcourts?" in P. Flensted-Jensen, T. H. Nielsen, & L. Rubinstein, eds. *Polis and Politics: Studies in Ancient Greek History*, 553–562, Copenhagen

Bers, V. (2002) "What to believe in Demosthenes 57, *Against Eubulides*" *Hyperboreus* 8: 232–239

Beyer, H.-V. (1968) *Über den Sachverhalt der demosthenischen Rede für Phormion*, Berlin

Biscardi, A. (1967) Review of Meyer-Laurin, *Gesetz und Billigkeit im Attischen Prozess*, *Studia et Documenta Historiae et Iuris* 33: 469–475

Biscardi, A. (1970) "La 'gnome dikaiotate' et l'interprétation des lois dans la Grèce ancienne" *Revue Internationale des Droits de l'Antiquité* 17: 219–232

Biscardi, A. (1979) "Diritto Greco e scienza del diritto" in H. J. Wolff et al., eds. *Symposion 1974: Vorträge zur griechischen und hellenistischen Rechtsgeschichte*, 1–31, Cologne and Vienna

Biscardi, A. (1982) *Diritto greco antico*, Milan

Blass, F. (1979) *Die attische Beredsamkeit, Vols. 1–4*, New York

Boegehold, A. L. (1972) "The Establishment of a Central Archive at Athens." *American Journal of Archaeology* 76: 23–30

Boegehold, A. L. (1991) "Three Court Days" in M. Gagarin, ed. *Symposion 1990: Vorträge zur griechischen und hellenistischen Rechtsgeschichte*, 165–182, Cologne, Weimar, and Vienna

Boegehold, A. L. (1995) *The Athenian Agora Vol. 28: The Lawcourts at Athens: sites, buildings, equiptment, procedure, and testimonia*, Princeton

Boegehold, A. L. (1996) "Resistance to Change in the Law at Athens" in J. Ober & C. Hedrick, eds. *Dēmokratia: A Conversation on Democracies, Ancient and Modern*, 203–214, Princeton

Boegehold, A. L. (1999) *When a Gesture was Expected: A Selection of Examples from Archaic and Classical Greek Literature*, Princeton

Boegehold, A. L. (2000) "At Home. Lysias 1.23" in P. Flensted-Jensen, T. H. Nielsen, & L. Rubinstein, eds. *Polis and Politics: Studies in Ancient Greek History*, 597–600, Copenhagen

Boegehold, A. L. & A. C. Scafuro, eds. (1994) *Athenian Identity and Civic Ideology*, Baltimore

Bonner, R. J. (1905) *Evidence in Athenian Courts*, Chicago

Bonner, R. J. (1907) "The Jurisdiction of Athenian Arbitrators" *Classical Philology* 2: 407–418

Bonner, R. J. (1912) "Evidence in the Areopagus" *Classical Philology* 7: 450–456

Bonner, R. J. (1916) "The Institution of Athenian Arbitrators" *Classical Philology* 11: 191–195

Bonner, R. J. (1919) "Apollodorus vs. Phormio, Criminal Assault" *CP* 14: 83–84

Bonner, R. J. (1994) *Lawyers and Litigants in Ancient Athens: The Genesis of the Legal Profession*, Holmes Beach

Bonner, R. J. & G. Smith (1930–38) *The Administration of Justice from Homer to Aristotle* 2 Vols., Chicago

Brooks P. & P. Gewirtz, eds. (1996) *Law's Stories: Narrative and Rhetoric in the Law*, New Haven

Brown, D. K. (2002) "Third-Party Interests in Criminal Law," *Texas Law Review* 80: 1383–1428

Burckhardt, L. & Ungern-Sternberg, J., eds. (2000) *Grosse Prozesse im antiken Athen*, Munich

Burns, R. P. (1999) *A Theory of the Trial*, Princeton

Butler, P. (1995) "Racially Based Jury Nullification: Black Power in the Criminal Justice System" *Yale Law Journal* 105: 677–725

Cairns, D. L. (1993) *Aidos: The Psychology and Ethics of Honour and Shame in Ancient Greek Literature*, Oxford

Cairns, D. L. (1996) "*Hybris*, Dishonour, and Thinking Big" *Journal of Hellenic Studies* 116: 1–32

Calhoun, G. M. (1914) "Documentary Frauds in Litigation at Athens" *Classical Philology* 9: 134–144

Calhoun, G. M. (1918) "Διαμαρτυρια, παραγραφη, and the Law of Archinus" *Classical Philology* 13: 169–185

Calhoun, G. M. (1919a) "Oral and Written Pleading in Athenian Courts" *Transactions of the American Philological Association* 50: 177–193

Calhoun, G. M. (1919b) "Athenian Magistrates and Special Pleas" *Classical Philology* 14: 338–350

Calhoun, G. M. (1919c) "Παραγραφη and Arbitration" *Classical Philology* 14: 20–28

Calhoun, G. M. (1999) *The Growth of Criminal Law in Ancient Greece*, Union

Calhoun, G. M. (1977) *Introduction to Greek Legal Science*, Oxford

Cantarella, E. (1975) "φόνος μὴ ἐκ προνοίας: L'elemento soggetivo dell'atto illecito nei logografi e nei filosophi" in J. Modrzejewski, D. Nörr, & H. J. Wolff, eds., *Symposion 1971: Vorträge zur griechischen und hellenistischen Rechtsgeschichte*, 293–320, Cologne and Vienna

Cantarella, E. (1976) *Studi sull'omicidio in diritto greco e romano*, Milan

Cantarella, E. & A. Maffi, eds. (1999) *A. Biscardi: Scritti di diritto Greco*, Milan

Carawan, E. M. (1983) "*Erotesis*: Interrogation in the Courts of Fourth-Century Athens" *Greek, Roman, and Byzantine Studies* 24: 209–226

Carawan, E. M. (1984) "*Akriton Apokteinai*: Execution without Trial in Fourth-Century Athens" *Greek, Roman, and Byzantine Studies* 25: 111–122

Carawan, E. M. (1985) "*Apophasis* and *Eisangelia*: The Rôle of the Areopagus in Athenian Political Trials" *Greek, Roman, and Byzantine Studies* 26: 115–140

Carawan, E. M. (1990) "Trial of Exiled Homicides and the Court at Phreatto." *Revue Internationale des Droits de l'Antiquité* 37: 47–67

Carawan, E. M. (1991) "Response to Julie Vélissaropoulos" in M. Gagarin, ed., *Symposion 1990: Vorträge zur griechischen und hellenistischen Rechtsgeschichte*, 107–114, Cologne, Weimar, and Vienna

Carawan, E. M. (1991) "*Ephetai* and Athenian Courts for Homicide in the Age of the Orators" *Classcial Philology* 86: 1–16

Carawan, E. M. (1993) "The *Tetralogies* and Athenian Homicide Trials" *American Journal of Philology* 114: 235–270

Carawan, E. M. (1998) *Rhetoric and the Law of Draco*, Oxford

Carey, C. (1989) *Lysias. Selected Speeches*, Cambridge

Carey, C. (1991) "Apollodoros' Mother: The Wives of Enfranchised Aliens in Athens" *Classical Quarterly* 41: 84–89

Carey, C. (1992) *Greek Orators VI: Apollodoros Against Neaira*, Warminster

Carey, C. (1994a) "Legal Space in Classical Athens" *Greece & Rome* 41: 172–186

Carey, C. (1994b) "Rhetorical Means of Persuasion" in I. Worthington, ed., *Persuasion: Greek Rhetoric in Action*, 26–45, London

Carey, C. (1994c) "'Artless' Proofs in Aristotle and the Orators" *Bulletin of the Institute of Classical Studies* 39: 95–106

Carey, C. (1995a) "The Witness's *Exomosia* in Athenian Courts" *Classical Quartlerly* 45: 114–119

Carey, C. (1995b) "Rape and Adultery in Athenian Law" *Classical Quarterly* 45: 407–417

Carey, C. (1996) "*Nomos* in Attic Rhetoric and Oratory" *Journal of Hellenic Studies* 116: 33–46

Carey, C. (1998) "The Shape of Athenian Laws" *Classical Quarterly* 48: 93–109

Carey, C. (2000) *Aeschines*, Austin

Carey, C. & R. A. Reid (1985) *Demosthenes. Selected Private Speeches*, Cambridge

Carter, L. B. (1986) *The Quiet Athenian*, Oxford

Cartledge, P., P. Millett, & S. Todd, eds., (1993) *NOMOS: Essays in Athenian Law, Politics and Society*, Cambridge

Cartledge, P., P. Millett, & S. von Reden, eds., (1998) *Kosmos: Essays in Order, Conflict and Community in Classical Athens*, Cambridge

Chambers, M., ed. (1994) *Aristoteles: Athēnain Politeia*, Leipzig

Chase, A. H. (1933) "The Influence of Athenian Institutions upon the *Laws* of Plato" *Harvard Studies in Classical Philology* 44: 131–192

Charles, J. F. (1938) *Statutes of Limitations at Athens* (Ph.D. dissertation, University of Chicago)

Christ, M. R. (1994) Review of Todd, *The Shape of Athenian Law*, *Bryn Mawr Classical Review* 94:6.6

Christ, M. R. (1998a) "Legal Self-help in Defense of the *Oikos*" *American Journal of Philology* 119: 521–545

Christ, M. R. (1998b) *The Litigious Athenian*, Baltimore

Clanchy, M. T. (1993) *From Memory to Written Record, England 1066–1307* Oxford

Clinton, K. (1982) "The Nature of the Late Fifth-Century Revision of the Athenian Law Code" *Hesperia* Supp. 19: 27–37

Cohen, D. (1983) *Theft in Athenian Law*, Munich

Cohen, D. (1984) "The Athenian Law of Adultery" *Revue Internationale des Droits de l'Antiquité* 31: 147–165

Cohen, D. (1985) "A Note on Aristophanes and the Punishment of Adultery in Athenian Law" *Zeitschrift der Savigny-Stiftung für Rechtsgeschichte* 102: 385–387

Cohen, D. (1989) "The Prosecution of Impiety in Athenian Law" in G. Thür, ed. *Symposion 1985: Vorträge zur griechischen und hellenistischen Rechtsgeschichte*, 99–107, Cologne and Vienna

Cohen, D. (1989) "Greek Law: Problems and Methods" *Zeitschrift der Savigny-Stiftung für Rechtsgeschichte* 119: 81–105

Cohen, D. (1991a) "Demosthenes' *Against Meidias* and Athenian Litigation" in M. Gagarin, ed., *Symposion 1990: Vorträge zur griechischen und hellenistischen Rechtsgeschichte*, 155–164, Cologne, Weimar, and Vienna

Cohen, D. (1991b) *Law, Sexuality, and Society: The Enforcement of Morals in Classical Athens*, Cambridge

Cohen, D. (1995) *Law, Violence, and Community in Classical Athens*, Cambridge

Cohen, D. (1998) "Women, Property and Status in Demosthenes 41 and 57" *Dike* 1: 53–61

Cohen, D. (2003) "Writing, Law, and Legal Practice in the Athenian Courts" in H. Yunis, ed., *Written Texts and the Rise of Literate Culture in Ancient Greece*, 78–96, Cambridge

Cohen, E. E. (1973) *Ancient Athenian Maritime Courts*, Princeton

Cohen, E. E. (1991) "Banking as a 'Family Business': Legal Adaptations Affecting Wives and Slaves" in M. Gagarin, ed., *Symposion 1990: Vorträge zur griechischen und hellenistischen Rechtsgeschichte*, 239–263, Cologne, Weimar, and Vienna

Cohen, E. E. (1992) *Athenian Economy and Society: A Banking Perspective*, Princeton

Cohen, E. E. (1994) "Status and Contract in Fourth-Century Athens: A Reply to Stephen C. Todd." in A. Biscardi, J. Mélèze- Modrzejewski & G. Thür, eds. *Symposion 1993: Vorträge zur griechischen und hellenistischen Rechtsgeschichte*, 141–152, Cologne, Weimar, and Vienna

Cohen, E. E. (2000) *The Athenian Nation,* Princeton

Comaroff, J. L. & S. Roberts (1981) *Rules and Processes: The Cultural Logic of Dispute in an African Context,* Chicago

Conomis, N. C., ed. (1975) *Dinarchi Orationes cum fragmentis,* Leipzig

Cover, R. M. (1986) "Violence and the Word" *Yale Law Journal* 95: 1601–1629

Cronin, J. F. (1936) *The Athenian Juror and his Oath* (Ph.D. dissertation, University of Chicago)

Crook, J. A. (1995) *Legal Advocacy in the Roman World,* Ithaca

Cunningham, C. D. (1992) "The Lawyer as Translator, Representation as Text: Towards an Ethnography of Legal Discourse," *Cornell Law Review* 77: 1298–1387

Damaška, M. R. (1986) *The Faces of Justice and State Authority: A Comparative Approach to the Legal Process,* New Haven

Damaška, M. R. (1997) *Evidence Law Adrift,* New Haven

De Brauw, M. (2001–2002) "'Listen to the Laws Themselves:' Citations of Laws and Portrayal of Character in Attic Oratory" *Classical Journal* 97: 161–176

Debrunner Hall, M. (1996) "Even Dogs have Erinyes: Sanctions in Athenian Practice and Thinking" in L. Foxhall & A. D. E. Lewis, eds. *Greek Law in its Political Setting: Justifications not Justice,* 73–89, Oxford

DeBruyn, O. (1995) *La compétence de l'Aréopage en matière de procès publics: des origines de la Polis athénienne à la conquête de la Grèce,* Stuttgart

Dilts, M. R., ed. (1997) *Orationes Aeschinis,* Stuttgart

Dodds, E. R. (2004) *The Greeks and the Irrational,* Berkeley

Dorjahn, A. P. (1927) "Poetry in Athenian Courts" *Classical Philology* 22: 85–93

Dorjahn, A. P. (1928) "Legal Precedent in Athenian Courts" *Philological Quarterly* 7: 375–389

Dorjahn, A. P. (1930) "Extenuating Circumstances in Athenian Courts" *Classcial Philology* 25: 162–172

Dorjahn, A. P. (1935) "Anticipation of Arguments in Athenian Courts" *TAPA* 66: 274–295

Dorjahn, A. P. (1941) "On the Athenian *Anakrisis*" *Classical Philology* 36: 182–185

Dover, K. J. (1968) *Lysias and the Corpus Lysiacum,* Berkeley

Dover, K. J. (1974) *Greek Popular Morality in the Time of Plato and Aristotle,* Berkeley

Dow, S. (1939) "Aristotle, the *Kleroteria,* and the Courts" *Harvard Studies in Classical Philology* 50: 1–34

Dow, S. (1961) "The Walls Inscribed with Nikomakhos' Law Code" *Hesperia* 30: 58–73

Dow, S. (1963) "The Athenian Anagrapheis" *Harvard Studies in Classical Philology* 67: 37–54

Due, B. (1980) *Antiphon: A Study in Argumentation,* Copenhagen

Eder, W. ed. (1995) *Die Athenische Demokratie im 4. Jahrhundert v. Chr.: Vollendung oder Verfall einer Verfassungsform?,* Stuttgart

Edwards, M. (1995) *Greek Orators IV: Andocides,* Warminster

Edwards, M. & S. Usher (1985) *Greek Orators I: Antiphon and Lysias,* Warminster

Ellickson, R. C. (1991) *Order Without Law: How Neighbors Settle Disputes,* Cambridge

Erbse, H. (1963) "Über Antiphons Rede über den Choreuten" *Hermes* 91: 17–35

Erbse, H. (1977) "Antiphons Rede (or. 5) über die Ermordung des Herodes" *Rheinische Museum* 120: 209–227

Euben, J. P., J. R. Wallach, & J. Ober eds. (1994) *Athenian Political Thought and the Reconstruction of American Democracy,* Ithaca

Evjen, H. D. (1970) "ΑΠΑΓΟΓΕ and Athenian Homicide Procedures" *Revue d'histoire du droit* 38: 403–415

Fallers, L. A. (1969) *Law Without Precedent: Legal Ideas in Action in the Courts of Colonial Busoga*, Chicago

Ferguson, R. A. (1996) "Untold Stories in the Law" in P. Brooks & P. Gewirtz, eds. *Law's Stories: Narrative and Rhetoric in the Law*, 84–98, New Haven

Fine, J. V. A. (1951) *Horoi: Studies in Mortgage, Real Security and Land Tenure in Ancient Athens*, Baltimore

Fingarette, A. (1971) "A New Look at the Wall of Nikomakhos" *Hesperia* 40: 330–355

Finley, M. I. (1985) *Studies in Land and Credit in Ancient Athens, 500–200 B.C.: The Horos-Inscriptions*, New Brunswick

Finley, M. I. (1999) *The Ancient Economy*, Berkeley (reprint of 1973 edition)

Fisher, N. R. E. (1976–79) "Hybris and Dishonour" *Greek, Roman, and Byzantine Studies* 23: 177–193 and 26: 32–47

Fisher, N. R. E. (1993) "The Law of *hubris* in Athens" in P. Cartledge, P. Millett, & S. Todd, eds. *NOMOS: Essays in Athenian Law, Politics and Society*, 123–138, Cambridge

Fisher, N. R. E. (1992) *Hybris: A Study in the Values of Honour and Shame in Ancient Greece*, Warminster

Fisher, N. R. E. (1998) "Violence, Masculinity and the Law in Classical Athens" in L. Foxhall & J. Salmon, eds. *When Men were Men: Masculinity, Power and Identity in Classical Antiquity*, 68–97, London

Fisher, N. R. E. (1999) "'Workshops of Villains': Was there much Organised Crime in Classical Athens?" in K. Hopwood, ed. *Organised Crime in Antiquity*, 53–96, London

Fisher, N. R. E. (2001) *Aeschines. Against Timarchos*, Oxford

Ford, A. (1999) "Reading Homer from the Rostrum: Poems and Laws in Aeschines' *Against Timarchus*" in S. Goldhill & R. Osborne, eds. *Performance Culture and Athenian Democracy*, 231–256, Cambridge

Forsdyke, S. L. (2005) *Exile, Ostracism, and Democracy: The Politics of Expulsion in Ancient Greece*, Princeton

Foxhall, L. (1989) "Household, Gender and Property in Classical Athens" *Classical Quartlery* 39: 22–44

Foxhall, L.& A. D. E. Lewis, eds. (1996) *Greek Law in its Political Setting: Justifications not Justice*, Oxford

Fuhr, C., ed. (1994) *Demosthenis Orationes*, Stuttgart

Frier, B. W. (1985) *The Rise of the Roman Jurists: Studies in Cicero's Pro Caecina*, Princeton

Gabrielsen, V. (1987) "The antidosis procedure in classical Athens" *Classica et Mediaevalia* 38: 7–38

Gagarin, M. (1978) "Self-defense in Athenian Homicide Law" *Greek, Roman, and Byzantine Studies* 19: 111–120

Gagarin, M. (1978) "The Prohibition of Just and Unjust Homicide in Antiphon's Tetralogies" *Greek, Roman, and Byzantine Studies* 19: 291–306

Gagarin, M. (1979) "The Prosecution of Homicide in Athens" *Greek, Roman, and Byzantine Studies* 20: 301–323

Gagarin, M. (1981a) *Drakon and Early Athenian Homicide Law*, New Haven

Gagarin, M. (1981b) "The Thesmothetai and the Earliest Athenian Tyranny Law" *Transactions of the American Philological Association* 111: 71–77

Gagarin, M. (1982) "The Organization of the Gortyn Law Code" *Greek, Roman, and Byzantine Studies* 23: 129–146

Gagarin, M. (1986) *Early Greek Law*, Berkeley

Gagarin, M. (1989) *The Murder of Herodes: A Study of Antiphon 5*, New York

Gagarin, M. (1990a) "The nature of proofs in Antiphon" *Classical Philology* 85: 22–32

Gagarin, M. (1990b) "*Bouleusis* in Athenian Homicide Law" in G. Nenci & G. Thür, eds. *Symposion 1988: Vorträge zur griechischen und hellenistischen Rechtsgeschichte*, 81–99, Cologne and Vienna

Gagarin, M. (1996) "The Torture of Slaves in Athenian Law" *Classical Philology* 91: 1–18

Gagarin, M. (1997a) "Oaths and Oath-Challenges in Greek Law." in G. Thür & J. Vélissaropoulos-Karakostas, eds. *Symposion 1995: Vorträge zur griechischen und hellenistischen Rechtsgeschichte*, 125–34, Cologne, Weimar and Vienna

Gagarin, M. (1997b) *Antiphon. The Speeches*, Cambridge

Gagarin, M. (1998a) "Women in Athenian Courts" *Dike* 1: 39–51

Gagarin, M. (1998b) "Series Introduction" in M. Gagarin & D. M. MacDowell, *Antiphon and Andocides*, ix–xxvii, Austin

Gagarin, M. (2000) "The *Basileus* in Athenian Homicide Law" in P. Flensted-Jensen, T. H. Nielsen, & L. Rubinstein, eds. *Polis and Politics: Studies in Ancient Greek History*, 569–579, Copenhagen

Gagarin, M. (2002a) *Antiphon the Athenian: Oratory, Law, and Justice in the Age of the Sophists*, Austin

Gagarin, M. (2002b) "La violence dans les plaidoyers attiques," Unpublished address (Paris)

Gagarin, M. (forthcoming) "Writing Athenian Law"

Gagarin, M. & D. M. MacDowell (1998) *Antiphon & Andocides*, Austin

Garlan, Y. (1988) *Slavery in Ancient Greece*, Ithaca

Garland, R. (2001) *The Piraeus: From the Fifth to the First Century BC*, Bristol

Garner, R. (1987) *Law and Society in Classical Athens*, London

Garnsey, P. (1998) "Grain for Athens" in W. Scheidel, ed., *Cities, Peasants and Food in Classical Antiquity*, 183–200, Cambridge

Gauthier, P. (1972) *Symbola: Les étrangers et la justice dans les cités grecques*, Nancy

Gauthier, P. (1974) Review of Cohen, *Ancient Athenian Maritime Courts*, *REG* 87: 424–25

Geertz, C. (1993) "Ideology as a Cultural System" in *The Interpretation of Cultures: Selected Essays*, 193–233, New York

Geertz, C. (2000) "Local Knowledge" in *Local Knowledge: Further Essays in Interpretative Anthropology*, 167–234, New York

Gernet, L. (1917) *Recherches sur le développement de la pensée juridique et morale en Grèce*, Paris

Gernet, L. (1938) "Sur les actions commerciales en droit athénien" *Revue des Études Grecques* 51: 1–44

Gernet, L. (1939) "L'institution des arbitres publics a Athènes" *Revue des Études Grecques* 52: 389–414

Gernet, L. (1964) *Droit et société dans la Grèce ancienne*, Paris

Gernet, L. (1981) "Capital Punishment" in *The Anthropology of Ancient Greece*, Baltimore 252–276.

Gernet, L. (1982) *Droit et institutions en Grèce antique*, Paris

Gilkerson, C. P. (1992) "Poverty Law Narratives: The Critical Practice and Theory of Receiving and Translating Client Stories," *Hastings Law Journal* 43: 861–945

Glendon, M. A. (1986) "Fixed Rules and Discretion in Contemporary Family Law and Succession Law" *Tulane Law Review* 60: 1165–1197

Glotz, G. (1973) *La solidarité de la famille dans le droit criminel en Grèce*, New York

Gluckman, M. (1973) *The Judicial Process among the Barotse of Northern Rhodesia*, Manchester

Golden, M. (2000) "Epilogue: Some Trends in Recent Work on Athenian Law and Society" in V. Hunter & J. Edmondson, eds., *Law and Social Status in Classical Athens*, 175–185, Oxford

Goldhill, S. (1990) "The Great Dionysia and Civic Ideology" in J. J. Winkler & F. I. Zeitlin, eds., *Nothing to Do with Dionysos? Athenian Drama in Its Social Context,* 97–129, Princeton

Goody, J. (1986) *The Logic of Writing and the Organization of Society,* Cambridge

Green, T. A. (1985) *Verdict According to Conscience: Perspectives on the English Criminal Trial Jury, 1200–1800,* Chicago

Gwatkin, W. E. (1957) "The Legal Arguments in Aischines' *Against Ktesiphon* and Demosthenes' *On the Crown*" *Hesperia* 26: 129–141

Hall, E. (1995) "Lawcourt Dramas: The Power of Performance in Greek Forensic Oratory" *Bulletin of the Institute of Classical Studies* 40: 39–58

Hall, F. W. & W. M. Geldart, eds. (1967) *Aristophanes: Comoediae* Volume I & II, Oxford

Hamza, G. (1991) *Comparative law and antiquity,* Budapest

Hansen, M. H. (1974) *Sovereignty of the People's Court in Athens in the Fourth Century BC and the Public Action against Unconstitutional Proposals,* Odense

Hansen, M. H. (1975) *Eisangelia: The Sovereignty of the People's Court in Athens in the Fourth Century BC and the Impeachment of Generals and Politicians,* Odense

Hansen, M. H. (1976) Apagoge, Endeixis, *and* Ephegesis *against* Kakourgoi, Atimoi, *and* Pheugontes: *A Study in the Athenian Administration of Justice in the Fourth Century B.C.,* Odense

Hansen, M. H. (1978) "Nomos and Psephisma in Fourth-Century Athens" *GRBS* 19: 315–330

Hansen, M. H. (1980a) "Seven Hundred *archai* in Classical Athens" *Greek, Roman, and Byzantine Studies* 21: 151–173

Hansen, M. H. (1980b) "Perquisites for Magistrates in Fourth-Century Athens" *Classica et Mediaevalia* 32: 105–125

Hansen, M. H. (1981a) "The Prosecution of Homicide in Athens: A Reply" *Greek, Roman, and Byzantine Studies* 22: 11–30

Hansen, M. H. (1981b) "Initiative and Decision: The Separation of Powers in Fourth-Century Athens" *Greek, Roman, and Byzantine Studies* 22: 345–370

Hansen, M. H. (1981–1982) "The Athenian *Heliaia* from Solon to Aristotle" *Classica et Mediaevalia* 33: 9–47

Hansen, M. H. (1983) "Two notes on the Athenian *dikai emporikai*" in H. J. Wolff, A. Biscardi, & J. Modrzejewski, eds. *Symposion 1979: Vorträge zur griechischen und hellenistischen Rechtsgeschichte,* 165–177, Cologne and Vienna

Hansen, M. H. (1985) "Athenian Nomothesia" *Greek, Roman, and Byzantine Studies* 26: 345–371

Hansen, M. H. (1989) "Solonian Democracy in Fourth-Century Athens" *Classical et Mediaevalia* 40: 71–99

Hansen, M. H. (1990a) "Diokles' Law (Dem. 24.42) and the Revision of the Athenian Corpus of Laws in the Archonship of Eukleides" *Classical et Mediaevalia* 41: 63–71

Hansen, M. H. (1990b) "The Political Powers of The People's Court in Fourth-Century Athens," in O. Murray & S. Price, eds., *The Greek City from Homer to Alexander,* 215–243, Oxford.

Hansen, M. H. (1999) *The Athenian Democracy in the Age of Demosthenes: Stuctures, Principles, and Ideology,* Norman

Hansen, M. H. & L. Pedersen (1990) "The Size of the Council of the Areopagos and its Social Composition in the Fourth Century B.C." *Classica et Mediaevalia* 41: 73.

Hansen, M. V. (1984) "Athenian maritime trade in the Fourth Century" C&M 35: 71–92

Hanson, V. D. (1998) Warfare and Agriculture in Classical Greece, Berkeley

Hardcastle, M. (1980) "Some Non-Legal Arguments in Athenian Inheritance Cases" Prudentia 12: 11–22

Harris, E. M. (1988) "When is a Sale not a Sale? The Riddle of Athenian Terminology for Real Security Revisited" Classical Quarterly 38: 351–381

Harris, E. M. (1989) "Demosthenes' Speech Against Meidias" Harvard Studies in Classical Philology 92: 117–136

Harris, E. M. (1990) "Did the Athenians Regard Seduction as a Worse Crime than Rape?" Classical Quarterly 40: 370–377

Harris, E. M. (1991) "Response to Trevor Saunders" in M. Gagarin, ed. Symposion 1990: Vorträge zur griechischen und hellenistischen Rechtsgeschichte, 133–138, Cologne, Weimar, and Vienna

Harris, E. M. (1994a) "Law and Oratory" I. Worthington, ed. Persuasion: Greek Rhetoric in Action, 130–150, London

Harris, E. M. (1994b) "'In the Act' or 'Red-Handed'? Apagoge to the Eleven and Furtum Manifestum" in A. Biscardi, J. Mélèze-Modrzejewski & G. Thür, eds. Symposion 1993: Vorträge zur griechischen und hellenistischen Rechtsgeschichte, 169–184, Cologne, Weimar, and Vienna

Harris, E. M. (1999) "The Penalty for Frivolous Prosecutions in Athenian Law" Dike 2: 123–142

Harris, E. M. (2000) "Open Texture in Athenian Law" Dike 3: 27–79

Harris, E. M. (2001) "How to Kill in Attic Greek. The Semantics of the Verb (ἀπο)κτείνειν and Their Implications for Athenian Homicide Law" in E. Cantarella & G. Thür, eds. Symposion 1997: Vorträge zur griechischen und hellenistischen Rechtsgeschichte, 75–87, Cologne, Weimar, and Vienna

Harris, E. & L. Rubinstein, eds. (2004) The Law and the Courts in Ancient Greece, London

Harris, W. V. (1989) Ancient Literacy, Cambridge

Harris, W. V. (1997) "Lysias III and Athenian Beliefs about Revenge" CQ 47: 363–366

Harris, W. V. (2001) Restraining Rage: The Ideology of Anger Control in Classical Antiquity, Cambridge

Harrison, A. R. W. (1955) "Law-making at Athens at the End of the Fifth Century B. C." JHS 75: 26–35

Harrison, A. R. W. (1998) The Law of Athens Vols. 1 & II, London

Hastie, R., S. D. Penrod, & N. Pennington, eds. (1983) Inside the Jury, Cambridge

Havelock, E. A. (1982) The Literate Revolution in Greece and Its Cultural Consequences, Princeton

Hedrick, C. W. (1994) "Writing, Reading, and Democracy" in R. Osborne & S. Hornblower, eds. Ritual, Finance, Politics: Athenian Democratic Accounts Presented to David Lewis, 157–174, Oxford

Herman, G. (1987) Ritualised Friendship and the Greek City, Cambridge

Herman, G. (1993) "Tribal and Civic Codes of Behavior in Lysias I." Classical Quarterly 43: 406–419

Herman, G. (1994) "How Violent was Athenian Society?" in R. Osborne & S. Hornblower, eds. Ritual, Finance, Politics: Athenian Democratic Accounts Presented to David Lewis, 99–117, Oxford

Herman, G. (1995) "Honour, Revenge, and the State in Fourth-Century Athens." in W. Eder, ed. Die athenische Demokratie im 4. Jahrhundert v. Chr.: Vollendung oder Verfall einer Verfassungsform?, 43–60, Stuttgart

Herman, G. (1996) "Ancient Athens and the Values of Mediterranean Society" Mediterranean Historical Review 11: 5–36

Herman, G. (1998) Review of Cohen, Law, Violence and Community in Classical Athens, Gnomon 70: 605–615

Heumann, M. & L. Cassack, (1983) "Not-So-Blissful Ignorance: Informing Jurors About Punishment in Mandatory Sentencing Cases" *American Criminal Law Review* 20: 343–392

Hillgruber, M. (1988) *Die zehnte Rede des Lysias: Einleitung, Text und Kommentar mit einem Anhang über die Gesetzesinterpretationen bei den attischen Rednern*, Berlin

Hölkeskamp, K.-J. (1992a) "Arbitrators, Lawgivers and the 'Codification of Law' in Archaic Greece" *Metis* 7: 49–81

Hölkeskamp, K.-J. (1992b) "Written Law in Archaic Greece" *Proceedings of the Cambridge Philological Society* 38: 87–117

Hölkeskamp, K.-J. (1999) *Schiedsrichter, Gesetzgeber, und Gesetzgebung im archaischen Griechenland*, Stuttgart

Holmes, O. W. (1997) "The Path of the Law" *Harvard Law Review* 110: 991–1009 (reprint of 10: 457–478 (1897)).

Hude, K. ed. (1979) *Lysias: Orationes*, Oxford

Humphreys, S. (1983) "The evolution of legal process in ancient Attica" in E. Gabba, ed., *Tria Corda. Scritt in onore di Arnaldo Momigliano*, 229–256, Como

Humphreys, S. (1985a) "Law as Discourse" *History and Anthropology* 1: 241–264

Humphreys, S. (1985b) "Social Relations on Stage: Witnesses in Classical Athens" *History and Anthropology* 1: 313–369

Humphreys, S. (1991) "A Historical Approach to Drakon's Law on Homicide" in M. Gagarin, ed. *Symposion 1990: Vorträge zur griechischen und hellenistischen Rechtsgeschichte*, 17–45, Cologne, Weimar, and Vienna

Hunter, V. J. (1994) *Policing Athens: Social Control in the Attic Lawsuits, 420–320 B.C.*, Princeton

Hunter, V. J. (1997) "The Prison of Athens: A Comparative Perspective" *Phoenix* 51: 296–326

Hunter, V. J. (2000a) "Policing Public Debtors in Classical Athens" *Phoenix* 54: 21–38

Hunter, V. (2000b) "Introduction: Status Distinctions in Athenian Law" in V. Hunter & J. Edmondson, eds., *Law and Social Status in Classical Athens*, 1–29, Oxford

Hunter, V. & J. Edmondson eds. (2000) *Law and Social Status in Classical Athens*, Oxford

Isager, S. & M. H. Hansen, eds.(1975) *Aspects of Athenian Society in the Fourth Century B.C.: A Historical Introduction to and Commentary on the Paragraphe Speeches and the Speech Against Dionysodorus in the Corpus Demosthenicum (XXXII–XXXVIII and LVI)*, Odense

Jebb, R. C., (1893) *The Attic Orators from Antiphon to Isaeus* Vols. I & II, New York

Johnstone, S. (1999) *Disputes and Democracy: The Consequences of Litigation in Ancient Athens*, Austin

Jones, J. W. (1977) *The Law and Legal Theory of the Greeks: An Introduction*, Oxford

Kahan, D. M. (1997) "Social Influence, Social Meaning, and Deterrence" *Virginia Law Review* 83: 349–395

Kahn, P. (1997) *The Reign of Law: Marbury v. Madison and the Construction of America*, New Haven

Kahrstedt, U. (1969) *Untersuchungen zur Magistratur in Athen*, Stuttgart

Kagan, D. (1987) *The Fall of the Athenian Empire*, Ithaca

Kaplow, L. (1992) "Rules versus Standards: An Economic Analysis" *Duke Law Journal* 42: 557–629

Kapparis, K. (1996) "Humiliating the Adulterer: The Law and the Practice in Classical Athens" *Revue Internationale des Droits de l'Antiquité* 43: 63–77

Kapparis, K. A. (1999) *Apollodorus. Against Neaira: [D. 59]*, Berlin

Katzouros, P. P. (1983) "Pollux et la Δίκη Συνθηκῶν Παραφάσεως" in H. J. Wolff, A. Biscardi, & J. Modrzejewski, eds., *Symposion 1979: Vorträge zur griechischen und hellenistischen Rechtsgeschichte*, 197–216, Cologne and Vienna

Katzouros, P.O. (1989) "Origine et effets de la παραγραφή attique" in G. Thür, ed., *Symposion 1985: Vorträge zur griechischen und hellenistischen Rechtsgeschichte*, 119–151, Cologne and Vienna

Kennedy, G. A. ed. (1991) *Aristotle. On Rhetoric*, New York

Koch, C. (1999) "The Athenian Syngrapheis in the Fifth Century B.C.: Ad hoc Drafting Committees or Elements of an Integrative Approach?" *Revue Internationale des Droits de l'Antiquité* 46: 13–41

Konstan, D. (1985) "The Politics of Aristophanes' Wasps." *Transactions of the American Philological Association* 115: 27–46

Konstan, D. (1997) *Friendship in the Classical World*, Cambridge

Konstan, D. (2000) "Pity and the Law in Greek Theory and Practice" *Dike* 3: 125–145

Kränzlein, A. (1963) *Eigentum und Besitz im griechischen Recht des fünften und vierten Jahrhunderts v. Chr*, Berlin

Kroll, J. H. (1972) *Athenian Bronze Allotment Plates*, Cambridge

Kussmaul, P. (1969) *Sunthekai: Beitrage zur Geschichte des attischen Obligationenrechts*, Basel

Lämmli, F. (1938) *Das attische Prozessverfahren in seiner Wirkung auf die Gerichtsrede*, Paderborn

Lanni, A. (1997) "Spectator Sport or Serious Politics? οἱ περιεστηκότες and the Athenian Law-courts" *JHS* 117: 183–189

Lanni, A. (2004) "Arguing from 'precedent': Modern perspectives on Athenian practice," in E. M. Harris & L. Rubinstein, eds., *The Law and the Courts in Ancient Greece*, 159–171, London

Lateiner, D. (1981) "An Analysis of Lysias' Political Defense Speeches" *Rivista Storica dell'antichità* 11: 147–160

Lateiner, D. (1982) "'The Man who does not Meddle in Politics': A *Topos* in Lysias" *Classical World* 76: 1–12

Lavelle, B. M. (1988) "*Adikia*, the Decree of Kannonos, and the Trial of the Generals" *Classica et Mediaevalia* 39: 19–41

Lavency, M. (1964) *Aspects de la logographie judicaire attique*, Louvain

Lawless, J. M. (1991) *Law, Legal Argument, and Equity in the Speeches of Isaeus* (Ph.D. dissertation, Brown University)

Lempert, R. (1991) "Telling Tales in Court: Trial Procedure and the Story Model" *Cardozo Law Review* 13: 559–573

Lentz, T. M. (1983) "Spoken versus Written Inartistic Proofs in Athenian Courts" *Philosophy and Rhetoric* 16: 242–261

Lévy, E., ed. (2000) *La codification des lois dans l'Antiquité: actes du Colloque de Strasbourg, 27–29 novembre 1997*, Paris

Liepold, A. D. (1996) "Rethinking Jury Nullification" *Virginia Law Review* 82: 253–324

Leisi, E. (1979) *Der Zeuge im attischen Recht*, New York

Lipsius, J. H. (1905–1915) *Das attische Recht und Rechtsverfahren*, Leipzig

Llewellyn, K. N. (1940) "The Normative, the Legal, and the Law-jobs: The Problem of Juristic Method" *Yale Law Journal* 49: 1355–1400

Llewellyn, K. N. & E. A. Hoebel (1983) *The Cheyenne Way: Conflict and Case Law in Primitive Jurisprudence*, Oklahoma

Lloyd, G. E. R. (1990) *Demystifying Mentalities*, Cambridge

Loening, T. C. (1987) *The Reconciliation Agreement of 403/402 B.C. in Athens: Its Content and Application*, Stuttgart

Lofberg, J. O. (1976) *Sycophancy in Athens*, Chicago

Loomis, W. T. (1972) "The Nature of Premeditation in Athenian Homicide Law" *Journal of Hellenic Studies* 92: 86–95

Lōpez, G. P. (1984) "Lay Lawyering," *UCLA Law Review* 32: 1–60

Loraux, N. (1986) *The Invention of Athens: The Funeral Oration in the Classical City*, Cambridge

Loraux, N. (1993) *The Children of Athena: Athenian Ideas about Citizenship and the Division between the Sexes*, Princeton

Luhmann, N. (1975) *Legitimation durch Verfahren*, Darmstadt

Luhmann, N. (1982) *The Differentiation of Society*, New York

Luhmann, N. (1985) *A Sociological Theory of Law*, London

MacCormick, D. N. & R. S. Summers, eds. (1997) *Interpreting Precedents: A Comparative Study*, Brookfield

MacCormick, D. N. (1994) *Legal Reasoning and Legal Theory*, Oxford

MacDowell, D. M. (1962) *Andocides. On the Mysteries*, Oxford

MacDowell, D. M. (1963) *Athenian Homicide Law in the Age of the Orators*, Manchester

MacDowell, D. M. (1971) "The Chronology of Athenian Speeches and Legal Innovations in 401–398 B.C." *Revue Internationale des Droits de l'Antiquité* 18: 267–273

MacDowell, D. M. (1975) "Law-making at Athens in the Fourth Century B.C." *Journal of Hellenic Studies* 95: 62–74

MacDowell, D. M. (1976) "*Hybris* in Athens" *Greece & Rome* 23: 14–31

MacDowell, D. M. (1978) *The Law in Classical Athens*, Ithaca

MacDowell, D. M. (1986) *Spartan Law*, Edinburgh

MacDowell, D. M. (1989a) "The *Oikos* in Athenian Law" *Classical Quarterly* 39: 10–21

MacDowell, D. M. (1989b) *Demosthenes, Against Meidias (Oration 21)*, Oxford

MacDowell, D. M. (1991) "The Athenian Procedure of *Phasis*" in M. Gagarin, ed. *Symposion 1990: Vorträge zur griechischen und hellenistischen Rechtsgeschichte*, 187–98, Cologne, Weimar, and Vienna

MacDowell, D. M. (2000) "The Length of Trials for Public Offences in Athens" in P. Flensted-Jensen, T. H. Nielsen, & L. Rubinstein, eds., *Polis and Politics: Studies in Ancient Greek History*, 563–568, Copenhagen

Mackenzie, M. M. (1981) *Plato on Punishment*, Berkelely

Maffi, A. (1992) "Écriture et pratique juridique dans la Grèce classique" in M. Detienne, ed., *Les Savoirs de l'écriture en Grèce ancienne*, 188–210, Lille

Markle, M. M. (1985) "Jury Pay and Assembly Pay at Athens" in P. A. Cartledge & F. D. Harvey, eds., *Crux: Essays Presented to G.E.M. de Ste. Croix on his 75th Birthday*, 265–297, London

McAdams, R. H. (2000) "A Focal Point Theory of Expressive Law," *Virginia Law Review* 86: 1649–1729

McKechnie, P. R. (1989) *Outsiders in the Greek Cities in the Fourth Century B.C.*, London

Meineke, J. (1971) "Gesetzesinterpretation und Gesetzesanwendung im Attischen Zivilprozess" *Revue Internationale des Droits de l'Antiquité* 18: 275–360

Meyer-Laurin, H. (1965) *Gesetz und Billigkeit im Attischen Prozess*, Weimar

Miller, W. I. (1990) *Bloodtaking and Peacemaking: Feud, Law, and Society in Saga Iceland*, Chicago

Millett, P. (1982) "The Attic *horoi* reconsidered in light of recent discoveries" *Opus* 1: 219–249

Millett, P. (1983) "Maritime Loans and the Structure of Credit in Fourth-Century Athens" in P. Garnsey, K. Hopkins, & C. R. Whittaker, eds., *Trade in the Ancient Economy*, See 36–52, Berkeley

Millett, P. (1993) "Sale, Credit and Exchange in Athenian Law and Society" in P. Cartledge, P. Millett, & S. Todd, eds., *NOMOS: Essays in Athenian Law, Politics and Society*, 167–194, Cambridge

Millett, P. C. (1991) *Lending and Borrowing in Ancient Athens*, Cambridge

Millett, P. C. (1998) "Encounters in the Agora" in P. Cartledge, P. Millett, & S. von Reden, eds., *Kosmos: Essays in Order, Conflict, and Community in Classical Athens*, 203–228, Cambridge

Mirhady, D. (1990) "Aristotle on the Rhetoric of Law" *Greek, Roman, and Byzantine Studies* 31: 393–410

Mirhady, D. (1991) "The oath-challenge in Athens" *Classical Quarterly* 41: 78–83

Mirhady, D. (1996) "Torture and Rhetoric in Athens" *Journal of Hellenic Studies* 116: 119–131

Mirhady, D. (2000) "The Athenian Rationale for Torture" in V. Hunter & J. Edmondson, eds. *Law and Social Status in Classical Athens*, 53–74, Oxford

Mirhady, D. & Y. L. Too, (2000) *Isocrates I*, Austin

Moore, S. (2000) *Law as Process: an anthropological approach*, Hamburg

Morrow, G. R. (1993) *Plato's Cretan City: A Historical Interpretation of the Laws*, Princeton

Mossé, C. (1973) *Athens in Decline 404–86 B.C.*, London

Mossé, C. (1975) "Métèques et étrangers à Athènes au IVᵉ-IIIᵉ siècles avant notre ère" in J. Modrzejewski, D. Nörr, & H. J. Wolff, eds., *Symposion 1971: Vorträge zur griechischen und hellenistischen Rechtsgeschichte*, 205–214, Cologne and Vienna

Murray, Oswyn, (1993) *Early Greece*, Cambridge (2d ed.)

Nader, L. & H. Todd, eds. (1978) *The Disputing Process: Law in Ten Societies*, New York

Noah, L. (2001) "Civil Jury Nullification" *Iowa Law Review* 86: 1601–1658

Nussbaum, M. C. (1993) "Equity and Mercy" *Philosophy and Public Affairs* 22: 83–125

O'Barr, W. M & J. M. Conley (1988) "Lay Expectations of the Civil Justice System" *Law & Society Review* 22: 137–161

O'Barr W. M. & J. M. Conley (1985) "Litigant Satisfaction versus Legal Adequacy in Small Claims Court Narratives" *Law & Society Review* 19: 661–701

Ober, J. (1990) *Mass and Elite in Democratic Athens: Rhetoric, Ideology, and the Power of the People*, Princeton

Ober, J. (1994) "Power and Oratory in Democratic Athens: Demosthenes 21, Against Meidias" in I. Worthington, ed., *Persuasion: Greek Rhetoric in Action*, 85–108, London

Oliver, J. H. (1989) *Greek Constitutions of the Roman Emperors*, Philadelphia

Osborne, R. (1985a) "Law in Action in Classical Athens" *Journal of Hellenic Studies* 105: 40–58

Osborne, R. (1985b) *Demos: The Discovery of Classical Attika*, Cambridge

Osborne, R. (1993) "Vexatious Litigation in Classical Athens: Sykophancy and the Sykophant" in P. Cartledge, P. Millett, & S. Todd, eds., *NOMOS: Essays in Athenian Law, Politics and Society*, 83–102, Cambridge

Osborne, R. (1996) *Greece in the Making: 1200–479 B.C.*, London

Osborne, R. (2000) "Religion, Imperial Politics, and the Offering of Freedom to Slaves" in V. Hunter & J. Edmondson, eds., *Law and Social Status in Classical Athens*, 75–92, Oxford

Osborne, R. & S. Hornblower, eds., (1994) *Ritual, Finance, Politics: Athenian Democratic Accounts Presented to David Lewis*, Oxford

Ostwald, M. (1969) *Nomos and the Beginnings of Athenian Democracy*, Oxford

Ostwald, M. (1973) "Was there a concept of *agraphos nomos* in Classical Greece?" *Phronesis Supp.* 1: 70–104

Ostwald, M. (1986) *From Popular Sovereignty to the Sovereignty of Law: Law, Society, and Politics in Fifth-Century Athens*, Berkeley

Paoli, U. E. (1974a) *Studi di diritto attico*, Milan

Paoli, U. E. (1974b) *Studi sul processo attico*, Milan

Paoli, U. E. (1976) *Altri studi di diritto greco e romano*, Milan

Parker, R. (1996a) *Miasma: Pollution and Purification in Early Greek Religion*, Oxford

Parker, R. (1996b) *Athenian Religion: A History*, Oxford

Patterson, C. (1994) "The Case against Neaira and the Public Ideology of the Athenian Family" in Boegehold, A. L. & A. C. Scafuro, eds., *Athenian Identity and Civic Ideology*, 199–216, Baltimore

Patterson, C. (1998) *The Family in Greek History*, Cambridge

Patterson, C. (2000) "The Hospitality of Athenian Justice: The Metic in Court" in V. Hunter & J Edmondson, eds., *Law and Social Status in Classical Athens*, 93–112, Oxford

Pearson, L. (1987) *Demosthenes: Six Private Speeches*, Atlanta

Pennington, N. (1981) *Causal Reasoning and Decision Making: The Case of Juror Decisions* (Ph.D. dissertation, Harvard University)

Perlman, S. (1964) "Quotations from poetry in Attic Orators of the fourth century B.C." *American Journal of Philology* 85: 155–172

Pettys, T. E. (2001) "Evidentiary Relevance, Morally Reasonable Verdicts, and Jury Nullification" *Iowa Law Review* 86: 467–531

Phillips, D. D. (2000) *Homicide, Wounding, and Battery in the Fourth-Century Attic Orators* (Ph.D. dissertation, University of Michigan)

Philippi, A. (1874) *Der Areopag und die Epheten*, Berlin

Piérart, M. (1987) "Athènes et ses lois" *Revue des Études Anciennes* 89: 21–37

Posner, E. A. (1997) "Standards, Rules, and Social Norms" *Harvard Journal of Law and Public Policy* 21: 101–117

Pringsheim, F. (1950) *The Greek Law of Sale*, Weimar

Pringsheim, F. (1955) "The transition from witnessed to written transactions in Athens" in *Aequitas und Bona Fides: Festgabe zum 70. Geburtstag von A. Simonius*, 287–297, Basel

Raaflaub, K.(1997) "Homeric Society" in B. Powell & I. Morris, ed. *A New Companion to Homer*, 625–649 Leiden

Rawls, J. (1999) *A Theory of Justice*, Cambridge

Reed, C. M. (2003) *Maritime Traders in the Ancient Greek World*, Cambridge

Rhodes, P. J. (1985) *The Athenian Boule*, Oxford

Rhodes, P. J. (1979) "ΕΙΣΑΓΓΕΛΙΑ at Athens" *Journal of Hellenic Studies* 99: 103–114

Rhodes, P. J. (1980) "Athenian Democracy after 403 B.C." *Classical Journal* 75: 305–323 (1980).

Rhodes, P. J. (1985) "*Nomothesia* in Fourth-Century Athens" *Classical Quarterly* 35: 55–60

Rhodes, P. J. (1991) "The Athenian Code of Laws, 410–399 B.C." *Journal of Hellenic Studies* 111: 87–100

Rhodes, P. J. (1993) *A Commentary on the Aristotelian Athenaion Politeia*, Oxford

Rhodes, P. J. (1995) "Judicial Procedures in Fourth-Century Athens – Improvement or Simply Change?" in W. Eder, ed., *Die athenische Demokratie im 4.Jahrhundert v.Chr.: Vollendung oder Verfall einer Verfassungsform?*, 303–319, Stuttgart

Rhodes, P. J. (1998) "Enmity in Fourth-Century Athens" in P. Cartledge, P. Millett, & S. von Reden, eds., *Kosmos: Essays in Order, Conflict and Community in Classical Athens*, 144–161, Cambridge

Rhodes, P. J. (2001) "Public Documents in the Greek States: Archives and Inscriptions" Parts I & II *G&R* 48: 33–44, 136–153

Rhodes, P. J. (2004) "Keeping to the Point" in E. M. Harris & L. Rubinstein, eds., *The Law and the Courts in Ancient Greece*, 137–158, London

Rhodes, P. J. & R. Osborne (2003) *Greek Historical Inscriptions: 404–323 B.C.*, New York

Richardson, M. B. (2000) "The Location of Inscribed Laws in Fourth-Century Athens. *IG* II² 244, on Rebuilding the Walls of Peiraieus (337/6 BC)" in P. Flensted-Jensen, T. H. Nielsen, & L. Rubinstein, eds., *Polis and Politics: Studies in Ancient Greek History*, 601–615, Copenhagen

Robinson, E. W. (1997) *The First Democracies: Early Popular Government Outside Athens*, Stuttgart

Robertson, H. G. (1924) *The Administration of Justice in the Athenian Empire*, Toronto

Robertson, N. (1990) "The Laws of Athens, 410–399 B.C.: The Evidence for Review and Publication" *JHS* 110: 43–75

Röhl, K. F. & S. Machura, eds. (1997) *Procedural Justice*, Brookfield

Röhl, K. F., (1997) "Procedural Justice: Introduction and Overview" in Röhl, K. F. & S. Machura, eds. *Procedural Justice*, 1–35, Brookfield

Rosen, L. (1980–1981) "Equity and Discretion in a Modern Islamic Legal System" *Law & Society Review* 15: 217–245

Rosen, L. (1984) *Bargaining for Reality: The Construction of Social Relations in a Muslim Community*, Chicago

Ross, W. D., ed. (1959) *Aristotle: Ars Rhetorica*, Oxford

Roy, J. (1988) "Demosthenes 55 as Evidence for Isolated Farmsteads in Classical Attica" *Liverpool Classical Monthly* 13: 57–60

Roy, J. (1998) "The Threat from the Piraeus" in P. Cartledge, P. Millett, & S. von Reden, eds., *Kosmos: Essays in Order, Conflict and Community in Classical Athens*, 191–202, Cambridge

Rubinstein, L. (1993) "Persuasive Precedent in the People's Court" Address delivered at the American Philological Association Annual Meeting (Washington, D.C.)

Rubinstein, L. (1998) "The Athenian Political Perception of the *idiotes*" P. Cartledge, P. Millett, & S. von Reden, eds., *Kosmos: Essays in Order, Conflict and Community in Classical Athens*, 125–143, Cambridge

Rubinstein, L. (2000) *Litigation and Cooperation: Supporting Speakers in the Courts of Classical Athens*, Stuttgart

Ruschenbusch, E. (1957) *"Dikasterion panton kurion"* *Historia* 6: 257–327

Ruschenbusch, E. (1966) ed. *Solonos Nomoi*, Weisbaden

Sauer, K. K. (1995) "Informed Conviction: Instructing the Jury About Mandatory Sentencing Consequences" *Columbia Law Review* 95: 1232–1272

Sarat, A. (1996) "Narrative Strategy and Death Penalty Advocacy" *Harvard Civil Rights -Civil Liberties Law Review* 31: 353–381

Saunders, T. J. (1991a) "Penal Law and Family Law in Plato's Magnesia" in M. Gagarin, ed. *Symposion 1990: Vorträge zur griechischen und hellenistischen Rechtsgeschichte*, 115–131, Cologne, Weimar, and Vienna

Saunders, T. (1991b) *Plato's Penal Code: Tradition, Controversy, and Reform in Greek Penology*, Oxford

Scafuro, A. C. (1994) "Witnessing and False Witnessing: Proving Citizenship and Kin Identity in Fourth-Century Athens" in A. L. Boegehold, & A. C. Scafuro, eds., *Athenian Identity and Civic Ideology*, 156–198, Baltimore

Scafuro, A. C. (1997) *The Forensic Stage: Settling Disputes in Graeco-Roman New Comedy*, Cambridge

Schaps, D. (1977) "The Women Least Mentioned: Etiquette and Women's Names" *Classical Quarterly* 27: 323–330

Scheibe, C., F. Blass, & N. C. Conomis, eds. (1970) *Oratio in Leocratem*, Leipzig

Scheppele, K. L. (1989) "Forward: Telling Stories" *Michigan Law Review* 87: 2073–2098

Schmitz, T. A. (2000) "Plausibility in the Greek Orators" *American Journal of Philology* 121: 47–77

Schofield, M. (1998) "Political Friendship and the Ideology of Reciprocity" in P. Cartledge, P. Millett, & S. von Reden, eds. *Kosmos: Essays in Order, Conflict and Community in Classical Athens*, 37–51, Cambridge

Schubert, C. (2000) "Der Areopag als Gerichtshof" *Zeitschrift der Savigny-Stiftung* 117: 103–132

Seager, R. (1966) "Lysias *Against the Corndealers.*" *Historia* 15: 172–184

Sealey, R. (1958) "On Penalizing Areopagites" *American Journal of Philology* 79: 71–73

Sealey, R. (1982) "On the Athenian Concept of Law" *Classical Journal* 77: 289–302

Sealey, R. (1983) "The Athenian Courts for Homicide" *Classical Philology* 78: 275–296

Sealey, R. (1984) "The *Tetralogies* Ascribed to Antiphon" *Transactions of the American Philological Association* 114: 71–85

Sealey, R. (1987) *The Athenian Republic: Democracy or the Rule of Law?*, University Park

Sealey, R. (1994) *The Justice of the Greeks*, Ann Arbor

Shear, T. L. Jr. (1995) "Bouleuterion, Metroon, and the Archives at Athens" in M. H. Hansen & K. Raaflaub, eds., *Studies in the Ancient Greek Polis*, 157–190, Stuttgart

Sherwin, R. K. (1994) "Law Frames: Historical Truth and Narrative Necessity in a Criminal Case," *Stanford Law Review* 47: 39–83

Sickinger, J. P. (1999) *Public Records and Archives in Classical Athens*, Chapel Hill

Sinclair, R. K. (1988) *Democracy and Participation in Athens*, Cambridge

Smith, G. (1924) "Dicasts in Ephetic Courts" *Classical Philology* 19: 353–358

Smith, G. (1925) "The Establishment of the Public Courts at Athens" *Transactions of the American Philological Association* 56: 106–119

Smith, G. (1927) "The Jurisdiction of the Areopagus" *Classical Philology* 22: 61–79

Smith, R. M. (1995) "A New Look at the Canon of the Ten Attic Orators," *Mnemosyne* 48: 66–79

Soubie, A. (1973) "Les preuves dans les plaidoyers des orateurs attiques" *Revue Internationale des Droits de l'Antiquité* 20: 171–253

de Ste. Croix, G. E. M. (1956) "Ancient Greek and Roman Maritime Loans." in H. Edey & B. S. Yamey, eds., *Debt, Credits, Finance, and Profits: Studies in Honor of W.S. Baxter*, 41–59, London

de Ste. Croix, G. E. M. (1961) "Notes on Jurisdiction in the Athenian Empire" *CQ* ns 11: 94–112, 268–280

Strauss, B. S. (1986) *Athens after the Peloponnesian War: Class, Faction, and Policy, 403–386 B.C.*, London

Stroud, R. S. (1968a) *Drakon's Law on Homicide*, Berkeley

Stroud, R. S. (1968b) "Aristotle AP 57.4 and the *Ephetai*" *Classical Philology* 63: 212

Stroud, R. (1991) "Response to Alan Boegehold" in M. Gagarin, ed., *Symposion 1990: Vorträge zur griechischen und hellenistischen Rechtsgeschichte*, 183–185, Cologne, Weimar, and Vienna

Stroud, R. S. (1998) *The Athenian Grain-Tax Law of 374/3 B.C.*, Princeton

Sunstein, C. R. (1996) "On the Expressive Function of Law" *University of Pennsylvania Law Review* 144: 2021–2053

Szegedy-Maszak, A. (1978) "Legends of the Greek Lawgivers" *Greek, Roman, and Byzantine Studies* 19: 199–209

Thalheim, T. ed. (1963) *Isaei Orationes cum deperditarum fragmentis*, Stuttgart

Thomas, R. (1989) *Oral Tradition and Written Record in Classical Athens*, Cambridge

Thomas, R. (1992) *Literacy and Orality in Ancient Greece*, Cambridge

Thomas, R. (1994) "Law and the Lawgiver in the Athenian Democracy" in R. Osborne & S. Hornblower, eds., *Ritual, Finance, Politics: Athenian Democratic Accounts Presented to David Lewis*, 119–133, Oxford

Thomas, R. (1996) "Written in Stone? Liberty, Equality, Orality and the Codification of Law" in L. Foxhall & A. D. E. Lewis, eds., *Greek Law in its Political Setting: Justifications not Justice*, 9–31, Oxford

Thompson, W. E. (1976) *De Hagniae Hereditate: An Athenian Inheritance Case*, Leiden

Thompson, W. E. (1978) "The Athenian Investor" *Rivista di Studi Classici* 26: 403–423

Thompson, W. E. (1981) "Athenian Attitudes Toward Wills" *Prudentia* 13: 13–23

Thür, G. (1991) "The Jurisdiction of the Areopagos in Homicide Cases" in M. Gagarin, ed. *Symposion 1990: Vorträge zur griechischen und hellenistischen Rechtsgeschichte*, 53–72, Cologne, Weimar, and Vienna

Thür, G. (1996) "Reply to D. C. Mirhady: Torture and Rhetoric in Athens" *Journal of Hellenic Studies* 116: 132–4

Todd, S. C. (1990a) *"Lady Chatterley's Lover* and the Attic Orators: The Social Composition of the Athenian Jury" *Journal of Hellenic Studies* 110: 146–173

Todd, S. (1993) "The Purpose of Evidence in Athenian Courts" in P. Cartledge, P. Millett, & S. Todd, eds., *NOMOS: Essays in Athenian Law, Politics, and Society*, 19–39, Cambridge

Todd, S. C. (1991) "Response to Sally Humphreys" in M. Gagarin, ed., *Symposion 1990: Vorträge zur griechischen und hellenistischen Rechtsgeschichte*, 47–51, Cologne, Weimar, and Vienna

Todd, S. C. (1993) *The Shape of Athenian Law*, Oxford

Todd, S. C. (1994) "Status and Contract in Fourth-Century Athens" in A. Biscardi, J. Mélèze-Modrzejewski & G. Thür, eds., *Symposion 1993: Vorträge zur griechischen und hellenistischen Rechtsgeschichte*, 125–140, Cologne, Weimar, and Vienna

Todd, S. (1996) "Lysias against Nikomachos: The Fate of the Expert in Athenian Law" in L. Foxhall & A. D. E. Lewis, eds., *Greek Law in its Political Setting: Justifications not Justice*, 101–131, Oxford

Todd, S. (1998) "The Rhetoric of Enmity in the Attic Orators" in P. Cartledge, P. Millett, & S. von Reden, eds., *Kosmos: Essays in Order, Conflict and Community in Classical Athens*, 162–169, Cambridge

Todd, S. C. (2000) "How to Execute People in Fourth-Century Athens" in V. Hunter & J. Edmondson, eds. *Law and Social Status in Classical Athens*, 31–51, Oxford

Todd, S. C. (2002) "Advocacy, Logography and *Erôtêsis* in Athenian Lawcourts" in P. McKechnie, ed., *Thinking Like a Lawyer: Essays on Legal History & General History for John Crook on his Eightieth Birthday*, 151–166, Leiden

Todd, S. & P. Millett (1993) "Law, Society, and Athens" in P. Cartledge, P. Millett, & S. Todd, eds., *NOMOS: Essays in Athenian Law, Politics and Society*, 1–18, Cambridge

Triantaphyllopoulos, J. (1975) "Rechtsphilosophie und positives Recht in Griechenland." in J. Modrzejewski et al. eds. *Symposion 1971: Vorträge zur griechischen und hellenistischen Rechtsgeschichte*, 23–67, Cologne
and Vienna

Trevett, J. (1992) *Apollodorus, the Son of Pasion*, Oxford

Trevett, J. (1996) "Did Demosthenes Publish his Deliberative Speeches?" *Hermes* 124: 425–441

Tulin, A. (1996) *Dike Phonou: The Right of Prosecution and Attic Homicide Procedure*, Stuttgart

Turner, V. (1996) *Schism and Continuity in an African Society: a study of Ndembu village life*, Oxford

Usher, S. (1965) "Individual Characterization in Lysias" *Eranos* 63: 99–119

Usher, S. (1976) "Lysias and his Clients" *Greek, Roman, and Byzantine Studies* 17: 31–40

Usher, S. (1999) *Greek Oratory: Tradition and Originality*, New York

Van Wees, H. (1997) "Homeric Warfare" in B. Powell & I. Morris, ed., *A New Companion to Homer*,
668–693 Leiden

Van Zyl, D. H. (1991) *Justice and equity in Greek and Roman legal thought*, Pretoria

Vatin, C. (1984) *Citoyens et non-citoyens dans le monde grec*, Paris

Von Reden, S. (1995) "The Piraeus – A World Apart" *Greece & Rome* 42: 24–37

Vélissaropoulos, J. (1980) *Les Nauclères Grecs: Recherches sur les institutions maritimes en Grèce et dans l'Orient
hellénisé*, Geneva

Vélissaropoulos-Karakostas, J. (1991) "Νηποινεὶ τεθνάναι" in M. Gagarin, ed. *Symposion 1990:
Vorträge zur griechischen und hellenistischen Rechtsgeschichte*, 93–105, Cologne

Vélissaropoulos-Karakostas, J. (2001) "Remarques sur la clause κυρία ἡ συγγραφή" in E.
Cantarella & G. Thür, eds., *Symposion 1997: Vorträge zur griechischen und hellenistischen Rechtsgeschichte*,
103–116, Cologne, Weimar, and Vienna

Vidmar, N. (1997) "Procedural Justice and Alternative Dispute Resolution" in K. F. Röhl & S.
Machura, eds., *Procedural Justice*, 121–136, Brookfield

Vinogradoff, P. (1922) *Outlines of Historical Jurisprudence Vol 2: The Jurisprudence of the Greek City*, Oxford

Volonaki E. (2000) "'Apagoge' in Homicide Cases" *Dike* 3: 147–176

Wallace, R. W. (1989) *The Areopagos Council, to 307 B.C.*, Baltimore

Wallace, R. W. (1991) "Response to Gerhard Thür" in M. Gagarin, ed., *Symposion 1990: Vorträge zur
griechischen und hellenistischen Rechtsgeschichte*, 73–79, Cologne, Weimar, and Vienna

Wallace, R. W. (1998) "Unconvicted or Potential 'Átimoi' in Ancient Athens" *Dike* 1: 63–78

Wallace, R. W. (2000) "'Investigations and Reports' by the Areopagos Council and Demosthenes'
Areopagos Decree" in P. Flensted-Jensen, T. H. Nielsen, & L. Rubinstein, eds., *Polis and Politics:
Studies in Ancient Greek History*, 581–595, Copenhagen

Wasserman, D. (1997) "The Procedural Turn: Social Heuristics and Neutral Values" in K. F. Röhl
& S. Machura, eds., *Procedural Justice*, 37–58, Brookfield

White, J. B. (1985) *Heracles' Bow: Essays on the Rhetoric and Poetry of Law*, Madison

White, J. B. (1990) *Justice as Translation: An Essay in Cultural and Legal Criticism*, Chicago

Whitehead, D. (1977) *The Ideology of the Athenian Metic*, Cambridge

Whitehead, D. (1986) *The Demes of Attica, 508/7 –ca. 250 B.C.: A Political and Social Study*, Princeton

Whitehead, D. (2000) *Hypereides. The Forensic Speeches*, New York

Whitehorne, J. (1989) "Punishment under the Decree of Cannonus" in G. Thür, ed., *Symposion 1985:
Vorträge zur griechischen und hellenistischen Rechtsgeschichte*, 89–97, Cologne and Vienna

West, W. C. (1989) "The Public Archives in Fourth-Century Athens" *Greek, Roman, and Byzantine Studies* 30: 529–543

Weyrauch, W. O. (1978) "Law as Mask–Legal Ritual and Relevance" *California Law Review* 66: 699–726

Wilson, P. J. (1991) "Demosthenes 21 (*Against Meidias*): Democratic Abuse" *Proceedings of the Cambridge Philological Society* 37: 164–195

Wolff, H. J. (1943) "The ΔIKE BΛABHΣ in Demosthenes, *Or.*, LV" *AJP* 64: 316–324

Wolff, H. J. (1944) "Marriage Law and Family Organization in Ancient Athens" *Traditio* 2: 43–95

Wolff, H. J. (1946) "The Origin of Judicial Litigation Among the Greeks" *Traditio* 4: 31–87

Wolff, H. J. (1966) *Die attische Paragraphe. Ein Beitrag zum Problem der Auflockerung archaischer Prozessformen*, Weimar

Wolpert, A. (2001) "Lysias 1 and the Politics of the Oikos" *Classical Journal* 96: 415–424

Wolpert, A. (2003) "Addresses to the Jury in the Attic Orators" *American Journal of Philology* 124: 537–555

Worthington, I. (1989) "The Duration of an Athenian Political Trial" *Journal of Hellenic Studies* 109: 204–207

Worthington, I. (1991) "Greek Oratory, Revision of Speeches and the Problem of Historical Reliability" *Classica et Mediaevalia* 42: 55–74

Worthington, I. (1992) *A Historical Commentary on Dinarchus: Rhetoric and Conspiracy in Later Fourth-Century Athens*, Ann Arbor

Worthington, I. (1994a) ed. *Persuasion: Greek Rhetoric in Action*, London

Worthington, I. (1994b) "The Canon of the Ten Attic Orators" in I. Worthington, ed., *Persuasion: Greek Rhetoric in Action*, 244–263, London

Worthington, I., C. Cooper, & E. M. Harris (2001) *Dinarchus, Hyperides, & Lycurgus*, Austin

Wycherley, R. E. (1957) *The Athenian Agora III: Literary and Epigraphical Testimonia*, Princeton

Wyse, W. (1967) *The Speeches of Isaeus*, Cambridge

Youni, M. (2001) "The Different Categories of Unpunished Killing and the Term ATIMOΣ in Ancient Greek Law" in E. Cantarella & G. Thür, eds., *Symposion 1997: Vorträge zur griechischen und hellenistischen Rechtsgeschichte*, 117–137, Cologne, Weimar, and Vienna

Yunis, H. (1988) "Law, Politics, and the *Graphe Paranomon* in Fourth-Century Athens" *GRBS* 29: 361–382

Yunis, H. (2001) *Demosthenes. On the Crown*, Cambridge

INDEX

proclamation (decree) v. Law p.18

||| relevancy as structure of mediation
    Universal & specific pp. 108-109   formalism
    in homicide court   v

            v

open relevancy of pp. 111-112   denociation
popular Court

social norm as mediator   democrati?
between specific & universal   v
in popular court   p. 117

            v

homicide courts   formalism